We Women
of Many Shades and Hues

Daily Common Ground for Survivors of
Childhood Sexual Abuse, Incest, and Rape

Shirley Phelps

SHIRLEY PHELPS

We Women of Many Shades and Hues

Daily Common Ground for Survivors of Childhood Sexual Abuse, Incest and Rape

Second Edition, May 2011
Copyright © 2011 by Shirley Phelps

ISBN: 978-0-9798633-8-7
1. Childhood Sexual Abuse
2. Rape 3. Incest 4. Women's Studies

Printed in the United States of America on acid free paper.

 Robertson Publishing
59 N. Santa Cruz Avenue, Suite B
Los Gatos, California 95030 USA
888) 354-5957 • www.RobertsonPublishing.com

Dedicated to my sons

Aaron and Donald
my heart's treasures

Acknowledgements

I know I'm going to miss mentioning a ton of folks who have helped and supported me in my life, my healing journey and in my writing. If you think you're one of those folks, hey…give me a call or write. Let's talk. Hey, that's you Vy!

To the folks I carry always in my heart, I want to thank my cousins Barbara and Anita, especially during my young adult years. Special thanks to my Aunt Irene for the attic, and to my Aunt Jeannie, my silver-lining during my youth. My late Godparents, Yosiko and Burton Delgado; my friends Stephen and Barbara Drier for traveling with me on a number of my spiritual journeys, often leading the way, and to my best friend when I was growing up and it was still safe to cut our fingers and be blood sisters, Diane Edison. At one time or another, all of these wonderful friends and relatives gave me shelter from "outdoors". Thank you Cecil Johnson for being my friend and saving me from making one of the most regrettable decisions I could have ever made against another human being.

Thanks to the ladies at the Middlesex County Detention Center during the mid-60s and mid-70s, and thanks to Frank Masi, the then director of the same center and who also gave me my first real job. Thanks to the junior high and high school teachers who epitomized the role of teacher by caring about my welfare as much as my academics. Many thanks to the nurses, therapists and counselors who helped me along the way and you know who you are.

To my sistagirls Juanita Molina and Charity Pritchard, I am always glad to call you friends for your support and just being who you are.

My heartfelt gratitude to Alice Molloy, founder of Mama Bears Store in Oakland, California who said, "Why don't you write a book review," and published my first public writing piece.

Thanks to my contributing editor for this book, Charlene Green of Punctuality Editing. Thanks Dr. Barbara Thomas for your review and kind words, and to Marilyn Moore for your time, support and our travels on the healing journey.

I could not have written this without the help of my friend, mentor and sistagirl, Teresa LeYung Ryan. Being the person who you are, your deep commitment to help, assist and connect those who cross your pathway, your spirit of community and honor, you have my gratitude and I am honored to call you friend. To my friend and former "boss lady", Cynthia Peterson, thank you for your support, and your invaluable work in the healing services. I know so few people as you who live the words of Jesus Christ, "Love one another as I have loved you."

To my kindred sisters and brothers at TSF and Survivorship I could not have completed this without your help along the way and especially towards the end of getting this published. I hold you all in my heart, visions and dreams and with a deep connection of gratitude that you all have been there for me.

Thank you Professor John Bishop for your patience and knowledge in answering my questions on publishing and other matters relating to Kajukenbo.

There is much healing in the martial arts. The founder of my school, the late Professor Coleen Gragen, was a visionary and I am thankful to have been her student even for a short season of my life. Special thanks to my co-Chief Head Instructors at Hand to Hand Kajukenbo Self-Defense Center, Sifus Jen Resnick and Sonya Richardson, my other teachers, my sistagirls Sifu Joyce Wong, Marcella Raimondo, Marion Gerlind, and the rest of my Kwoon community where I have a place to practice my martial arts training, and have sanctuary from an insane world. I would be remiss without a shout out to Professor Barbara Bones, Great Grandmaster Charles Gaylord and my Ohana at the Kajukenbocafe.com.

Special thanks to my older brother, Vincent, who has always been an ardent supporter of my healing. Your commitment, care, duty and responsibility to our family are unsurpassable in my book of life, and I am proud to call you my brother. To my sisters, Lorna and Janice, may you continue to hold fast to your dreams and the visions of your hearts.

Most especially, thank you Mother. You gave me the invaluable gift and lesson of living the courage of my convictions and shared with me your great love for music, pens and books. More importantly, I am and have been touched throughout my life in words I cannot explain, each time you lay your hand upon my shoulder and say, "daughter."

Juan: Thank you for the years we had together as husband and wife, and for being the wonderful father you are to our sons.

Donald and Aaron: I hope one day to find the perfect words, the perfect phrase, the perfect story, the perfect poem, the perfect way to express the gift of love you both are to me, and I thank the Holy Mother Spirit for such a bestowal of love into my life. I am so proud of the young men you are today, of your strength and integrity of character, your deep capacity to love and of your compassion you express in your lives and to the world. I thank you both for being my sons and for loving me. If you know nothing else in this world at any time during the journeys you take in your lives, know that I carry you both always in my heart.

Preface

When I first wrote this a few years ago, a 20-year old Black woman was rescued and treated for injuries sustained from at least a week's torment of sexual, physical and emotional maltreatment by a group of White adults in West Virginia. Her ordeal began with kidnapping and abduction, and then further acts of sexual abuse and assault such as hot water poured on her while being raped and other atrocities throughout her captivity. It is a given that her healing journey will need all the help and assistance society can make available to her. In one way, she is not unlike the majority of sexual assault victims of whom 72-77% of victims are acquainted with their perpetrators.

Society appears to believe this woman because of the heinous people involved who have history of a combined total of 108 criminal charges, including one perpetrator who served time for murder. We believe her because there is evidence to support her story. We believe her because her first "outcry" was to a law enforcement officer. We also believe her because her perpetrators "look" like rapists or other images we hold in mind for what rapists look like. On the other hand, had the law enforcement officer not discovered her in the tortured shed she had been imprisoned in, had she told this story after escaping on her own and in a body that looked healthy, we probably would not believe her. Such are the more realistic experiences of many survivors.

The trial of Michael Jackson is a classic example of why children are not believed when they say a trusted person has sexually abused, assaulted or incested them. It is my opinion Michael Jackson was acquitted, despite the testimony of a survivor to whom Jackson made a financial settlement with, along with testimony from other alleged victims and witnesses, because society *did not want him to be guilty*. We knew Michael from the time he was a little boy. We loved him as a musical genius even with his eccentricities and were proud of his charitable works visiting hospitalized children and inviting children to his Neverland Ranch with its amusement park rides and its various domesticated animals. And so the jury, the public and especially his fans, went into denial mode. Reasonable doubt? Hardly. Deep denial is more the case. Not wanting to believe Michael Jackson has done anything wrong to sexually hurt a child because he's talented and also has done a lot of good in other areas of his life.

The most recent trial of incest and childhood sexual abuse (CSA) to come to public attention has been the criminal charge and conviction as an accomplice to incest and rape against Warren Jeffs, considered to be the prophet of the Fundamentalist Church of Jesus Christ of Latter-day Saints (FLDS), which is a polygamist religious sect located in Utah and Arizona. After investigations by law enforcement and the media, it has been proven that child marriages were arranged by Jeffs for older male members in their 50s and above to girls as young as 14-years old in his sect. Additionally, as another indicator of child abuse, many of the young teen males, now commonly known as "The Lost Boys", were ex-communicated from the community so that there would be less competition to the older males for marriage to the limited number of available young women. It is the belief of this religious sect that in order to get into heaven, a male must be married to at least three women. Unfortunately, and despicably so, these are the types of communities where incest, child sexual abuse and rape flourish in a conspiracy of silence by the collective community-at-large including some politicians and law enforcement.
(See page XXIX in the back for updates on Williams, Jackson and Jeffs.)

Unlike the young woman mentioned earlier, most perpetrators do not look like the pictures of her alleged perpetrators. The overwhelming majority of pedophiles, rapists and sexual abusers look like regular people. Perhaps it is because they are regular people. They are fathers, stepfathers, mothers, stepmothers, brothers, sisters, stepsiblings, cousins, uncles, aunts, grandparents, and/or trusted people in the community such as caregivers, lawyers, doctors, teachers, coaches, and religious leaders, etc. They have a public face and they have a special private face for their child victims.

Childhood sexual abuse differs from incest only by the nature of the relationship of victim to perpetrator. Any and all sexual violations may happen in either category. Traditionally, incest has been described as sexual interactions with members of blood relatives and extended family members. Some modern day definitions are now including primary caregivers, school authorities, or others who have care of children, including babysitters. However, the word "incest" as used in this book is confined to family and extended family members including temporary partners who take up residence with a woman or man who have children and become part of the family whether married or not. Other children are considered victims of CSA. For example, if a neighboring adult sexually abuses or rapes a child when she goes over to play with the neighbor's child that is not incest just because they live close to the family. It is a neighbor committing a sexual crime against a child. [1]

CSA and incest can be perpetrated as covert sexual actions of inappropriate sexual language with a child, showing pornographic photos and/or videos to expressed fondling and molestation of genitals and rape of a child. Sexual assault does not always include rape; rape, definitively includes forced vaginal and/or anal penetration by a penis or other bodily parts or an object without the consent of the other person. Depending on the State one lives in, consent depends on age and different age spans. For example, in California it is illegal for anyone over the age of 18 to have sexual intercourse with anyone under the age of 18. In fact, it is technically illegal for anyone under the age of 18 to have sexual intercourse. Nonetheless, it is unlikely that two juveniles, where one is 16-years old and the other is 15-years old, will be charged with rape or sexual assault if it is consensual on the part of both parties.

Incest can involve one person or multiple people in the same family or occur with the family in child sex rings, religious sects and cults. It can happen once or it can happen intermittently throughout a childhood. It can be on a weekly or daily basis until the child leaves home or until the child reaches a certain age and is no longer attractive to the offender. The perpetrator may approach the child with kindness and by making her feel special by saying, "This is our little secret." Or, she can be approached with threats and violence. The end result is still the same— the child is sexually assaulted with admonitions and/or threats not to tell or else the child or someone she loves will be hurt or killed. It is not unusual that the child keeps the "secret".

My experience with sexual assault was CSA in the home of a primary caregiver, incest by a close family member and assault, battery and rape by a fiancé after I said I wanted to discontinue our relationship. The incest was a family member who had access to me on a regular basis for a number of years and as he stated to the authorities, for every accusation I made, someone was

---

[1] The words "partner, lover or beloved" is used interchangeably throughout this book regardless of sexuality in marital or intimate relationships unless otherwise noted..

always around. In those days and what is still similar today, when there are no witnesses, when it is one person's word against another, and a sexual assault accusation is made, law enforcement is reluctant to press charges, especially if they do not have evidence to prove it.

Nonetheless, since the 1960s society has made some progress in the protection of children and youth from predators, familial or otherwise. They do take the accusations of youth and children more seriously than they did a couple of generations ago; there are new therapeutic ways to interview children for an uncontaminated report of what happened to the child. Also, minors are entitled to be represented by an attorney. During the 1960s in my youth, there were no child interview centers and children had no rights except as decided by the courts. Now, if the perpetrator resides in the home of the child or is a regular visitor, the perpetrator is removed from the home and/or the visitor is no longer allowed in certain proximity of the child, especially the child's home and restraining orders are available for further protection. Too, for those who report being raped a sexual assault examination can be conducted within a 96-hour window from the time of the assault to collect DNA as evidence for the use of the district attorney's office in deciding which cases to charge with a criminal offense. (Collection of DNA began with a72-hour window: recently some states, like New Jersey have changed it to a 5-Day window.)

American society currently provides substantial preventative education to children and teenagers through the public education system, presenting to both male and female students what is safe touch and what is not; what is rape and what is not. As part of some of the programs, self-defense workshops are also offered at no costs to the participants. Health care-givers such as therapists and counselors, and anyone who is entrusted with caregiving of children and youth are nationally court-mandated reporters, especially physicians as well as teachers and other professionals. Additionally, social agencies provide telephone numbers and agencies that people can contact anonymously if they suspect a child or teenager is being abused in any manner— sexually, physically, emotionally, neglectfully and/or abandonment. Along with the preventative educational measures, society has a campaign for public awareness through different media to help parents, educators and other healthcare personnel to recognize probable indicators of sexual abuse with children and youth in terms of their behaviors, sleep patterns and other signs that the child is not acting in her usual manner in a given span of time and circumstances.

Rape cuts across all societal divisions of race, creed, religion, class, gender, etc. Some victims are more at risk than others in all the groups. The majority of sex offenders are male, and 2% of sex offenders are women. After reviewing overall statistics it can be said unequivocally that rape is a crime against youth as 83% of rape victims are 24-years old and under.[2] 21.6% of females under the age of 12 are raped; youth between the ages of 12-17 are the highest group of rape victims at 32%, while women 18-24 are 29% of rape victims. The remaining 17% are 25 years and older. Additionally, women with disabilities are twice as likely to be sexually assaulted and raped as other female population groups; and approximately 20% of elderly citizens are raped.

A significant point that statistics reveal is that girls who have been sexually assaulted or incested in childhood are twice as likely to be raped in adulthood as other women. Some statistics are even higher for re-victimization by rape depending on the number of childhood incidents and the severity of the sexual abuse in the adult's childhood personal history.

Current research has yet to come up with a comprehensive national study on the scope of incest compared to statistics on rape and other sexual abuse crimes. While some stats might show that fathers, stepfathers, live-in lovers or uncles are frequent perpetrators in incest, my experience with victims and survivors suggests that there are numbers of children that are being incested by mothers, brothers, sisters and cousins much more frequently than indicated by current data.

Perhaps one of the reasons there are so few in-depth studies is the fact that many victims of incest do not disclose until they are adults. Additionally, incest may be disclosed on the basis of the comfort level of the victim, that is, the incest can no longer be tolerated by the victim and the victim is willing to risk asking for help despite any threats or fears of retaliation she may have internalized from the perpetrator. Presently, most of the research information on CSA seldom delineates how many children are sexually abused by incest or by non-family members, nor the length and span of time in regards to incest.

---

[2] *2007 REPORT: Research on Rape and Violence*, California Coalition Against Sexual Assault.

Also, many children in early childhood who are incested have difficulty remembering the event or do not have the language skills to tell someone what happened.

Sometimes child victims of incest do not know that what is happening between themselves and the abusers is sexual abuse since it may have been happening over a long period of time, and so they find a way to incorporate the incest as a "normal" part of their lives. For these non-reporting incest victims while they may develop a deep sense of powerlessness and helplessness they also develop deeply embedded psychological defenses to handle their suffering and distress such as emotional withdrawal, disassociation or amnesia. Such a thing is a tremendous strength for a child, but can be a great handicap for an adult healing from that experience.

As recently as the 1980's, incest was considered to be uncommon and as a result, there were few forums or social agencies to which an incest victim or survivor could seek help. Victims of incest tend not to report as frequently as non-incest victims because of the internalized shame attached to the act and to the family. Incest may also not be reported because a child may go to a parental figure and receive the message not to tell anybody else, that the family will handle the problem. It is this last reinforcing message of "don't tell", whether it comes from a family member or the perpetrating family member, which seems to settle into the psyches of victims and survivors.

In a sample study of 263 adolescent females, one of the findings is the closer relationship to the perpetrator, i.e., a family member, made the reporting of sexual abuse an unlikely immediate disclosure. In another National Survey of Adolescents, 86% of those who were sexually assaulted did not report at all. And in a 1994 survey of 243 American women, with significant numbers of Black, Latina and Asian women, with CSA histories were 3 times as likely in adulthood to be raped than women without CSA histories.[3] Neither of these studies separated their figures between general CSA and incest.

In the 1990's there was an upsurge of disclosure by adult survivors of CSA and incest, both of which became a topic of societal controversy and remains so to this day. Controversial or not, it allowed many victims and

---

[3] 2007 Report: Research on Rape and Violence, California Coalition Against Sexual Assault.

survivors of CSA to find their voices and to "break the silence" of speaking about the taboo of incest, CSA and rape that happened or is happening to them. What we also know about incest survivors is that a variety of studies and research suggest that in American culture about 10 to 20 million people are victims or survivors of incest at any one given time. Also, girls are reportedly more often the target as the ratio of boys to girls being incested is about 10 to 1.[4]

Violence against women and girls is a health concern world-wide: 1 woman in every 3 has been beaten, coerced into sex, or otherwise abused in her lifetime and more often than not the abuser is a member of her own family.[5] As to sexual assault, the statistics for convictions and reporting are somewhat discouraging at this time. Only 16% of rapes are reported to the police and, according to the U.S. Senate Judiciary Committee: Conviction and Imprisonment Statistics, 1993, only 2% of rapists are convicted and imprisoned.[6]

There are so many variables when considering these statistics depending on what social strata is being studied, the numbers of the research participants and who is doing the research. For instance, Black women tend to have a slightly higher percentage of rape than White women, and lower income women tend to have higher statistics than other income levels.[7] The question then arises as to what is the overlap of women who are Black, poor, and have been raped? Or additionally, do Black women lack private resources so that they must turn to law enforcement or other agencies with more frequency than other racial and ethnic women?

In my twenty years of counseling, with eleven years experience as a crisis intervention counselor and advocate for victims of sexual assault, I can not recall any of my primary clients of any race who were lawyers, doctors or dentists and who underwent a sexual assault examination as a result of a police report for rape. However, the children of the afore-mentioned professional groups have been brought in by their parents for examinations, support and

4 *Incest*, Free Health Encyclopedia: http://www.faqs.org/health/topics/68/Incest.html.
5 *2007 REPORT: Research on Rape and Violence*, California Coalition Against Sexual Assault.
6 Rape Trauma Services: http://www.rapetraumaservices.org/rape-sexual-assault.html.
7 Op cit.

counseling. Also, there are numerous boys and men who are raped but such citing of those statistics would be for another book. I mention the statistics that I have cited to give the reader a sense of how pervasive CSA, incest and rape are in American culture and committed against females.

What is most important in the experience of victims or survivors is that we believe our own truths for there will always be a person, a family member, a group and in a number of cases a jury that will not believe the truthful stories we have to tell. As an adjunct to the belief in our own truths, we who are survivors in healing know that the healing comes in our own time and that others who have walked the path are willing to help and walk with us on our journey. No matter what our experience has been with CSA, incest and/or rape, one of the most salient points to remember is that none of it is our fault. A pedophile, a rapist or a molester makes the decision to commit a sexual crime and we have been their target. The person who commits the illegal act is a person who has committed a crime regardless of how a victim was acting. The only one responsible for the act of violation is the perpetrator. It is the perpetrator's fault, the perpetrator's shame and the perpetrator's crime. It is the perpetrators who walk a path of harm, destruction and offense. And it is our path as victims and survivors, should we choose, to walk a path of healing.

PLEASE NOTE: While my personal and professional experience counts for much of the knowledge and healing I have gained, *I am not a medical doctor nor am I a clinical psychologist or therapist.* For victims and survivors reading this book, please take care of yourselves as some of the material can be triggering, may remind you of your own past experiences, or tap into issues you may be working on in your present healing. Please take time to breathe, to have your support, friends and phone numbers nearby and a way to ground yourselves if the reading gets heavier than you anticipated. *If for any reason you feel you need medical attention as a result of anything you have read, please call 911 or if you have a therapist or counselor please do not hesitate to contact them. And remember you can always call a hotline which you will find in one of the resources listed in the back of the book.*

The writing of this book is part of my healing journey and it is my hope it will be helpful to other victims and survivors who say "yes" to another day of living and to a promising journey of healing.

Shirley Itím Melo Phelps
January 10, 2008
2nd Edition, January 1, 2011

Foreword

Shirley Itím Melo Phelps has written a book which aims to help all victims of sexual assault, including groups frequently omitted from such discussions such as women of color. The author offers words of encouragement to help the rape "victim" feel like a "survivor" instead of a victim. Speaking directly to the survivor, Phelps takes her through the post-rape recovery challenges, emphasizing both how one can help oneself and how others can aid in the recovery process.

This daily guide speaks directly to the multitude of issues, concerns, and feelings of survivors of sexual violence. Phelps provides emotional honesty about the impact of sexual violence and represents the reality of the issues often faced by survivors of sexual violence through insight, inspiration and hope. Thus, the book may also be a resource for family and friends who are affected by sexual violence, helping them better understand what the survivor may be experiencing.

Ms. Phelps has dedicated many years to the completion of this project. She has worked with hundreds of sexual assault survivors who have shared their experiences of sexual violence. Combined with her personal knowledge of sexual violence and her professional experience as a counselor and advocate for victims of sexual assault, she has captured their pain by being sensitive and compassionate and in return through her book, provides them with a tool to continue moving forward in the healing process.

Ms. Phelps' words are strong and powerful as she evokes daily survival techniques that victims may draw upon. She has spent many hours of reflection, research, and meaningful consideration on the impact of sexual violence to survivors. Her book provides readers with the tools to address some of the overwhelming emotions and feelings of helplessness that may arise from the experience of being sexually assaulted or raped and are now working towards healing their lives.

In this wonderful resource, Phelps offers day-to-day words of encouragement that will support anyone who has experienced sexual violence in their lives. I highly recommend this book to anyone who has been the victim of rape and is working towards becoming a survivor!

Cynthia Peterson, Director of Crisis Counseling
Community Violence Solutions
January 2008

Introduction

We Women of Many Shades and Hues is about and for women who have experienced CSA, sexual abuse, sexual assault, rape and/or incest, and who are now, as adults, healing from the myriad repercussions such as chronic depression, fatigue, despair, anxiety, panic attacks, and phobias. While especially written with women of color in mind, it is not exclusive of other co-survivor sisters traveling this road of healing, hence "Shades and Hues." It is about acknowledging the pain of violation in the core of the soul and healing these particular wounds we carry into every facet of our lives. And, it is about wrestling with the salient she-monster of our thoughts and feelings as we seek to find happiness within our lives and with our loved ones.

There are no shortcuts on the healing journey, but as in all healing there is a formula: recognition of an injury or wound, correct diagnosis of the problem, treatment plan, and time and care to allow for healing. Companions are part of our journey. Some in the form of other people— no one heals in isolation; and some in Spirits— Courage, Hope, Faith, Wisdom, Patience, and Love.

As to these Spirits of Courage, Hope, Faith, Wisdom, Patience, and Love— they will turn up throughout our journey of healing; without them there is no healing. We all have these spirits embodied within our being, as they are our undeniable spiritual heritage and it is how many of us survived.

It takes the Spirit of Courage to dismantle defenses that have defined most of our lives, and to face fears we have been running from since our earliest memories. When one develops a lifetime of powerful coping mechanisms to survive an assaultive environment, it takes the Spirit of Hope that we can reconstruct, restructure, redeem, and reclaim all that was stolen or lost to us.

It is possible to heal— even though everything we know about ourselves leaves us disinclined to believe it because, after all, we know ourselves better than anybody else. So, amongst other things, we need to tap into the Spirit of Faith, faith that no matter what happens on this journey, we shall, can, and will heal.

Once Hope and Faith are on board, it is a matter of time before the Spirits of Patience, Wisdom and Love show up. We need the "wisdom to know the difference" between what is useful on our journey and what we can throw out— things that no longer serve, such as defenses that were useful and now only work against us. We need wisdom to know when to trust, when to risk, when to say yes and when to say no, wisdom to know which of our defenses to keep and which ones to let go, which people help us grow and sustain our lives, those that just pretend to, and those who simply take and never give anything except bad advice.

Walking with the Spirit of Wisdom, we learn patience and love, especially for ourselves and the parts of ourselves we have rejected, ignored, or thrown away in order to survive from one day to the next as we continued to cling to the Spirits of Hope and Faith to lead us to a healing in our lives.

In terms of people we choose to go on this journey with us, there is only one requirement: who we are must be accepted unconditionally. Now, this does not mean that whatever we do or say is behaviorally acceptable. It simply means that, bottom line, we are individuals worthy of having a place in this world, our "selves" have a right to exist as much as the sky we look to above, and the grounds we walk upon with our dreams. It also means that in reclaiming our voices, we have a right to be heard. The companions we choose are people we select because they give us the dignity, recognition, witness, and respect we deserve— something that was often missing in our lives as we traveled the road from childhood into adulthood. These folks can be our family members, spouses, partners, friends, counselors, therapists, people in a survivor's group, or a 12-step group, online internet groups— any one or group who supports us.

Incest, CSA, and rape wreak havoc with anybody's psyche. If left unaddressed and buried in the deep recesses of the brain, it still has the ability to generate chaos in the everyday relationships of those of us who survive the experiences. There are as many forms, variations, and stories of survivors as there are the children that are its victims. Each woman has her own story to tell. However, we all share common ground for healing: rage, anger, fear, terror, sadness, powerlessness, helplessness, and hopelessness. There are also defenses: phobias, chronic anxiety, panic attacks, depression, hyper-vigilance, psychosomatic diseases, disassociation, and more. The fallout of this sexual violation of self is the long-lasting imprint of being overwhelmed by circumstances (internally and externally), and most of all, the deep wound of betrayal. And so, one of the hardest and principal parts of our journey, is learning to trust in the unassailable power of the Spirit of Love.

And why do any of this except for love of ourselves and others? We who are of the human race crave love, long for reciprocating love, and want to give away the love born to us within our hearts. Of course we know of many people who exist without love. Their lives are excruciatingly empty, painfully lonely, and most of the time they get through the day, if they get through the day, on numbness— be it by drugs, alcohol, or denial. This is not what we want for ourselves. We want love and we want it fully in our lives. We want to heal the rift within ourselves, to bring ourselves back into this kismet called life, the healthy, pulsing dance of humanity. It is our Spiritual Birthright.

This book covers a wide range of feelings and issues experienced by survivors. It does not matter where any one is on the spiral of healing— whether beginner or someone with much experience traveling the healing path. It has many uses such as daily reading and self-reflection, a reference resource to where we are in our specific journey, or for group discussion.

To heal fully is possible. It does not mean that we will be "cured" of all our problems. However, healing does mean we can have a healthy, loving life to live. It means we can have a job we enjoy doing. It means we can release the creativity that has so long been imprisoned by our defenses. It means we can honor all that we have gone through and will go through. It means we will be able to depend on ourselves, and that we will take care of ourselves in healthy and loving ways. And lastly, it means in all its hopeful promise, we can be all of which we are— evolving soul/Women meant to live in the truth, beauty, and goodness of life.

January 1

DRAGON'S DEATH

She who gives birth
is destined
a dragon's death

"Can this year be different?"

It is the New Year. Again. And once again, many of us will make new year resolutions— "I will not run away from my fears...my memories...my demons...my nightmares," or something along the lines of "I will not allow my family to drive me crazy by pretending that nothing happened. I will not, in fact, spend any time with my family as long as they are in denial."

Many times we make resolutions based on what we will not do. We might be better off with resolutions of what we will do, i.e., "I will face my fears...my memories...my demons...my nightmares," and/or "I will take care of myself by spending time with others who validate and love me."

Just as every new day gives us a chance to try all over again, a new year gives us the opportunity to plan out long-term projects and more realistic perspectives with which to view the growth of our lives.

Sometimes when we are just beginning our healing, a year seems too long to wait to be able to process our journey. But suddenly the year is over, and we look back and see just how far we have come, just how much we have progressed in *only* a year's time.

Defending ourselves from our abuse and our history takes a lot of work. Many of us have fortresses that are almost impenetrable not only to others, but also to ourselves. Think about it— isn't it a gift that the New Year gives us more room and more space to breathe and change and grow? And if we so choose to risk a new step in our healing, then it's possible we can begin to tear down at least one of our walls so we no longer have to use it to separate ourselves from others or the desires of what we want in our lives.

* * * * * * * * *

"I welcome the New Year like a long-awaited and wanted guest."

"When will my life happen?"

Some of us are taught not to want much from life, to let our desires and longings smolder to ashes in our thoughts. Even when our souls burn with desire, it is not enough to bring our deeply-felt yearnings and visions to fruition. And when the flames of our desires are extinguished, our souls are empty and wanting, sometimes buried in a dead dream. This sense of hopelessness and despair can be so overwhelming at times that getting out of bed is in itself a real achievement, not a matter to be scorned or belittled.

Looking into the eyes of others, we see our fears confirmed in the clear and undeniable reflection of what we are not. Some of us can not look for fear of what we will see. Nonetheless, nothing will change just because we wish it so. It is in these desperate moments of being that we must trust ourselves to do what only we can do, and that is to live our lives as only we can.

If we want changes in our lives, then we must make them so. If we would have our dreams come true, then we must allow ourselves to dream. If we would believe in ourselves, then it is by taking that first step that only we can take to make our new beginning, and new beginnings can start at any time.

* * * * * * * * *

"Like the sun, I rise every morning to a new day."

"How will I learn to slow down?"

Our lives can make us feel like a living yo-yo. One day we can experience intense joy and happiness for the lives we lead, and then the very next day we slip down the steps of despair. Caught off balance, we tumble to the bottom of the floor scattering everything in our hands. Then the very next day, we're on top of the world again; and the day after that, we're slipping down those same stairs again. It is mind-boggling, crazy-making, and dizzy enough to make us run screaming from our own lives.

We who are women who have spent a lifetime recovering from frequent crises in our lives, must learn how to live and lead lives of balance. We can do this by making a commitment to ourselves to indeed live more in balance with Spirit. To have a stretch of routine is not a bad thing. To have our days envisioned peacefully is a good thing. Only good can come out of good.

* * * * * * * * *

"Viewpoints change when we look at life from different angles."

"Can I get a witness?"

Validation from self and others is an indication that we are, indeed, healing. Healing should not be some esoteric awakening or a year's work in a garden that yields no fruit. Validation from family, friends, and community sends out individuals prepared for the many journeys that only they can take alone.

A number of us live lives of missed opportunities, necessary sacrifices, and the overcoming of great odds and obstacles in meeting the vicissitudes of life. And, it is validation from our loved ones and ourselves that makes our struggles worthwhile, especially in our healing.

While validation from others is important, real validation must come from within the self. When that is not forthcoming, such a life lives in a state of constant craving to be filled by otherness, and if we can not find that fulfillment of validation from within ourselves, many of us will turn to drugs, alcohol, TV, and any other kind of addiction to alleviate the awful pain of filling the void of non-validation.

It is not wrong to want to see some kind of change as a result of our healing work. Whether it is a lessening of nightmares, a ridding of old flashbacks or the ability to try new ways to meet old and ingrained problems, moving forward in our healing is validation that we are on the right path. In healing there may not be any wrong ways to heal, but rest assured there is a right way to heal. Such healing should yield a validation that we are getting healthier and better. If we are not, then we should look again to the path we are walking for our healing.

* * * * * * * * *

"The human spirit does not survive well in isolation."

"Why do I seem to crave the touch of another person?"

We who are women of color are desperate for safe touch. Sometimes we have children just so that we can have someone safe to love. Who is hungrier for touch? Who commonly reaches out to bring another human being closer? Who takes hands and lovingly traces facial features, pulls gently on strands of hair, and sticks fingers into ears? Who freely grasps the fingers of another and holds on until the need to hold is satisfied? Who laughingly runs up to its mother or father and gives great big knee hugs? Who plops down unabashedly and wraps arms around necks and upper torsos? Who but that of a loving child?

When we are adults our agendas change, and our touch is jealously reserved for special people or special occasions. We give out hugs and kisses to other adults on holidays. We parcel out hand-holding for weddings and funerals, and we only give out spontaneous hugs and touches when our emotions threaten to burst from within us, and the body demands we express ourselves. And, then of course, we reserve the unabashed touching for our most intimate moments of sex. Is it no wonder so many of us are addicted to sex? The body craves touch and if coupling is the only avenue we think we have, then that's the road we'll take!

If we would attend to that part of ourselves that craves the human touch, then we could easily take lessons from the children of the world. Without shame or unintended harm, they reach for one another. What a great space to occupy.

* * * * * * * * *

"Nothing's so electric as the touch of another human being."

"What would it be like to live without my phobias?"

We may have acquired certain phobias to help ourselves defend against the real terror in our lives: feelings and realities. The reality of being trapped and powerless may be too much for a child's mind to handle and so to function, we place the real fears of our life situation on substitutes: fear of heights, fear of being in small, enclosed places; fear of open places, fear of certain animals such as spiders, cats, dogs, or birds.

The real object of our fear is displaced. How is it possible that the ones that love us can forget and strike out against us in a moment of violence? Their violence. Our vulnerabilities. And many times we didn't even feel the pain. Some of us may remember experiences of life moving on an even keel and then suddenly, out of nowhere, a hand roughly slips between our legs or we are struck by a hand on our head, maybe knocked down to the floor or continually being hit all over our body while frantically searching through our mind and asking, "What'd I do? What's happening? Why can't I think? Why doesn't this hurt?" For others, the slightest touch caused excruciating pain.

Living a life in the shadow of fear and casting that fear off so the power is no longer there presents us with the new and extremely difficult challenge of looking at life differently, going to places previously closed off to us, and trying new activities because now these fears are no longer with us. Just as it took time for these fears to develop into full-blown phobias, it will also take time for us to reclaim the lost freedom and the joys such freedoms bring to our lives. Let us be as patient with ourselves in adjusting to our newfound freedom as we were in accepting our all-encompassing fears.

* * * * * * * * *

"There are places in my heart waiting for me to fly free."

"What is this compelling need I have to love?"

What do we who are women and who love and want to be loved actually know of love? Is it an attraction? Is it the person we claim we love? Is it a feeling by itself that we can call up whenever we think we've found someone we want to share our lives with intimately? Or can we put it away when we don't want to be hurt at our deepest core?

We who are women with bandaged wings never think we can soar as high as others who seem to love so easily, who accept faults of their lovers, who roll with the waves of stormy times, and can withstand even the most threatening of all hurricanes. Rather, we are like the participants of earthquakes. We hold onto whatever is available, which in non-earthquake times is patently useless or dangerous, but in the earthquake it's the only place to be.

We are all babes to the world of love. We have so little of it on a constant basis. We are all learning. But the little that we do have is enough to build a strong and unyielding foundation, unabated by storms or hurricanes or even earthquakes. True love, with its simple truth of unconditional acceptance, is foreign to many of us, bandaged wings or not. But true love, as spoken by the poets of time, comes to us all whether we are cruising on a wind song or delicately perched on the branch of a willow tree. When love presents itself will we once again hold ourselves back? Or, will we take a risk and fly into its arms?

* * * * * * * * *

"We are drawn like magnets to a world called love."

"Why am I so restless sometimes?"

There are days when the spirit of the soul will not be soothed, will not calm itself, will indeed not be appeased. Such restlessness produces soul agitation. It happens when we are clearly stuck with who we are and know it. We know who we are and know we are dissatisfied with what we have. We know something is keenly missing, know we are the only ones who can find it, and don't have one iota of a thought of the first place to look for it. When we look in askance and wonder what "it" is all about, it is then that our most inner selves are giving a message of terrific import to us. We want more in our life. We are not happy with the way things are. We want change. And most of all we are not listening to our inner selves. Such "self" will not go away. Such "self," if not met, will enter a path of destruction— drugs, alcohol, gluttony or maybe just pure inner ugliness spread out to the world.

At these times, our life can seem unbearable. It is then that we must exercise all the patience we know, and then wait. For if we are kind to ourselves, if we will extend the necessary moments and do what we need to do, we will learn what it is we want from ourselves. We who are women often choose to turn a deaf ear to our own inner longings. It is one of the terrible choices one can make and one we needn't make. We are worthy of hearing and obeying the truths of our soul. So for today, we can be kind and take a moment or two to really hear what we have to say to our *own* selves, and then take a step on acting on that knowledge.

* * * * * * * * *

"We must feed our souls or spend energy denying we are hungry."

"What's wrong with me?"

Some days it seems as if there just isn't anything right about ourselves, so wrong that we don't even want to look in the mirror to see the person we know we will see, knowing a thing hasn't changed since the last time we looked.   Self-rejection is a mighty foe and is a number of years in the developing of its grip upon our inner self. If we reject ourselves who else is left to count? If we have not found a way to make ourselves count as much as anyone else, why should any one else's value count? Some of us won't say or do a specific thing because we are afraid of the opinion of others. And then we hate ourselves and afterwards, when we look in the mirror, can not meet our own eyes.

On those days when we can not look ourselves in the eyes for no good reason, yet still we have kindness for everyone but ourselves, it is best if we leave most of that day alone, going on about our business as necessary. Perhaps a simple spiritual holding of ourselves is all that is needed. Perhaps, like the child that whines and will not be placated except by being held, there is something we do not understand, but that nonetheless needs to be addressed with kindness and patience from our inner voice or a spiritual holding from our soul. This is, perhaps, the most simple and true thing to be done.

* * * * * * * * *

"Today I claim every part of me as mine."

"Why don't I know what's going on in my life?"

Some of us don't plan for a future because at some point we accepted the belief that whatever future there was for us, no good could come of it. Come to think of it, there was a good possibility that there was no future, and if there was a possibility, we just didn't think of our future in terms of goodness.

Then one day it happened. We were free. Free to make our own decisions and plans for our own life. And some of us found that we couldn't. We found that the days would arrive so suddenly and that we had no plans. We didn't know how to make our ideal day actually happen. In futile desperation we raged. And time passed, and our activities passed— a career, a child, a relationship, and there we were with our lives passing and not quite sure how all of it happened so quickly. We met many of our short-term goals and still we were dissatisfied and right around the next moment, the future was coming. Actually it is here, and we do not know what to do with all this time we have to form and shape the vast frontier of space in our lives.

Let us not throw the proverbial baby out with its bathwater. Each day we are given the grace to start exactly from where we are to get where we want to go, no matter who we are, what we are, or where we come from. Perhaps that is one of the supreme secrets of life— each day we are given a chance to create our lives as we so wish them to be.

* * * * * * * * *

"The future I want is in my capable hands, waiting only on me."

"Why am I always on a roller coaster of emotion?"

It would appear that some of us have grown up thinking that feelings just happen to us. We are given at birth and at different seasons in our lives different temperaments in which to mobilize within the world. Yet some of us are definitely inclined, whether from experience or biology, to ride the roller coaster of life's emotional ups and downs. So while we are riding this carnival-like vehicle, it behooves us to find a safety strap as we take the ups and downs, sometimes experiencing the thrill, though mostly hanging on for dear life. It is not so much the periodic mood swings that bother us. In fact, we are culturally accepting of them as women because of our menstrual cycles and our pregnancies and sometimes because we have been programmed by society to be this way.

For many of us, mood swings are a regular staple of life, and if not harnessed, they add greatly to burdens we may already be carrying. Making the mood swing adjustment does not have to entail great deeds of enormous, emotional work. It is enough sometimes to accept that this is the way our life is for the moment. Self-stroking at such times is a necessity. Simple contact with friends, sea salt baths, a trip to the gym, an evening of reading or watching a favorite video, can sometimes be just the activity to bring us back to balance. Sometimes it helps to get a physical exam as we may be suffering a biochemical imbalance and medication can be helpful with mood swings. If those do not shift us, it is always a good idea to check in with our Creator Spirit, who constantly encourages our souls, regardless of what our minds may be saying, back onto the trail of a healing path.

* * * * * * * * *

*"I can tame the strong emotions I have that seem as
if they have a mind of their own!"*

"No matter what, why can't I seem to fill up?"

When we underestimate the little things in our lives, we do a disservice to ourselves. When we spend most of the day and night attending to other things, even necessary things, we ignore the quiet voice in our hearts telling us to come listen, and we skyrocket off the path of self-satisfaction. Our days seem edgy and jagged and we are not fit people to live with. As we go about our daily tasks and the voice gets louder, and still we don't bother to hear it, it is almost as if our spirit separates from us and a restlessness beyond our control seems to sink in and take its place, and then we have two things do deal with: not listening to ourselves, and the knowingness of not listening to our souls. The soul does not take kindly to this situation. In fact, it does everything it can to bring harmony and healthy functioning to the person it embodies. Suddenly, nothing that is simple to do is simple anymore. We are inner-fighting on too many levels to function properly in our daily lives. Nothing that needs attending to will simply get better on its own. Nothing grows without nurturing. Chaos doesn't stop on its own accord. What it leaves behind is debris that has to be cleaned up.

What we know from experience is that when we attend to the insistent voice of our soul, it is almost as if magic has appeared in our inner lives. Externally nothing may have changed, but almost immediately our inner landscape is renewed. The hunger of the soul will not be pacified with substitutions. Starving appetites require real food.

* * * * * * * * *

"I can start listening to the whisperings of my soul."

"What does it mean that my cup is half-empty?"

We have all heard of the proverbial pessimist and optimist. Despite all the bad press, the pessimist really does have strengths. We just have to look for them. Truthfully, the pessimist may start off on an unhopeful path. It is what contributes to her pessimism and depression— the beginning path. But as the beleaguered warrior comes through her travails, she learns not only about the wisdom of life's teachings, but also about another dimension of herself.

The pessimist learns she can withstand the most raging storms, the rockiest earthquakes, the most frigid blizzards, and the sweltering day of almost no air. She learns to see the personal challenge of an obstacle, and knows by her experience she can be successful even in the most difficult of times. She knows that if she is successful, it is an experience no one can take away from her. The pessimist knows that a situation is going to be difficult, but she has also learned that she can survive the difficulty with success.

* * * * * * * * *

"Sometimes it's all about how we handle the struggle itself."

"I wonder if they knew the real me would they still be my friends?"

When we are children, we sometimes dream of being naked in front of our friends or classmates. Some of us continue to have that same little nightmare into our adulthood. It is almost a universal dream. The fearful part of such a dream is that if people see us as we really are then we may be found wanting, that there is something wrong about us not only in our own eyes, but in the reflection of others. Despite our fears, some of us manage to masquerade in costumes we feel quite comfortable in. It is really a silly cover-up for ourselves. It is not like our friends do not see the way we are dressed or do not know who we really are under the costume.

Unlike children who pretend and dress up and take delight in being discovered and found out that it is really them and not the person they are pretending to be, we adults take it in the opposite direction, hoping with our fingers crossed that no one we know will guess who we really are. The truth of the matter is that our friends and loved ones do know who we are. Often they know of our fears before we even address them, choosing not to say anything because *we* deem it so important not to talk about it. It is one of the nonverbal things we communicate and is often picked up on by those closest to us. But they also know our strengths and in spite of this combination, they love us because we are who we are. We who walk this sometime, fragile path of never being sure of why we are liked, or why anyone would really want us for a friend, must grasp in a wholehearted way that we are lovable human beings, even with all our faults, imagined or real.

* * * * * * * * *

"My true friends love me just as I am."

"Why is the word "joy" such a stranger to my ear?"

Sometimes the word "rejoice" rings empty in our lives. When we have distanced ourselves from our feelings and our inner children, we can not tap into the magic of such a state. To rejoice, to give in to the feelings of joy in our lives, is something we are often blinded to, beset as we are by the many problems of our daily lives and of our personal histories. Sometimes all of it seems too much, so how could we possibly rejoice? Sing with a choir of angels? Take flight on the edge of one of their soaring wings?

No matter how deep the pain, a moment will come in the day when we've forgotten how badly we feel. Maybe it's something one of our children said or did. Maybe it's the way the sun is setting at night and all of a sudden, we can actually feel the peace of the Universe, and no matter what is going on in our daily lives, we are truly connected to something greater than ourselves. Sometimes it's just a matter of letting go, of being uplifted for a moment, and then we can see and feel the tremendous joy of simply being alive. We, every one of us, have the inner resources to do that, no matter what is currently happening in our lives. No matter how old the saying or the concept, truly, the answer lies within ourselves. There is joy in the Universe and it is ours to wonder and behold.

* * * * * * * * *

"The same joy that lives in the Universe can live in my heart.."

"Why must my healing always be one step at a time?"

Sometimes it's as if some of us never had a chance. How does one bring love and trust to a relationship when you may have spent your childhood warding off the very person you should have been able to trust? Without question? Without hesitation? Without doubt? Without fear of betrayal? Once the hideous disease of incest begins for a child, the outcome is almost predictable. This is a no-win situation. In its best scenario, the offending party, who would stay in the family, would get help and offend no one anymore. The child's trust would be restored, the family would be salvaged, and all would go on to lead productive lives.

Rare are the families that can do this work. It is a societal problem whose "die is cast." Its worst scenario is to leave a child in the same environment, who will grow into an adult whose capacity for deep feeling, love, and trust is miserably disabled. The energy and resources it will take to restore healing to this future adult is short of a miracle. This is not to say that these future adults will not have happiness and love or are permanently incapable of relationships. But it is to say, with substantial predictability, that until we eradicate this heinous crime, we will all pay— the future husbands and wives, future children, future bosses and co-workers, future significant others, future key intimates, future neighbors— everybody in the band will have a chance to hear the solo note. Sometimes it will be heard as an eerie, bone-chilling scream, sometimes as a hoarse whisper, sometimes it will even be boldly blown, but it will be nothing we want to hear again.

* * * * * * * * *

"I am capable of reaching out and trusting people again."

"Can getting what I want actually be a problem?"

It is possible to come to that which you love, and then abhor what you meet. It is possible to face the very thing you want, to *have* the very thing you want, and have to spend energy fighting every destructive impulse you've ever had not to ruin what you've work so hard to achieve. It is possible that the same desire that produced that which you love will be met from the other side of you that doesn't think you are worthy to have it. We see it every day. The woman who finally finds the perfect mate then sets out to destroy the relationship, however unconsciously, is quite common.

Too, we sometimes mobilize ourselves to the best of what we have and then tread the path of compulsion to blithely destroy it, crying the next morning about the damage we have done— the awful word said that can never be retrieved, the awful act done that can not be denied— the awfulness of the other side of our being human. We are so afraid to accept the act of self-sabotage as part of our human condition, that when it slips out, we are horrified to even name it. It is the human faux pas of being a human being and it is not the end of our world when it happens to us. It is called a mistake.

All is not hopeless. We may not be able to retrieve that "awful" word or change the erroneous act. Understanding is not condoning. We do what we need to do to pick up the pieces and in doing so, take a bite out of our inner monster so its strength is depleted until finally, its strength is totally broken by our continuous choices to make healing the victor. This is our victory.

* * * * * * * * *

"Life is not always a struggle."

"Why does it seem to take so long to do what I want?"

Hope is not fed by our dreams alone. "We live not by bread alone," is still apropos some 2,000 years after the words were first uttered. If we keep our vision to include only our world and only in this time frame, we are surely fated to see life through a myopic tunnel of light. We are all interconnected to things in past history and even to moments of the future that we have not yet stumbled upon. Being cut off except for contact with creatures like us makes it difficult to believe that there is indeed a high purpose to our being in this world. And despite the theory of the creative bang, spontaneous combustion never created anything that didn't immediately self-destruct. Its opposite— evolutionary growth— is what we know and live.

It takes one lifetime for a human being to grow in the stomach of its mother, another lifetime to grow into an adult, and even another lifetime to grow into a balanced human being. And we grow, because we are driven to grow by our inner gardener. Like a seed that is planted and that roots underground in darkness, we have no idea of the evolving beauty that lies above us. It is all a matter of time, a lifetime for our soul to grow.

* * * * * * * * *

"Time is a measurement, not a race."

"Is it time to move on or should I stay?"

How do we know when to stick with a relationship or when it would be better all the way around, regardless of the consequences, to move on? How do we, who have so little experience with trusting the goodwill of anyone, make the distinction between sticking with a relationship because it's the best thing to do, and staying because we're afraid if we don't, we might be making a mistake? Living, loving, and sharing a life with someone is surely one of the tasks we are supposed to learn while we are here in this world.

Some people are better skilled at being in relationships than others. Trusting the care of ourselves to another person is no light matter. Expecting another to love us as we love ourselves, to have our best interests at heart just as they have their own, and vice versa, is almost a superhuman event. How long do we wait for our partners to take heed to the saying, "Do unto others..." where we're concerned? We have had many signposts and guidelines along the way, but no one has come up with a foolproof plan on when to exhaust our love on another person, or keep the love alive.

As always, the answers lie within our hearts and with what we truly know about ourselves and the person we love, and no one can answer this question except our own knowing and loving soul. It is in the heart of our soul that we can lay trust.

* * * * * * * * *

"Whenever I stop doubting, I'm in touch with the answers carried within my soul."

"How did I get backed into this corner? Ugh!"

Some of us are not surprised that we are backed into a corner and that the corner is of our own making. It's not surprising that considering our abuse history, we were often backed into a corner. For some of us, being backed into the corner was a daily experience. We were trapped in an untenable situation and powerless to stop the events, the abuse, that took place when we were children. Despite the pain and the experience, we eventually got out of the corner, whether by our own means and cunning or because the abuse ran its course, and we had to pick ourselves up and move onward to the next step in our lives.

But it is different now that we are no longer victims, but instead survivors, and habitual, surviving patterns die hard. We sometimes back ourselves into corners of our own making and then feel helpless to get out of them. We are not. We have choices today and it really doesn't matter what the current corner is. What does matter is that we truly accept that we have the power to take ourselves out of such corners. We made them. We can undo them. We are the decision makers of our own lives. *We own our lives.* We are our own power brokers, our own agents, our own rescuers and sisters. We have the power to do it.

* * * * * * * * *

"Simple, but true, there is always a way out!"

"How is it I look in the mirror and see tears I don't feel?"

There are days when tears simply spill from our eyes without a hither and yon for our permission. We have no idea why these tears are falling. We simply know that they come of their own accord. Many of us can remember a time when we made the decision not to cry anymore. It hurt too much to cry and long for something that was never going to happen— the abuse to immediately stop, our abuser to go back to being the loving person we thought he or she was, our families to embrace and love us and acknowledge what happened to us. One day we recognized that was never going to happen, and we vowed never to cry again so no one could ever hurt us again, could ever rip out our hearts, stomp on it and watch us watch it be destroyed. And for a while, that helped many of us to survive.

But one day, payback time comes around, and the body will not be ignored by anyone, including ourselves, without accepting payment in kind. And if we as holistic women will not recognize what needs to be done, then the body itself will begin to respond and take care of itself. And if we won't on an emotional level take care of ourselves, unacknowledged feelings will. Our body will cry for us even if we won't. It is a wake up call, sisters. Our body is telling us we need to take care of scary, unfinished business. We are survivors. We can do this.

* * * * * * * * *

"If I do not take care of these tears, who will?"

"After all this time, has all been said that can be said of everything?"

It seems a simple enough task, a simple enough thing to do. We open our mouths and speak. Some of us talk in paragraphs and chapters. Some of us can even talk the length of a book if our audience would let us. Some of us chatter on and on, in spite of what our audience says or thinks. We fill the air with words to cover an empty space we can not tolerate. Who knows what would happen in the next moment if silence were allowed to occur. But, then, some of us can not form a sentence and fear disturbing the silence. Would the one word we utter somehow change the course of human events? Would the next word turn our world upside down? Again? Would certain words destroy our loved ones, destroy our world?

Perhaps even more frightening is the possibility that there would be no one out there to hear what our lips would utter.

Everyone needs to be heard; everyone needs to be acknowledged. We need validation. It is part of the human experience. We are social animals and we do not thrive in isolation. Without other human beings, we wither and die. And yes, people do die of lonely hearts.

Despite our deepest fears and doubts, our friends and loved ones really do want to hear what we have to say. We only have to take the risk and say what lives within our hearts. No matter what the situation, and especially when all else fails, we can always speak from our hearts.

* * * * * * * * *

"Today's truth is that I am worthy of being heard."

"Who will help me collect the scatterings of my broken heart?"

It's been said that it is easier to pick up the pieces of a shattered mirror than those of a broken heart. Really, we don't know where to begin. We'd just as well as grab a teddy bear critter and curl up in a corner, rather than touch that first piece of a broken heart. How do we begin to explain? The words won't even come; the pain is so great. And who would care to listen?

Sometimes we don't even know our heart is wounded until it becomes affected by some event in our lives, and like salt on an open sore, it screams for us to do something. And we try. God knows we try, and still the pain of that open wound won't go away— and we haven't the slightest idea where the soothing, healing ointment might be.

To say that the healing might be in our Higher Power or in another person is to bring alive all the disbelief we keep at bay. We haven't come this far in life just to be tricked again like we were as children. And yet, therein lies our solution. It is only with our child's heart that we pick up the pieces and make them fit again. We might use our adult woman mind to make the pieces fit, but it is our child's heart that needs mending. If we don't see that, who will? We mother enough people. Certainly it is time we mother the broken hearts of our inner children.

* * * * * * * * *

"All the king's horses...could've tried a loving heart"

"During the din and noise, why can't I can't hear my own voice?"

It is often difficult to hear our own inner voice with all the noise and chatter constantly taking place in our daily world. We know there is a voice deep inside that knows, the voice that speaks the truth, if only we could hear it. Sometimes, along the way, we lose that voice, not knowing we've lost it until it comes time for us to speak and we can't find the words to express ourselves, to say the things our hearts long to be heard. For many of us, that voice was stolen along with all the other stuff encompassed in our personal history. And luckily, for many of us, the first thing we reclaim in our healing is our voice. After all, we have to break the silence, and that can be done only if *we* speak our truth. It is no one else's but ours, so it doesn't have to fit anybody else's life. It is our life. It is our truth. It is our voice.

It is in speaking our truth that we see how silenced we were. To own what once was ours is to reclaim yet another part of ourselves that went into hiding so that we might survive another day of an intolerable situation. To speak the truth after holding back so long is to truly make the body human again, and rejoin the spirit of our soul.

* * * * * * * * *

"I speak for me now and in my own voice."

"Why aren't there any guarantees to loving?"

Let us not confuse loneliness with solitude. Solitude is that which we seek when we need to retreat from an all-too-busy world, even our busy inner worlds. Solitude is a gift we give ourselves as we nurture our soul for an inner time of rest and peace. It is something we look forward to.

Loneliness is a formidable enemy. It is not being alone with ourselves, but rather, it is being alone when we really want to be with others and when we think we can't find another soul we want to be with or that we can talk to. It is a yearning and desire to fill the void of a space in our hearts that wants contact, yet can't find it anywhere. It is an uneasy and unsettling feeling, perhaps even a break from grace provided freely by the Universe. Loneliness is poison, for often it speaks of an unnecessary void in our lives, our unwillingness to take the risk we need to connect with another being, whatever our reasons may be, righteous or not. Loneliness now is an unworkable defense. It keeps us at a distance and separate from others.

We are lucky. Loneliness is one of our easier defenses to dismantle. With the dial of a number or a walk down the street, we can break the hold it has upon us. We can fill the void. It is one of our weaknesses we can readily and actively give up. A simple hello to a stranger or a call or a visit to a friend can help remove the invisible wall that says no one cares. They do.

* * * * * * * * *

"The heart is always one step ahead of the mind."

"How long is the vigilance of the hand that rocks the cradle?"

Not infrequently, a child dies because of the thoughtlessness and desires of its parent, its guardian of decisions until the child is old enough and independent enough to make life decisions for herself so she doesn't die.

Those of us who may have had our desires snuffed out when we were children, those of us who remember so clearly what it was like not to be able to pursue our dreams because of the seemingly arbitrary decisions of our parents, are perhaps in danger of being such a parent, especially if we were denied unless we cooperated with an exchange for sex. It is difficult to withstand a child's expressed heart's desires, but then again, that is why we are parents. It is our job to exercise wisdom and love in all its many forms and manifestations, whether deeply heartfelt and free from strings, or culled and tempered with discipline that comes from our own wisdom of living.

We who raise children are bound to make mistakes. This learning is part of the reason we exist, here on earth and at this time. But one of the lessons we should surely master for the good of all concerned is not making reckless mistakes that seem okay in a moment, but in time demand a payoff when our children become adults and must face the obstacles and challenges that life presents to them, just as life does with us. We should be as diligent in our role as parent in teaching our children survival skills as other species in the animal kingdom; even moreso.

* * * * * * * * * *

"When raising children, small decisions can be as hefty as big decisions."

"How risky is it to trust myself with another person?"

We who are women who come from backgrounds of abuse knew our greatest fear was to be alone with the abuser. We knew, regardless of whatever facade was working while others were around, our abuser had a face and personality just for us, and we couldn't see how others could miss what we so familiarly knew. As a consequence, we learned to isolate ourselves, even in the midst of large family gatherings. We knew wherever the abuser was, we needed distance, and distance meant being alone. In many ways, we learned to depend on ourselves, on our decisions to live with the many mini-crises we experienced in our daily lives. Some of us learned, exquisitely, how to implant and build upon invisible boundaries so that if physically we were assaulted, emotionally and spiritually we were left intact...or so we thought.

We may find that our independence has made us quite capable of performing in roles we have attained in society— mother, manager, PTA president, etc. But despite the many contacts we have, we may find ourselves wanting a connection that isn't there.

Closeness requires that we step beyond our self-imposed boundaries and take risks, risks to trust that the person we want to connect with wants to connect with us as well. It is sometimes as simple as making a friend— a real friend. Sometimes the risk requires that we ask more of ourselves and our life partners, to go into emotional and spiritual territory that might have been too threatening a week ago, but in the now, is just the right time to reveal something tender, something vulnerable about ourselves to our partners or a possible new friend.

* * * * * * * * *

"I am entitled to have close and intimate relationships."

"What kind of life is this, anyway?"

After all is said and done, where do we get the extra energy to do simple housecleaning? When it seems that it takes all our energy just to get out of bed, the idea of actually tackling drudge housework can seem like the last thing we want to do. But then, we may wake up one morning, look all around in our living spaces, see that every area needs the energy of spring cleaning work and ask, "Where have I been?" We may become discouraged knowing the labor and time it will take just to bring a semblance of order back into being. And we may find that we can't do anything else until our refuge world is brought back to order and cleanliness.

Healing from our abuse history can be like that. We may wake up in the morning and feel that it is all too much, no matter how well we convinced ourselves the night before that the next day was going to be a better day. The next day comes and we are, face-to-face with the demon we thought we left behind the day before. Our depression is still there, twisting around in our stomach or hovering in our mind, giving us a headache. And nothing has changed from the night before.

Sometimes there is nothing we can do. Like the housework, we may have to let it go one more day, not because we want to, but for whatever reason, we can't do it. At these times, we simply do the best we can. We take care of the stomachache or the headache or the backache, or just the blues. And as for the house, we do little things, picking up one room at a time, or maybe just an area of a room. When we are ready, and when we can, we will do more.

* * * * * * * * *

"Every stride of progress starts with one step, and then another."

"Why can't everything be okay with my family and me."

During our healing, our families can be one of our strongest sources of support or our most difficult barrier to overcome. Healing is individualistic. Some of us who have children may find that they are welcome diversions and lifesavers when it comes to our healing. Our children may be a source of hope and inspiration when our own inner children are connecting positively with our own young offspring. Partners may also be strong, supportive people. Or not. We may find our partners to be the life-saving force to our healing, providing the comfort and space we may need to let ourselves go to fully heal. Our partners may be the ones to bring us back to safe touch and safe love. Our partners may be the steady lighthouses in the hurricane storms as our emotions go thundering about us, and like stormy waves, come crashing down upon us. It may be the lone light which our partners shine that keeps us hopeful that all is not lost and that sometime soon the storm will abate. Or not. Some of us may have partners just waiting for us to get better and leave us be to hold our own until the storm moves elsewhere.

If our partners are with us on this healing journey, then all the better. If not, it is a sad state of personal affairs, and yet another obstacle to overcome or addressed so that at least our partners are not a hindrance to our healing. We can never do enough talking and honest communicating of where we are on this journey, even if it's only to say we can't talk or we hear that our partners can't be there for us. It is in dealing with truth, with whatever aspect is presented, that we make our most progressive steps. If we have partners and children, then our relationships with them are an integral part of our healing.

* * * * * * * * *

"My family, along with my healing, is my priority."

"How can I find my center?"

Sometimes we really don't know who we are, and we just become nonplused in the face of the masked rider that comes skidding out during certain periods in our lives, just when we thought we knew who we were. Suddenly, we don't know our belief systems for being here in this world, and it seems we're skating on treacherous ice no matter what direction we spin in.

No matter how prepared we think we may be, we are still taken by surprise by the apparent crack in a foundation we once thought was so solid. We may find ourselves caught in the moment and find ourselves slumping down. We may want to throw our hands up in the air and give up.

Better yet, we should simply stop and take a deep breath. Perhaps we need to take a look and make another assessment; after all, a crack is not the same as a wide-open hole. Cracks can be filled, mended, rebuilt, and even be skated away from or circled around.

* * * * * * * * *

"Falling down doesn't mean I can't get up— again."

February 1

FIGHTING
I am so tired
of the raping
the threats
the guns
and bullets
and knives
the lack of
peaceful warriors
with boundless visions
and valiant dreams
to heal
the sick
the hungry
the wounded
vanquishing poverty
ending evil
increasing warriors
renewing life

"What can open my eyes to my untapped power?"

Most tasks come with instructions and many goals are developed with well thought-out planning. However, when it comes to reclaiming our self-power, there are no instructions. The human machine, unlike other equipment, comes with those rather ethereal rules and regulations. Much is contingent on not how we work, but rather, tapping into unknown resources we didn't know we had, usually as a process of elimination.

Learning powerlessness is a complicated process. Some of us were more powerless than others because of our experiences, and too, vice versa. But all of us have the potential to reclaim all of our personal power. It is no secret that our perpetrators took that power away. In fact, that is what makes our personal abuse history our reference point in life— everything from that point on is related to that experience.

If we are willing to look specifically at how that power was stripped from us, then our chances are extremely good at getting it back. After all, you can't reclaim something if you don't know where it is. And sometimes in reclaiming our power, we must see how we are giving it away. Those of us who suffer from panic disorders, life-long anxieties, phobias, and post traumatic stress disorder know only too well the power-makers of intense fear, learned helplessness, and inculcated powerlessness.

If we want to move forward in our healing, then we must put ourselves in positions where these areas can be challenged and where they are deeply entrenched in our minds. That is the scary part: to risk what we know to chance, even though now we are very different than when we were children. We must have the courage to take a chance on ourselves, for if not us, then who? And who does any of this matter to anyway, except ourselves? For those who would give up immediately and say, "I can't," the answer, of course, is "I can."

* * * * * * * * *

"If faith can move a mountain, I can reclaim my own power."

"Why is my life filled with so many crises?"

It is hard to trust peace when it becomes more frequent in our lives. Many of us learned that crisis was a lifestyle. We carried it over into our workplaces. We took jobs that were demanding, knowing we could handle whatever came up. It didn't matter that maybe inside ourselves we were in turmoil and freaking out. What mattered is that we handled the external crisis and got the job done.

Some of us also carry that into our relationships. We attach ourselves to partners that, in some way, allow us to play out the pattern of which we grew up in. This may be someone who, just by their nature, unconsciously sets off triggers from our past and we try to find a way to accept that person, somehow hoping that this time, we can find resolution to that past time.

Many of us don't trust peace and goodness. We think that somehow it will be taken away from us, that it is untrustworthy to believe that happiness and goodness can reign for long periods of time within our lives. The truth, which we have a hard time accepting, is that our lives can have goodness in it. The truth is that if we look around, especially at children, we will see that we are embodied with the gift to experience happiness and peacefulness within our lives. It may seem funny to have to encourage anyone to trust happiness and peace, but for we who are women of color and survivors, that, too, takes courage— the courage to believe that such joy can come into our lives, that it is real, and a substantial part of our being.

* * * * * * * * *

"The more I trust in peace and happiness in my life, the more real it is."

"If my healing is possible, what's taking so long?"

Believing we can heal from our abuse is one of the harder truths for us to accept. Given a process that often calls for one step forward and twenty back, the possibility that we might be fully healed seems slim to narrow, if at all. Some of us have been consciously working on our issues for years and nothing seems to have significantly changed. We still feel that basically, our lives, even though manifesting some differences, remain untouched by our search for the "Holy Grail" of healing.

Healing often means that our old wounds do not interfere with our functioning in our daily lives. Let us not mistake healing for perfectionism, as some of us often do. Healing means that the dynamics of our issues have changed. We may still occasionally have flashbacks and intrusive thoughts and the occasional memory retrieval, but if we are on our healing path, they are not the same as when they first appeared. We may be able to distance ourselves from the flashbacks, may be able to banish the intrusive thoughts and may be less threatened by the return of a few painful memories.

To the skeptic in us, the fact that much of this is not an immediate conversion to health may indicate that our time and investment in our healing is overdrawn. It might be helpful to remember that many of our defenses have come from a lifetime of abuse. Sometimes it takes almost another lifetime to gain a healthy and balanced life. The skeptic in us must be willing to look at the small steps we are taking and not just how long the journey is taking to heal.

* * * * * * * * *

"Unfounded skepticism is just another voice in my head from the past."

"Where is it?"

She slipped and fell again. Just as she was doing so well, she thought. Losing her balance in the pouring rain, her backpack dropped and everything came tumbling out as she lurched forward and fell flat on her face. Searching around for all her things, the rain fell even harder and she wiped her eyes with her arms and struggled to see where everything had landed. She could not see the one thing she'd so lovingly protected throughout her journey. What if it had rolled down the hill into the river and sank to the bottom? Getting up, she stumbled and immediately fell again, learning she had sprained her left ankle in the fall. Crawling around on her knees, she began grabbing at her things, stuffing them in her backpack, regardless of their condition. Gingerly, she stood up and looked around. She could see a little better, and this time the rain seemed to be washing her face clear. Still, her heart sank. The most important item was missing and there was only one in the world like it and it was hers. It was irreplaceable. Why bother going on? She would not be the same. Nothing could be the same. When she realized her object was gone for good, that there was no way she could retrieve it, she slid to the ground on the back of a tall tree and let the rain fall upon her as it willed. You couldn't tell her tears from the pouring rain upon her face.

Time dripped as did the rain, and not knowing how long she had been sitting, she stood up; and as she walked there was a slight limp to her left leg. She had to complete her journey. She adjusted her backpack and began walking again. The rain was easing up, the ground wasn't as muddy as before, and her ankle seemed to get stronger with each step she took. Sighing, she stuck her hands in her pocket and suddenly a smile came upon her face. It was right there in her side pocket. Perhaps her gem had a life of its own. With pure joy, she jumped up and shouted, twirled herself around and hugged her body, forgetting the pain from her ankle. Suddenly, nothing seemed impossible. She could travel forever down the crooked, muddy path, knowing she would go where she must.

* * * * * * * * *

"What we truly need is always with us."

"Is anybody worthy of my trust?"

Survivors do not have a monopoly on pain and suffering. However, it is true that those whose paths may offer a great deal of difficulty to heal are those who have a personal history of CSA, especially if the abuser is not a stranger. If anything is severely damaged in the life of a survivor, it is the ability to trust the very people who are closest to us in relationships and proximity. Oftentimes, healing is not addressed until the survivor is an adult. And to heal this betrayal wound, to be able to love and to attach and to connect with another human being, we have to be willing to trust others we wish to be close to.

Imagine if everyone went to sleep one night and, upon the morning, awakened to the fact that daylight had not yet come. Can we imagine the disorientation...the shock...the disbelief...the denial? Suppose the daylight didn't return until 13 years had passed? Would it be possible to explain to those born afterwards and when daylight returned, exactly what it was like to not have daylight for a number of years? Would those who didn't experience it understand? Would those who did experience it ever go to sleep again with the security and knowledge that upon waking up, they would be greeted with daylight? Of course not. They would always be expecting the *possibility* that daylight might go away again, simply because it happened once.

People are much more unpredictable than nature. Nature has law and order, and natural things are not thrown out of balance unless something is artificially introduced. Trusting again is not cart blanche for "blind" trust. It does, though, mean taking calculated risks on the people we choose to be in our lives and who we allow ourselves to be closest to: lovers, spouses, partners, key intimates, and significant others. All of us make mistakes and any loved one can betray a trust. It is up to us to decide which violated trust can be mended, and that which is not. Only we can do that for ourselves, and it *is* something we can do.

* * * * * * * * *

"Like all my stakes, I can claim my trust."

"Who am I today?"

The moment of our incest, rape, or molestation— whatever form the abuse took— it was a moment that forever changed our lives. It forever changed how we as children related to other members in our families, and who we became. And regardless of who it was— a brother, a sister, a mom, a dad, an uncle, an aunt, a trusted family friend, a neighbor who visited frequently, a minister who often came to dinner, a teacher, a coach, a babysitter— we desperately tried not to be alone with them again. Much to our chagrin, our dismay, and our health, this was not possible. And the closer to us in relationship, the harder it was to escape. Even if we did escape (and a number of us did), it still did not change the rupture of our relationships and, most importantly, our personal feelings of safety. It began a chain of behaviors all adopted to make sure *no one* could ever hurt us again.

Some of us chose various personas to handle our abuse. Some of us were not successful at all, and our perpetrators became the bane of our existence. If we could not escape physically, then we made mental and emotional escapes and, in the process, cut off not only our feelings, but whole parts of ourselves. We created parts of ourselves to deal with different situations and different people; and in the process, we lost contact with our core selves. We lost touch with what it meant to have a personal opinion, to be separate from others while at the same time maintaining who we were. *And,* we who are women of color would *never* tell anyone about these splits unless we lost control of these protective parts and they came out on their own, and then it was chalked up in our communities to something like, "You know, she's not all there, po' chile."

We have the opportunity in our healing to reclaim all the parts of ourselves. Some of us have literally split off. We can choose to integrate the parts, or to accept them as being separate. In our healing, what we do on our journey and how we do it is up to us. We are the ones, now, to make all of our choices.

* * * * * * * * *

"Regardless of who I present to the world, I know who I am."

"Why did I do what I did?"

Sexual abuse steals authenticity. It steals our soul's feelings. Some of us decided it was too painful to laugh, that we had no right to joy, and so seldom did smiles play upon our faces. Some of us thought crying left us too vulnerable, and so despite the pain, we allowed no tears. Some of us thought our anger is what caused our abuse, that we were bad children with bad tempers, and so we pretended to the world that we were the nicest people on earth. And some of us thought we were abused because of our bodies, and therefore, we hid them behind huge clothing; or we stuffed ourselves with food; or we didn't eat at all, hoping the perpetrators couldn't see the real us, and wouldn't want us for their sexual desires.

When it came to the abuse, it didn't matter. Our perpetrators didn't care what disguises we were dressed in. Their job was to go beyond our clothes anyway. Our perpetrators waited only for time and chance to commit their various acts of assault. So despite what we did to hide the "real us" they came and violated us anyway. And because nothing we did worked to stop them, we blamed ourselves. To our child-youthful mind, that is the only thing that made sense. If this ugly thing kept happening, then it must have been something we were doing. Short of removing ourselves from our environment, there was nothing we could have done to change the behavior of the perpetrators.

Our healing demands that we remove our self-blame. There is nothing we did to encourage the abuse, no matter how we acted or what we did. If, as children, we acted inappropriately, then it was up to the adult to set the boundaries and limits. Abuse is always the onus of the perpetrator. In removing our self-blame we allow other parts of our souls to heal and come forth. We allow into our consciousness self-acceptance, self-esteem, self-confidence, and most of all, self-respect. We allow ourselves to exist with the rest of the world, and we need not hide anymore.

* * * * * * * * * *

"We can not expect children to take responsibility for the actions of an adult."

"When will this winter ever end?"

Seasons of time may be triggers for any number of us. For some, the winter is the time a severe depression may set in because it was wintertime when we seemed most trapped. It was cold out, it got dark early, and our abuse may have seemed to have started early in the night. For others, it may be the summer, with its long days stretching ahead and with our perpetrators having more time off from work to make our lives miserable. It could be that for others, it is spring that brings inexplicable sadness with its promise of new beginnings, when in our lives the same ugly things were happening over and over again. And still for others, it may be autumn that makes us feel like crying all day. Autumn with its promise that the old year is ending, and so is the possibility of our abuse. But, of course, abuse was never contingent on the seasons, only on the time of day.

We need not be prisoners of the past even if events and seasons remind us more at some times than others the places we have been, the lives we have lead, and that we may wish to change. In a life without abuse history, there are still feelings of despair, depression, and sadness. In a life free of abuse history, these are normal feelings that spear on change for a person's life.

Here we are in the stronghold of winter. We need not be afraid anymore of its early nights. In fact, we can wrap ourselves up in its covering and lie before a fire, basking in the truth that we are no longer children suffering at the hands of our abuser. We are not miracle workers, not even in our own lives. But wondrous and good things can happen regardless of where we have been in our past. Our present says that much of what happens is now up to us, the seasons notwithstanding.

* * * * * * * * *

"There is a season of time transcending even my past."

"How do they sleep at night?"

Perhaps it was the way evening fell. And, too, maybe it was the soft pelting of the rain upon her rooftop and the walls of her house. Or maybe it was the low lighting. It could have been the combination of all of that and the strong, harmonic voices of the group Sweet Honey in the Rock singing, "We who believe in freedom can not rest...," keeping time with the beating of her heart and the rhythm of her arms mopping the floor. Whatever it was, it made her think of blankets and velvet, and long, black arms that saved her life. It made her think of the underground railroad of women saving other children just like her.

The night of her escape came back to her as sure as the voices transforming her present. She stood up slowly, letting the dizziness pass her and steadying her body for the moment. She took nothing for granted. Being in her own home and being with her loved ones were things she had worked hard for. They did not come easy to her. And so she was grateful to the many loving women who had helped her be free.

She squinted out the window, looking through misted pane. She wondered how many other children in chilly, dangerous homes were in need of freedom. She wondered how many would sleep undisturbed without the creak of the floor awakening their anxiety for what only they and their perpetrator knew lay secreted in the unfolding night.

Turning deliberately, she continued cleaning, wiping her stove and wished, for perhaps the hundredth time, that all the problems of all abused children could be as easily wiped and cleaned out of existence. She couldn't save all the children, but she might be able to save one or two. Now, if everybody else joined in, wouldn't that be a human revolution? She scrubbed at the stain on the oven glass and pondered how she might begin her cadre of healing revolutionaries.

* * * * * * * * *

"Freedom is not a bestowal for a select group of people, but to everyone."

"What is this feeling that keeps screaming to get out?"

Rage. In its best light, it is like the ferociously revered mother bear protecting her cub. However, on its own it is like a tornado sweeping an open field with a lone homestead surrounded only by a wooden fence. Sometimes we must learn how to harness this powerful defense or, like the beast, we will eat our own young inner selves.

We who are women of color know only too well its presence embedded in our bodies. After all, we spend much time staving it off and hoping it will stay dormant before it does destruction, or rather, further destruction. We are attracted and repelled by it at the same time.

Let us not fool ourselves, for it may be the last bastion we hurdle to be truly free. It may be the final layer of ourselves that says we have a right to a healthy and safe life from those that would prey upon us. The world of human beings is not always user-friendly, and we can transform our rage into righteous indignation against true enemies. Untamed, our rage makes enemies of everyone, including those closest to us, and those that would love us.

Rage is no lightweight instructor. If we do not quell it healthily, give it sanction, it will eat us alive. We can not destroy it, for we would destroy ourselves in the process. We must make peace with it. And so we must acknowledge it, must give credence to its birthright, must give place to its legitimacy to exist, and must give space for its reason to be. Our rage knows of the awful depths of our isolation and silence due to our personal histories of incest and/or CSA; and so must we respect, it just as we must respect all other parts of our being. If it is in us, then it is there to tell us something about ourselves. Something about us needs healing, which is something only we can do for ourselves

* * * * * * * * *

"If nothing else, my rage tells me when I think I've been violated."

"What is this new experience?"

It is okay to have nothing exciting to do for the day. It is okay to become part of the daily or weekend routine of everyday living. We do not have to experience highs and lows all the time. Sometimes we are like the ocean, simply moving about as nature intended us to. We are like the waves that wash up on the shore with the ocean receding back with yet another wave to wash upon the shore. We do not have to have a cloudy sky in the backdrop threatening to break the oceanic waves. It is really okay to have the sun spreading its warmth and promising a gorgeous day. Sometimes we just need to be without signals and triggers.

Perhaps that is the hardest part for us. Few of us can remember having long stretches of time that didn't mean the world was coming to an end or that we were about to have our peace disturbed by an unwanted and fearful act. Peace and moving about within our own rhythms was not part of our everyday living. In fact, by the time we became independent adults, everything we heard and saw portended possible danger to our space.

Finally, we have arrived at a point where life is what it is like without the abuse, without the memories, without the flashbacks full of fears and anxieties, and we now find ourselves in a new situation calling for us to just be and go on about our daily business. We may find that this is exactly what we've wanted all along— the space and time to be and to do little, piddly things. Nothing is wrong with that. In fact, we have to learn to acknowledge that all might be right, despite old voices of fears and doubts, in our own little worlds.

* * * * * * * * *

"Some days are just for piddling around."

"How does a person sustain hatred in their heart?"

In 1963 in Birmingham, Alabama, four little Black girls were killed by a bomb thrown into a church where families were attending Sunday worship service. In one split of a second of a moment, the lives of all the people in the town were changed. In fact, the lives of many people across the nation were changed, and this act of hatred motivated many people to eradicate such animosity out of the country's heart. And for the families of those little girls, their lives were irrevocably changed forever by the racial hatred that burned in the hearts of not a few actively hating men and women.

In some ways, this act of hatred has no color boundaries. In some ways, this act of hatred has no "ism" boundaries— sexism, racism, nationalism. In some ways, it is pure hatred looking for a form to express itself. In the lives of survivors, it is in the arena of sex and children. Like the survivors of that Birmingham bombing, survivors of CSA remain perplexed years later at how such hatred could burn in the heart of someone else, and cause such a person to strike out at another in the form of sexual molestation and assault. While a number of abusers leave their victims physically scarred, and some even murder their victims, most of the damage abusers do is in the form of emotional and psyche abuse.

We may never know how evil takes root in the heart of one person. We may never know how it is that that person comes to live with his or her evil thoughts and remains untouched by the damage they do to others. What we do know is that in our anger and our rage and our pain, that we can not allow, under any circumstances, that hatred to become a part of us. We must find ways to safeguard our hearts from such self-embraced hatred. It leaves nothing in its wake but death. A healing journey, difficult as the path may be at some many turns, offers us life

* * * * * * * * *

"Thankfully, and there but for Spirit of Truth, I am not my perpetrator."

"So, what's with this cupid stuff anyway?"

Valentine's Day is mainly for lovers. While couples run around reminded by 5th Avenue that their significant other should be the most important person in their life today, this day provokes much anxiety, anger, and snorting from survivors.

Some of us are angry at ourselves and our perpetrators on this day. We are angry with ourselves because we are not in a relationship, something we yearn to have more than anything else; and yet we know that it is because of who we are at the moment, that we do not have a relationship, do not have that intimacy and closeness that others around us seem to have. Some of us are thoroughly angry with our abusers because we know that much of the residue has to do with what they perpetrated on us.

Some of us have nothing but scorn for advertisements selling love and happiness with a box of chocolates or a diamond ring, and we snort each time we see them. We have no room in our hearts for such feelings and such sentimentality. And we are glad we are not part of the crowd looking for symbolic gifts with which to proclaim our love for someone who may or may not exist.

For other survivors, this day is anxiety-filled because we do not have a lover in our life and think that's the way it will always be. The commercials on TV and on the radio and all the brouhaha are reminders of how we are failing in the love and sex departments.

And for others, this is a fun day, a day to celebrate love with a special person whom we love and who loves us. And we are glad that we can celebrate these gifts that we have received, especially the ability to love another person, when once we thought it was impossible.

* * * * * * * * *

"Today is my day to celebrate or not."

"Why can't I accept my own feelings?"

Deeply feeling our emotions can be overwhelming. Having spent much of our life keeping feelings at bay, embodying them once again can be scary. We don't know what this new energy is about. We don't know if we can control it like we used to. Some of us experienced sexual pleasure during our abuse, so we cut off our feelings and disappeared deep inside, lest we become like our perpetrators. When we heal and let those feelings back in, some of those same feelings with their accompanying conflicts arise; for example, pleasure and guilt. "I shouldn't be feeling like this," we say to ourselves. "I must be a bad person if I feel this good," we think.

Sometimes, underneath all those feelings are our feelings of rage; and we think if we acknowledge or feel that rage that we, too, may become like the abuser and hurt others, not unlike the way we were hurt.

We can find appropriate outlets for our feelings, appropriate people with which to share our feelings: friends, loved ones, our support group, our therapists— people who will understand and recognize the person who we really are. But first we must recognize that we have the right to all of our feelings. We have the right to exist even though we were taught early in our lives we had no rights, and it was a bad thing that we existed. None of that was true.

The truth is that we're different now, and we're in a different time and space. We can acknowledge all our feelings, pleasurable and rageful, and whatever other feelings come up and that does not turn us into our abusers. It is up to us to choose when and how we want to express these newly reclaimed emotions and feelings.

* * * * * * * * *

"To be human is to give myself permission to accept all of my feelings."

"Who am I to a child?"

We are role models to every child we come into contact with, be it on our jobs, at home, with the neighborhood children, or just chance-passing through stores and other places where we humans tend to congregate.

We never know in a chance passing what our affect will be on a child. However, many of us have memories of how the smile of one adult in our childhood has always stayed with us. We remember how that person, even in a chance passing, became an indicator of what we could expect from other adults or what was possible from other adults.

At every point of contact with a child, we are either a parent or teacher, and in some instances, both. If we have children of our own, we are both and we are always on duty even when we tell them, "Give me a break...I'm on time out."

Children are creatures of resiliency. It seems to be part of their hidden genetic code to disregard those people or things that cause them pain and to move on to those activities and people that make them feel good.

We women who have known what it is to be a child who has constantly had her boundaries broken and/or have learned that adults can be extremely dangerous living beings, know the power an adult has over a child. We also know what it is to be the beacon of safety, what it means to have an adult you can trust and who will let you be yourself. At any given time, we send that message out to all the children we have contact with, especially the children in passing. In one moment, we can teach an abused child that there is hope and love in the world, rather than a life already present with a reality they are resigned to accept to survive in their child abuse-filled world.

* * * * * * * * *

"One adult can make all the difference in the life of one child."

"Why can't she just 'get over' this?"

There's a lot of talk about having a victimized mentality, and a great deal of it is pointed at survivors. "Why can't those folks just get over it? Why don't they go ahead and accept it and move on with their lives?" These things are said as if survivors want nothing more than to be: depressed, despairing, fearful, panicky, anxiety-ridden, disassociated, hyper vigilant and just generally overwhelmed by the stresses of daily living. Nonetheless, we wake up everyday and face whatever fears, anxieties, panic attacks, or any of the other post traumatic stress disorders that play upon our minds and our lives.

One thing we can agree upon: Survivors do want to "get over it" and move forward in our lives. We don't want intrusive thoughts from the past invading our present lives. We don't want the memories and the flashbacks. We are extremely tired of living depressed lives, tired of the despair that, at times, can seem like part of our everyday routine, tired of the anxieties that creep up on us as we go about our daily tasks; and we are extremely tired of the fearfulness that invades our lives by external forces. It is not safe to be a woman in this society. It is not safe no matter where you go; and coming from a background where our personal safety, for some of us, was attacked daily, we are quite aware of the unsafe, life-threatening possibilities now in our daily present lives.

We survivors are some of the bravest people walking the earth. Many of us have been walking this healing path a long time, and we are familiar with it. Knowing the strength of spirit in survivors and in we who are women of color, we gladly give a hand to others following, and reach for those who walk ahead of us. We don't have to "get over" this, don't have to do it alone, but we can move forward towards healthier, and yes, happier lives.

* * * * * * * * *

"I will continue my journey as long as necessary for my healing."

"Why do I feel worse than before?"

There are times in our healing when we may start backtracking, when we will feel worse than when we first started on our healing journey. We find ourselves doing all the "right" things and still, we seem to be sinking even lower than when we first started. Frantically, we start searching our minds for any hint that we are not healing "right," that we are forgetting to do something, or that we are being punished because we can not understand why. We wonder, *Why did this happen to me? Why was I chosen? What did I do wrong? Why am I being punished?* In a world where there seems to be so much law and order in the natural scheme of life, where most of us find there is rhyme and reason "out there," we are perplexed as to why there seems to be no rhyme or reason to our lives. We get stuck, thinking, *"Why did the perpetrator choose me?"*

No matter the various situations of how we came to be a survivor, *we did nothing wrong. It is not our fault*. We are not being punished for anything or even for being born. We have this pain and we are survivors because some perpetrator chose to act a certain way in regard to us, and that is the only reason this exists in our lives. The only part we have in any of this is to heal ourselves from its impact and after-effects in our daily lives.

There are about three phases to any layer of our healing. First, recognizing the problem; secondly, accepting the problem for what is; and lastly, committing ourselves to healing our wounds. Nothing more. Nothing less.

* * * * * * * * *

"Put the blame where it belong— at the feet of the perpetrators."

"Why is this happening to me?"

Seldom are survivors who have been incested or sexually assaulted and/or abused by a family member, vindicated, validated, and accepted fully back into their family of origin no matter how clear the truth and facts are. There comes a point for some survivors when the truth of what they are saying can not be denied anymore to any of their family members. Even if and when this truth is accepted, there seems to always be a barrier that can not be crossed over back into the fold before the incest or assault happened.

We know we can not change the past. Those who have the most to lose want nothing to do with us. It is important to us that there are family members that accept our truth, but it does not lessen the pain of those in the family who the know truth and still want nothing at all to do with us, or who just tolerate our presence. And each time we come into contact with them, hopefully looking for some sign that perceptions have shifted, that feelings have shifted, we are disappointed that it is all still the same.

In contrast, the perpetrator may continue to have acceptance in the family, particularly with incest. Yet we who are survivors and women of color are still somehow blamed for the pain that has fallen upon the family. In fact, we may be become the symbolic icon from the old adage, "killing the messenger because of the message." Through time and wisdom, we learn to accept the truth and all the ramifications of accepting such a truth. That's why our friends, loved ones, significant others, support groups, etc. are so important in our road to healing. Eventually we learn to "accept the things I can not change," and to "change the things I can," and in our healing, gain "the wisdom to know the difference."

* * * * * * * * *

"Our wisdom comes from living our truths."

"Why?"

His prey, deep in thought watching the evening sunset was easy and weak. He thought. It did not matter to him who she was. She was simply his. He would do what he want, and wait for however long it would take. In his world it was timeless, and he waited only for opportunity.

At first she looked into his glassy eyes, saw its evil gleam and instinct told her to immediately close hers. When he was finished, he thought he'd left her for dead. He thought he'd silenced her forever. Humming to himself, he pulled up to his full height, zipped his pants, turned and sauntered away as if what he'd done was a high achievement instead of the unspeakable acts of atrocities upon the woman he'd left on the ground. He gave no more thought to the dead he left behind than when he first came upon her and implemented his attack.

He did not see her rise. It would take almost a lifetime to get to her feet. But get to her feet she did. She would gingerly put one foot down and then the other. She would stand, shakily at first. Sometimes she would fall as soon as she stood up straight. But each time she got back up, she stood up straighter and, more firmly grounded. Eventually, she would stand her full height, shaking out her arms and hands— parts of her she thought had been broken. She could move and that was what counted. She would walk to the edge of the park where she saw the headlights of cars speeding by. She did not know how, but somewhere in the recesses of her mind, she knew it was possible. She looked down the long road that would lead her to help and began her first step on her particular path of healing. It would not be her last. He might have damaged parts of her body, violated her most inner, physical life force, but in her shock during the attack, her mind removed itself from the duration of the assault; and her spirit, as always, began its immediate ministry of healing her embodied soul.

* * * * * * * * *

"There are parts of me that are absolutely indestructible."

"Why isn't there anything to do?

15 THINGS TO COMFORT AND MAKE HAPPY ALL OUR INNER CHILDREN:

1. Drink a hot cup of chocolate milk with marshmallows on top.
2. Curl up to a favorite (safe) person and lay your head on their lap.
3. Color, draw, paint, or write.
4. Have a tea party and invite your favorite toys.
5. Chew as many pieces of bubble gum as you like.
6. Watch a favorite video again and again and again.
7. Play and sing a favorite song again and again and again.
8. Read a favorite book in bed or on the sofa.
9. Take a warm bath.
10. Find a friend and go for a walk on the beach, or on a hiking trail.
11. Go outside and sit in the sun and do nothing.
12. Indulge yourself and buy a favorite toy you've always wanted.
13. Go shopping and buy something you don't need, but want.
14. Buy cotton candy, or red or caramel candy apples.
15. Make popcorn and eat it.

* * * * * * * * *

"Our inner restlessness is often a cry from one of our inner children."

"Was ever I a child?"

With no blame. With no right or wrong. A newness to each experience. With purity. Undefiled. No injuries. In complete form. To be as meant in creation. Sleeping unaware.

Bright, shimmering paleness in midnight blue. The darkest hour before dawn. Undisturbed, protective silence. Red sun setting in on the large western sky. Morning's air after the first night's blanket of snow. The untouched, fallen leaves and pine needles in the deep of a forest, awaiting a nap from a deserving creature. The ocean at noon on summer's hottest day. The beginning arch of an ethereal rainbow peeking out of the clouds.

The first taste of ice cream we remember. The love of anything just because it's beautiful. The wind blowing softly through our hair. The first time we hear music. The first time we pray and connect with Spirit.

The love of music. The love of song. The love of laughter. The love of people sharing and giving and being included.

Was ever I a child so free?

* * * * * * * * *

"I can be free as a child anytime I want to be."

"Well, how long will this take?"

Okay. Everybody who thinks healing is easy work and done quickly, raise your hand.

As time goes on and our lives move forward, we can see a number of changes. For those of us beginning our healing journey, just the fact that we are now willing to accept and look at the abuse that happened in our lives is a move forward, even if it appears we don't have a clue as to what's going on in our outer and inner lives.

Regardless of where we are on the healing path, there are days of discouragement, seemingly underscored by a need to wait for further unfolding from our Higher Consciousness. There are days when we wake up to our same lives where it seems nothing much has changed, and we wonder if our healing efforts are in vain. Some of us may think that we will always be stuck with our old feelings and behaviors. Some of us may simply be stuck in that difficult place where we are unable to see the many changes we have made and the progress we are making.

We must learn to live not only by new measuring sticks, but also with the insights we have gained to old problems no longer existing. Our need to wait may be a difficult marker for us to accept, however we may now be in a place where waiting is what our healing is about. To let our bodies and our subconscious minds do their work while we go on about the daily tasks before us is one of our necessary steps in the healing process, regardless of our impatience. At one time, waiting may have been something we didn't want to do since it meant anticipating something painful and unwanted happening to us. Now, sometimes waiting *is* the healing mode, and its length of time is different for each one of us as we are all unique individuals.

* * * * * * * * *

"Waiting can be nature's way of giving us respite on our journey."

"Does it matter if I hurt?"

Hurt and love, pain and joy, have no color. We who are women of color with CSA personal histories spend much of our energy denying our feelings, especially those that hurt and cause pain. And we who are women of color seldom have the luxury nor the space nor the permission from our inner selves or our communities to say, "I hurt." We will, at times, readily acknowledge that we are angry, that we are depressed, that we are outraged, that we are happy, and sometimes even that we are afraid. But few are the lips that utter, "I hurt."

Children say they hurt. A child stumbles and falls, scrapes its leg and gets up crying and runs over to its mother and says, "I hurt, mommy." When was the last time we fell and scraped some part of ourselves and ran to someone and said, "I hurt"? No doubt, it was some time when we were children.

We are no longer children and yet, even unto the oldest adult in the world, our pain can still cause us to hurt. We who are women of color, who have often given so much to the outer world, perhaps even in disregard to our own personal problems, must take personal time and honor our own pain and give ear to the part of ourselves that say, "I hurt." We can learn and acknowledge that we are as worthy as any other individual and deserving of love and nurturance to that part of ourselves that wish to express the hurt. Often that means the expression of our emotions; and the self-recognition of our pain and its validation by ourselves and those who sincerely claim to love us, support us, and care about us.

* * * * * * * * *

"Love and its expression has a domino effect to any and all in its proximity."

"What do I do when the 'ties that bind' are broken?"

Family is the first social unit that we are all part of. It causes many of us sadness when these family bonds are broken. Even if the abuse took place outside our family of origin, the perpetrators may have strong ties to our families, and therefore, affect our contact with our families.

There are numbers of survivors who have no contact at all with their families. Some of us have made the decision that it is in our best interests to have no contact whatsoever. Even when we are adults the abuse can continue, and so we remove ourselves totally from this unhealthy situation. Nonetheless, it does not change our feelings of loneliness and isolation from the rest of our family members. We may have brothers and sisters who can not maintain contact with us, even if they believe in us, because of their loyalty to the family. There are other brothers and sisters who do not maintain contact with us simply because they do not believe us, or like our perpetrators, pretend it didn't happen. Some of these same brothers and sisters may have experienced similar abuse, but choose not to remember and/or deny it happened so that they may maintain contact with family members who are abusers.

Then, there are the family members that are our advocates and who support us. For those folks we are grateful, because many of these people were important to us during our childhood when the abuse was happening, and perhaps were the only ones who believed in us. Some of them were pivotal in our seeking help with the incest problems in our families.

These lasting family relationships need our nurturance and sustenance. For those whom we can not continue to have relationships with, we need to grieve our loss. The ugly legacy of CSA or incest can be just as terminal as death itself. We survivors are given the task to know and learn where the flicker of the candle is still lit, and when the wind has blown it out totally.

* * * * * * * * *

"Loss of family, regardless of reason, requires honoring our grief."

"What's in it for me?"

What does it mean to take a risk and change behaviors we do not like or want for ourselves? These behaviors we wish to change were/are rooted in our personal make-up because at some point they worked in our survival. Acting a certain way, closing ourselves off from others, putting distances between ourselves and other people, denying there is anything wrong, disassociating from the world going on around us or accepting that this is the way life is— that this is the way we are— all have their foundation as a means for us to survive a situation that was ego and life threatening to us.

While many of us may have been terrified of anticipated abuse events, others of us experienced them as life/death situations because our lives were indeed threatened. Some of us lived with horrific, abusive people passing themselves off as our caretakers and/or parents. The old saying, "Nobody knows what goes on behind close doors," speaks well to the issue of CSA in our societies. So our defenses served a purpose to see us through intensely hostile living environments.

In our healing, to take a risk means exchanging new behavior for old behavior and dealing with the feelings they ultimately will bring up. Some of these feelings will be freeing and welcomed as we begin to get in touch with feelings that express our joy and happiness. Other feelings will be extremely threatening because they will be ones of sadness, hurt, and grief— feelings we ran away from during the abuse because we experienced them as intolerable. As a child, they were intolerable because we were powerless to change our situations. But as adults, these cut-off feelings are the way back to our wholesome selves; they are the way for reclamation of self.

* * * * * * * * *

"Taking risks I choose means the possibility of getting what I want for myself."

"What would it be like to be unafraid?"

Our fears we embody are often simple ones. Mostly, though, it seems as if we fear what people will think and say about us. We fear others will tap into what hurts us most and mirror it back to us in words, or use it against us, or reject us totally— they will want no part of us.

Being survivors, this is not difficult to understand. When abused, we have no idea of why someone would want to cause us that kind of pain and so, especially because we are usually children when it happens, we internalize their actions to become our thoughts. If someone is hurting us it must mean that we are "bad." If they are treating us badly then it must be because of something we did. If someone suddenly starts yelling at us because of something we said, then our words must have caused that person to be that way. If someone starts verbally abusing us and calling us out of our names and telling us we are stupid, dumb, selfish, useless, worthless, a whore and a bitch, we take it in and all of it sort of settles within us. Internally, we become all the negative things that were projected our way.

Fear, of course, can be paralyzing and can stop us from progressing in our lives. It can also be our motivation to change. There doesn't seem to be anybody on the human record who has said, "Hey, I really like living in fear all the time. It keeps me on my toes!" We can make fear work for us as it is intended— for fight or flight survival. Anything else along the fear lines is simply excess baggage.

* * * * * * * * *

"When I give up my fears, suddenly I discover a world I didn't know existed."

"Why isn't there a manual to help me with my decisions?"

Uncertainty is a good defense. It keeps us from committing and moving forward or making mistakes. As long as we are uncertain about something, say a decision we need to make, then we stall the inevitable, perhaps learning something we are afraid to know.

Survivors of CSA can spend a lot of our energy being uncertain about our environment and who we are. We continually question our motivations, as well as those of other people. We learn that nothing can be taken at face value, and that perhaps others, like our perpetrators, have hidden agendas. Any time a person we have learned to totally trust crosses a boundary, then everybody afterwards becomes suspect in our minds. We think, *Um, it happened once, it could happen again.*

There are no guarantees in life and no absolutes, even though we may wish fervently that it were true. But it is not and we can not stand still in life. Human beings either grow or they stagnate, but they do not stand still. Not making a decision is, in fact, making a decision not to make a decision. Not making a decision is to decide to put things on hold, and when we do that, we put our lives on hold. In some sense, we continue our own abuse by punishing ourselves by not doing for ourselves.

It is okay for us now to make decisions, even if it means we make mistakes. By making mistakes we learn to choose what it is we really want to do, and we get to see ourselves in another way.

* * * * * * * * *

"I don't have to run away anymore."

March 1

WAR

They love
have children
he goes off
to war
and now
she goes, too
leaving their children
with others waiting
for a war to end
perhaps if she came home
and he did, too
they would
put down their arms
and fight no more
and find the peace
waiting for the death
of their weapons

"Is anybody else tripping like me?"

Everybody's healing journey is different, just as everybody's life is individual and diverse. Still, there comes a point in all journeys where it becomes exceedingly tempting to give up. We want to forget it all, and put all our longings and yearnings for a complete healing to rest. We may find it hard to believe that we can get past this, that no matter how hard we try, we will never be able to overcome the legacy of our sexual abuse. We may fear that the ghosts from our experiences will never leave us in peace, that they will continue into our dreams and our relationships, never leaving us alone and totally seeming to appear of their own accord.

Actually, there are many who have gone before us and taken the worst of their lives and their experiences and transformed that which was incredibly destructive to the soul. They transformed that energy into a sword for healing, living in its glimmering energy with its two-edged cut.

Going through the fire may get us burned, but it can also cleanse the wound and give us a burning desire to show others that there is a bestowal of healing that reaches deep into the guts of our souls. Going through the fire can show us how to make our fears work for us. Our fears can motivate us to change. Our anger and rage can transform a listless and depressed life. Our longings and desires can move us beyond an everyday existence to one that literally pulsates with activity that we choose to create and actualize into deeds of change— for the good of ourselves and others who come into contact with us.

Our healing gives us compassion for all others who suffer, regardless of circumstance and reason. Our healing teaches us to listen with our hearts instead of just hearing with our ears. And most of all, just as we are about to give up on all that we have worked for and transformed, our healing reaches deep down within to show us we need never give up on ourselves...ever.

* * * * * * * * *

"Even the seemingly worst of a journey
can afford the most opportunity for healing."

"What does it mean this time?"

When we are in our place of darkness, it is difficult to appreciate just how much healing we have done in our lives. This darkness has a way of making us forget, momentarily, the many strides we have made in our journey, the many obstacles we have overcome, and the many issues we have faced and resolved.

Entering such a place is usually an indicator of, not a setback as some of us may think, but of another part of ourselves that needs healing. We are able to face our issues only when we are mentally and emotionally ready, and sometimes, the most difficult and painful ones are at the bottom of our darkness, and it takes peeling layer after layer to reach it.

When we slide into the darkness, again, we can be heartened (yes "heartened") that we have been here before and we have come out with new revelations, and sometimes new memories from our past that need healing and will make our present more real and sensible to us.

It is tempting when we come to these passages in our lives, to say, "Oh no. I'm not going *there*!" However, in doing so, we may be committing a disservice to another part of ourselves that needs healing, and so, we must once again be courageous, brave and have faith that there is an inner part of us that knows exactly what she is doing, that knows exactly what needs to be done and will lead the way for more progress in our healing.

In many cases going into the darkness it is yet another step forward in our unfailing promise of healing. One day we will not be on this particular path anymore. We will carry our experiences with us, but it will no longer be the road we constantly travel. Learning to meet and honor ourselves on any ground, including the darkness, is a sure sign that we are on the right healing path.

* * * * * * * * *

"When we venture into our darkness, it teaches us not to be afraid."

"What are these gifts of the Spirit?"

We can not travel our path without spirituality in some form or another. Those who have the most difficult time in our healing do not recognize the reality of Spiritual forces at work in our lives and in the world in which we live.

The difficulty with accepting spirituality is that it is often confused with accepting religious organizations as religion itself; and many religions, while sharing redemption, salvation and love, often go hand-in-hand with punishment, retribution and damnation. True spirituality is not punitive. True spirituality tends to teach by discipline and repetition of a lesson unlearned until we "get it."

Our childhoods may have been chaotic and arbitrary, but spirituality presents us with law and order in a far-reaching Universe of which we are a small, but certainly significant part. Our job is to learn the role of spirituality in our lives and to live our lives to the fullest, which is why many of us seek a healing to harmonize with the higher energies of life.

Religions give us beliefs and creeds, but true spirituality gives us truth and transcends any man-made beliefs and creeds. When we transcend our everyday woman lives, we see the possibility of connecting with the unassailable Spirit of Love. And if we are to pursue such a life, then we must remember that part of our makeup is spiritual, and therefore, we travel with certain spiritual companions on this healing journey— mainly Courage, Hope, Faith, Wisdom, and of course, Love.

It is up to us as individuals to learn the spiritual side of our existence. We may find groups in which we share with other people the same spiritual outlook, but our traveling in this world and at this time suggests that in the healing of the wounds of our survival, we all have our own spiritual, individual truths to learn, live, and love.

* * * * * * * * *

"Even in my darkest moments, I have not traveled alone."

"How do I move forward now?"

Pushing our limits is another one of the main tasks of our healing. While growing up in an abusive environment, we learned many techniques and defenses to protect ourselves from our CSA. As many of us know, these defenses are not something we can turn on and off at will. They become part of us; they are a mainstay of our personas that we project into the world.

As we seek more authenticity in ourselves and from other people, as we seek to make more real our connections with self and others, we find ourselves running smack into those defenses whose job were to protect us; and protect us well they did. But now these defenses need modification; long-held anxieties, phobias and panic-attacks, which no longer serve as real warnings of dangers to ourselves, need letting go. Awful and as useful as they are to our psyches, they now serve no purpose except to cover up issues and events from our past that, as adults, we are now equipped to handle.

When we choose to accept the challenge of dismantling old defenses for new ones (we don't want to be doormats!), we may find ourselves frequently stuck. It is not easy to give up something that has not only worked in the past, but is now almost as habitual as getting up every day. We must push our limits to change that which we want to see make a difference in our lives. At that moment when we think, *I can't do this now,* we must take a chance and risk and do that one thing we think we can not do, be it at home, at work, or in our intimate relationships. Pushing our limits means being willing to wade through the muck and mess to reach a clarity that will replace a much worn out defense mechanism. Pushing our limits can bring us no more harm than maintaining old defenses that are hindrances to our healing. We all have inner-limits we can push to the max, and we are lucky that the we can now make these choices.

* * * * * * * * *

"Personal growth is sometimes only made with excruciating effort."

"Was it all my fault if I'm the only one with no contact with my family?"

We survivors, no matter how much progress we make, continue to want to protect our families. Few are the people who have "innocent" childhoods, albeit, there are a number of folks who grew up with wonderful childhoods and wonderful parents.

We survivors did not experience this "wonderfulness." We may have accepted the goings-on in our families as the way all families were. While it may be true that other families had their problems, not all families were physically, emotionally, and/or sexually abusive to their children. Not all families neglect the inner gardens of their children's lives, and not all families meet the inquisitiveness of a child's interest with a loud "Shut the hell up," a dismissal with the wave of a hand, or a slap to the face.

Despite these awful actions, numbers of survivors continue to protect their families and the perpetrator in the families. This, of course, is a defense, and a useful one at that for a child. Who can believe that the person who walks around during the day smiling, joking and laughing is the same monster that enters a child's bedroom at night for molestation and/or rape? Therefore, during daytime many of us automatically went into denial about what happened the night before. Sometimes we went so far into the denial that we totally disassociated, cutting off parts of ourselves so we could continue a daily co-existence with our family.

While cutting off vital parts of ourselves, we were able to pretend our parents were "good" mothers and fathers, despite the fact that one might have been a perpetrator and the other knew, yet was in denial about the abuse. In the face of all this, some of us still love these same parents. Nonetheless, our healing is predicated on facing realities, and that means letting go of protecting these people and stopping our self-blame of accepting that the heinous crimes committed against us within our homes was in any way our fault.

* * * * * * * * *

"Difficult as it is to accept, some of us may have to create new families for ourselves."

"Why can't I be a normal human being?"

Does anyone know what "normal" is? When we are at a gathering of folks who are survivors, every now and then someone voices the fact that they wish they were "normal," and then the talk goes on as to what "normal" is, as if, were it not for our personal histories of sexual abuse, then everything in our lives would be a smooth ride. However, so many women and men have been abused in one way or another, that there aren't any statistics to say how many are "normal". If we were to suddenly be "normal" what would that be like?

Do normal people have rages? Do normal people wish they were somebody else? Do normal people have horrendous problems in their intimate relationships and work environments and/or with family and friends? If normal is a definition of what the "average" or "majority" is, then who's to say that survivors are not "normal"? Do normal people have sexual problems? Identity problems? Do they have trouble making decisions? Do they carry ambivalent feelings about any and everything?

Perhaps "normal" is simply what works and what is functional in a person's life, regardless of circumstances. What's normal for a blind person is not for a sighted person. What's normal for an only child is not for a person who has siblings. What's normal for men is not what's normal for women. And what's normal for people of color is not for those who are not.

Actually, the only "normal" thing about living is that we share the human experience of being born, making a life for ourselves with the gifts and talents we've been blessed with and then, we all at one time or another, die. Everything in between is individual. And, even if we are all survivors, each of us has an individual story to tell. We may be connected by the experience of "survivor," but each one of us has traveled a different path on the same journey. The only "normal" in our life is our own gauge: Are we living the lives we want, or someone else's?

* * * * * * * * *

"I am as individual as a unique single snowflake."

"Why can't I find medium ground?"

If anything drives a survivor batty on the healing jaunt, it's the ups and downs and the extremes of our feelings, both within ourselves and towards other people.

We may find ourselves in relationships where we have deep feelings of love one moment, and in the next, we find ourselves raging at this very person we love so much. One minute we're ecstatically happy, and then an hour later we sink into the depths of despair. We may find ourselves starting our day off in a cesspool of depression, and by afternoon feel as though the world were created to do our bidding.

Being a feeling creature is part of the human experience. Even if we go to great lengths to shut off our feelings, as many of us have done, they still seep through in some fashion or another— positively and negatively. We human beings are created with a deep capacity to feel love, anger, and fear. And one of our major tasks in healing is to reclaim that part of us that shut down in order to survive— our feelings. To not feel is to not live. If we shut down one part of our emotions, it includes almost all the other parts. Some of us may give into rage only for a time, some to only positive feelings, and some only to fear. Whichever one it is we choose, we are still out of balance.

There is medium ground. Instead of fighting our feelings, we can be willing to ride the roller coaster, knowing what we passed through is temporary. We must take new steps to see a new picture and accept who we are at a given time, knowing when we continue to travel our healing path, our ride will find its balance from within ourselves with our new and continuing growth.

* * * * * * * * *

"Even feelings can have minds of their own,
so it is our task to bring them into balance."

"Will this gray depression ever lift off of me?"

Depression among survivors is legendary. For many of us just beginning our healing, it is a constant state of being. For those of us already walking the healing path, it is something less in our lives, but can still be a daily battle. And there are those of us who do not know how not to be depressed.

Still, we needn't be so hard on ourselves. Our personalities may take to depression for good reason, aside from any biochemical considerations. When we begin exploring our issues and our histories we come face-to-face with our abuse. We bring to consciousness the details and specifics of what happened. Our healing calls for us to confront the memories that linger in our minds in the present, and to confront them so that we can progress. Of course, exploring these memories brings up our feelings, feelings that we ran away from because they were intolerable as children and teenagers who were stuck in environments where there was no escape, only endurance. And oftentimes we endured by shutting down, by shutting off, by numbing out and by disappearing from the actions that were violating our bodies and minds by the perpetrator(s). We did all of this so that we could depress what we were feeling in order to deflate and/or avoid the pain of such an experience.

We do not have to remain depressed. In taking the steps to confront the aspects of our past, to look honestly into our inner selves, we come into contact with the pain that causes the depression, and such contact is not an easy task. We may spend a lot of time in this area healing ourselves, for this is a mutilated space in our hearts. At one time our depression was a good defense for us, but we do not need it any longer. We are capable now of handling such pain in healthy ways and we do not have to be alone anymore with it if we do not wish to. We have friends, loved ones, support people, and the inner tools to help us move beyond the pain and our depression. We need only remember to be gentle with ourselves as we face the opening and healing of this wound.

* * * * * * * * *

"I shall be released".

"And what of my sisters and me?"

We women of color are often personally affected by the dominating White supremacy culture, most often in our jobs but also in our daily activities such as shopping, going places and doing things outside of our personal homes. Few of us are allowed the luxury of not having to make a living, and many times we find ourselves in the minority of our workplaces or agencies and institutions we must have contact with, such as hospitals or schools. We may find that our abuse histories make us incredibly sensitive to behaviors of racism because we are used to dealing in silence, using intuition and nonverbal language. We are attuned to reading attitudes and body language because one of the many ways we survived was by hearing what was not being said by the perp's behavior. We learned to trust our perceptions in order to protect ourselves. We still carry those same survival skills with us now, and many times our perceptions of racist attitudes and behaviors are correct. Even in our support groups, though we may be kindred spirits to all survivors, we are, after all, human, and we encounter racism even in some of our safety zones.

It is helpful to have support from other women of color. It is within our supportive groups with other sisters that we can totally relax and not be concerned that on a racial level we will be misunderstood. Unconditional support is a must, and sometimes we can only get this from other women of color. It does not mean that we will not be challenged, but it does mean that we can be supported in ways we can not be in a mixed group. It is a validating experience to be affirmed by our sisters and to be supported by them, and in doing so we are empowered to continue in our healing on another level. This does not mean we need negate others in order to affirm ourselves, but rather, we need to seek common ground. Just as CSA is a reality, though many deny it, so is racism; and support from our sisters is a gift we can give to ourselves.

* * * * * * * * *

"Sometimes, there is nothing like the support of my sisters."

"What must I do to heal?"

3 STEPS IN HEALING:

1. First, we must make a commitment to our own healing. If we find ourselves wavering in our healing, chances are we are ambivalent about our healing. It is necessary to go back and reassess our commitment to our recovery process of healing, and where such healing may lead us to exploration of the deepest levels of our psyche's mental, emotional, and spiritual levels.

2. Secondly, although this may be controversial for some, as soon as possible, get a competent, professional healer. Our hidden memories are unknown territory to us. When we come upon them, it is helpful to have a guide who knows how to help us maneuver in such territory. It is not enough to have just a friend, a support group, or a significant other as a resource. Although some survivors have healed without such a step, a lot of us need to work closely on our personal issues with someone trained in the familiarity of the psyche, memories, sexual abuse and assault, and the long-term affects of such a personal history, especially post traumatic stress disorder.

3. Third and lastly, never give up on ourselves. Perhaps this is the most important step in our healing. We must be our own best advocates; our own best coaches; and our most faithful believers in our healing. We must remember that no matter how many times we get turned around we can make it out of the mazes back to our path of healing. In never giving up on ourselves, it is an axiom— a forgone conclusion that our healing is inevitable. We are our own best fans. We can be, and many of us are, the Olympic champions of our survivor healing journey.

* * * * * * * * *

"In the Records of Life, I am the champion for my healing."

"Why is this taking so long?"

The mind is an incredible fortress. Its job is to take care of and protect us. We might not like all our defenses; in fact in our eyes they may work against us. But rest assured, our defenses hold purpose— usually to protect against traumatic experiences. In fact, not only will the mind go into shock when assaulted by events, so will the body. Some folks who were injured in a terrible physical accident have said in retrospect that at the time they didn't feel a thing although they witnessed everything that was happening at the time.

People who are bodily injured receive treatment for physical rehabilitation. They must learn to use their old muscles again, or exercise other parts of their bodies to compensate for their losses. They are often admired by society for doing the work necessary to heal, and in many cases if they can not afford to pay, society somehow makes provisions for them to get the help they need.

In matters of survivorship, our injuries are viewed as the "invisible wounds." Short of suing one's perpetrator and winning, most financing of therapy and help must come from the survivor, and our treatment is often interrupted because we run out of funds. Some of us make the sacrifice and pay anyway because our healing is a high priority in our lives. But not all survivors can do this. Some therapists and counselors reduce their rates knowing our healing takes time. There are Survivors of Incest Anonymous groups and others like that where the plate is passed around and a person can give what they can. And some social agencies have sliding scale fees. But maybe in the future, society will have survivorship clinics like we do for Planned Parenthood or drop-in centers like we have for drug addicts. Maybe there will be clinics and inpatient programs where we can get the necessary therapeutic help we so desperately want and need. Perhaps we who are women and are healing will eventually organize a treatment resource or agency so that healing for adult survivors is not so heavily dependent upon our finances, but upon our choice to heal.

* * * * * * * * *

"I make the decisions for what I am willing to do to reclaim my soul."

"Who are these non-protectors?"

Healing the non-protector in us is immense work. Inhabiting our bodies is difficult, especially when our feelings are running high. Some of us may take to self-harm and self-abuse, thinking we have no alternative to the pain that won't go away and the pain we can't seem to tolerate at the moment. It seems as if one more conscious moment of this psyche pain will drive us stark-raving mad, and so we seek to eliminate it by stabbing at ourselves, cutting at ourselves, picking at ourselves, and perhaps knocking ourselves about. When this happens, we have run into the "non-protector." It is as if our feelings of powerlessness and helplessness that we experienced as children who were locked in an inescapable situation, became "stuck" in a certain segment of our brain. We feel as if there is no release, no escape from our present situation until we do something to hurt ourselves, to stop the pain by symbolically cutting on ourselves and releasing it, even if only with the smallest trickle of blood.

If we wish to stop this self-harming behavior, we must be willing to look at these underlying feelings of powerlessness and helplessness and how we accept it in our lives today. What is going on presently that we feel there is no escape from and have not identified it? Many of us think we are dealing with the pain, but often what happens is that we allow the painful feelings to come up and then internally we run away from them. We say, "Yes this happened." We feel something and then we run because it is too painful to deal with. Or the feelings themselves come up, unattached to any thoughts, and their frightening presence makes us want to stop them from being in our minds. And like before, we feel alone.

If we are to stop this self-harm behavior, we must be willing to take a risk and share our pain with someone else— someone safe in our eyes; someone who can help us see that we are not alone, that we are not powerless and that we are not helpless. We need no longer be under the rule of the "non-protectors." Not today.

* * * * * * * * *

"We can stop the cycle of abuse, especially the self-afflicted violence against ourselves."

"And who is it that needs forgiveness?"

No one can make another person forgive any one. Forgiveness, as many of us have been taught, comes from the heart. If we wish to see the act of forgiveness in action, we can watch children when they think they have hurt another person. Their request for forgiveness is authentic. Their expression literally matches their feelings. They are genuinely sorry they have hurt another person and they say so. All of this can be conveyed to the receiver in moments, and that, too, is why children who are not sorry will also tell another person that they're not really sorry.

In order to forgive, one has to be rid of the aftermath of fear and rage we experienced at the hands of the perpetrators. It can not course unconsciously through our blood as we offer forgiveness, for then it is not forgiveness that we are offering; it is a deal. One has to come to an understanding from a clear healing knowledge that people make horrendous mistakes. After all, it is not the easy things we have trouble forgiving. It is that which reaches deep into the heart that makes us fearful, hesitant, and resistant to extend our forgiveness. Truly forgiving means that we harbor no attachments for ill feelings towards the person under consideration for forgiveness from us; that we have "let go" of the *acts* that caused the harm they perpetrated upon us, and moreover, it means that we extend a spiritual gift to another human being that truly is ours to give.

Sometimes just letting go of the need to forgive can bring forth forgiveness. We are not bad people if we find we can not forgive our perpetrators. And some of us may transcend our histories, may move forward to a spiritual level that goes beyond our understanding, and actually be able to forgive those who have trespassed so grievously against our souls.

* * * * * * * * *

"To forgive another also means we receive another gift of freedom."

"Is that another reason I don't say what I really think and feel?"

Uncontainable rage? Is it? That is, uncontainable? Once, a comic made some comments about being a man and knowing not to piss off a bigger man, because the bigger man might get a bit ruffled and take a swing. All that to say, most of us can put our rage in check. We sometimes think it permissible to go off on our loved ones and/or friends. But we know it's not possible to do with our boss on the job, and we don't do it. We don't do it to a police officer, judge, medical doctor, or the clerk at the grocery store. But we really let go on the home front, offering the excuse that we can't help ourselves, that those near and dear to us push our buttons like others don't. Whether that is true or not, we still have the final say so of when we let go. Our families don't deserve the unfair weight of our baggage.

When we first release pent-up rage, we are sometimes shocked. These feelings may seem more powerful than other feelings we express because, generally, it isn't a feeling that is encouraged or used a lot and the key to expressing rage is "permission." We just have to find safe ways to express them; safe ways that don't hurt our loved ones and that don't hurt us. The following are several avenues to explore:

- Write and vent.
- Call a friend and tell them you want to rage for a few minutes.
- Call a hotline and tell them you want to rage for a few minutes.
- Take some glass soda bottles, line 'em up in a safe place and throw baseballs or rocks at 'em.
- Get a desktop punching bag and some sparring gloves and have at it.

So goes the way. Our rageful feelings need expression, but our loved ones don't need them expressed upon them.

* * * * * * * * *

*"Every day is testament to the fact that my rage
is controllable and approachable for me to express."*

"So, what's real and what's not?

The technological information has been a boon to many folks, and that includes survivors. Networking has never been easier or more accessible. The "Information Highway" has done more than any other tool to "break the silence" and to connect with others.

Genuine relationships can be developed as a result of discussion lists and chat groups. It's a step in between pen pals and phone calls. We can get to know another by writing and responding to different concerns and issues we all share. For folks who can not afford individual therapy and/or may be too frightened or distrustful to go to support groups (or if there are no support groups in a given area), survivor discussion groups and chats may be the saving lifeline and support. And many groups are tailored to address the concerns of specific ways we deal with the world.

But just like in the real world, in the virtual world we still have to be careful and recognize boundaries. We still have to make decisions about whom to trust and whom to be careful with. Just because people are friendly doesn't mean they are our friends. We have to use the same skills we use in real life in virtual life. If a discussion group or chat group doesn't meet our needs, then we should move on and look for other groups. A discussion/chat group should be respectful of each member. Just because we are physically invisible doesn't mean it's a free for all. The safest groups are those that are moderated by facilitators or owners and have specific rules that the groups abide by.

The virtual world is another resource for our healing. In fact, for some of us, it may be our only source of support in the beginning.

* * * * * * * * *

"The virtual world is as close as my fingertips."

"What do I wish for now?"

Learning to say *yes* to ourselves is another one of the stepping stones to our healing. We must learn to say *yes* to our feelings, our dreams, our goals, our aspirations, and our innate goodness. Sometimes the *yes* part of us seems like the hardest resister of all to our healing. That part of ourselves just doesn't want to hear it and it seems will not be moved by anything we say or do. That *yes* part always seems to come with its counterpart *but* as in "Yes, but..." and then we come up with a zillion reasons why we can not say *yes* to ourselves.

As children, many of us were not allowed to say *yes* to ourselves. Sometimes, our wanting to do something was denied because we would not willingly participate in our abuse. Sometimes, as a form of punishment for not cooperating with a perpetrator or for causing our families problems, when we asked to do something we wished for ourselves we were met with a resounding "No!" So we put our desires, wishes, wants, and dreams on hold, denying some of our most precious feelings and dreams until we could get out of that situation.

We no longer have to put our wants, desires, and dreams on hold. We are free now. We may have problems, may have limitations in the ways of skills or finances, but there is nothing stopping us from beginning the actuality of our dreams, wants, and desires. We can now say *yes* to that which our hearts long for. We can now begin to find ways to pursue many of the things we wish to see come to fruition. We are victims no longer. We are survivors, and today we are free.

* * * * * * * * *

"I have the freedom to pursue my goals, dreams, and desires."

"How can I possibly face this day or my feelings?"

It's another day. Outside the sun is shining gloriously, beckoning everyone to come outside and do something with the day. Birds are whistling and fussing. Cars and trucks sound their noise through closed windows. Neighbors' voices ring out muffled laughter. A dog barks.

Despite the calling of the day, some of us awaken and are immediately filled with the sense of dread, with the sense that something terribly wrong has happened and we are the blame for it. There is nothing we can do to fix the damage; and we are overwhelmed with a sense of shame and guilt that all of it is our fault.

Many of us were separated from our families, either literally or figuratively, and became the scapegoat, the "outsider," the one to cause the family all the problems. Any closeness or acceptance as being a valued member of the family, or the illusion of it, was quickly dispelled and broken. In one moment of time, everyone recognized the ugly truth, that indeed there was sexual violation going on with a child in the family, and the one being violated was one of us. And nothing was done. And life went on as before.

This time in our healing is a hard step. Feeling the terrible feelings of "It was my fault," and accepting the truth that "None of it was my fault," that no matter what happened there was nothing we could've done to change any of it, is a difference of thought patterns and changes. To honor our feelings and aid in our healing, what we can do now is give back the blame/shame and the guilt to the perpetrator, and anybody else who knew what was going on but looked the other way during our abusive living situations. In our healing, we recognize that we were children given central casting in the drama of a sick adult world. We have an inalienable right to live our lives as wholesome, loving women— without fear, guilt, shame, and blame. We have a right to wake up and answer the call of the day.

* * * * * * * * *

"No matter how badly I feel, today I remember that none of the abuse was my fault."

"How can I heal the unreachable me?"

How do we move forward in our healing when we are stuck in the same old places? Knowing healing is change means we must actually transform some things about ourselves. Even when we say we want to change ourselves, still we have old inner enemies, old defenses we've spent a lifetime cultivating to protect ourselves in the only way we knew how. Fortresses do not come apart easily, and few are the souls that are privy to spiritual epiphanies, psychic healings, and magical wands, even when we cry desperately for a laying-on of the hands and immediate relief. For the majority of us, healing means that sometimes we push the recalcitrant part of ourselves that does not believe healing can take place. It means to risk taking a chance on some type of new behavior on our part.

Even though some of us may have different support groups and individual therapists, the real healer in our lives is ourselves. Our support groups are invaluable because they let us know we are not alone and that healing is possible for us all if one of us can heal; and our therapists aid in the speed of our healing because they can see parts of ourselves that we are blinded to. But, it is the healer in us that has the most important role in our journey. We must believe that we can heal, and we must also do the work. Sometimes that means pushing ourselves beyond our limits, even if we are afraid, discouraged, angry, depressed, fearful, or dreading a new choice we need to make.

Over and over again we see that our healing takes place one step at a time. We know it can not be rushed, and we also know the impetus to move forward must come from our own individual selves. When there is something we want to do but we think, "I can't do it, I'm afraid," we can act as if we can do it anyway. We can do it with the fear, for after all, it is only a feeling. We try new behaviors so we can move forward. The act is difficult, but the truth is simple.

* * * * * * * * *

"Today I will take a risk and try one new behavior I am always afraid to do."

"Is therapy worth the expense I incur?!"

Professional therapy, at some point, is almost a requirement for most of us healing from CSA. For the majority of us, our healing requires our obtaining a therapist to work with us as we heal from our personal histories. This is too bad because professional therapy, even in its shortest length of time, is fairly expensive. Even those of us who have health insurance may find ourselves paying part of it, since many policies only cover a certain number of the therapy sessions. Or else, we must see therapists in the health plan, and not one of our own choosing. And then of course, there are many of us who have to pay for therapy ourselves, and given the nature of our diagnosis and treatment plans, this is a service that can cost us financially, at least, for a two year period, and that's being optimistic. If we go to a clinic, we often end up with interns or with people who don't stay very long.

Historically speaking, we know that there were slaves in America who would do anything for freedom, making their escape the top priority in their life, risking capture and punishment to themselves and their loved ones while they answered the call of their Spirit to be free of tyranny and fear. We CSA survivors are not unlike slaves, trapped and wishing to break free from the tyranny of our fears, anxieties, phobias, and PTSD (post traumatic syndrome disorder) symptoms so that we might be "freeborn" and live a healthy life. We may find that, like the slaves seeking freedom, we must make a total commitment to our healing, and that commitment may include using our finances to pay for the help that we need and want. It would be great if all of our perps had to pay our therapy costs, but that seldom happens, although a few of us are eligible for State's Victim funds. Like slaves, our freedom may call for a guide, someone who knows the way to our freedom. Those survivors who have effective and caring therapists don't regret a penny they spend. It is up to each of us to decide whether such a way of traveling our healing path is the way for us. In the long run, we may find the cost expensive, but if we do our work, it is well worth its payment to our healing and freedom.

* * * * * * * * *

"Healing is my priority, no matter the cost."

"Is this not the way?"

When we start our healing journey, it really does not matter at what age we start. The phases of healing are pretty much the same for all: a willingness to look at what happened, the emergency stage where we think we're going crazy; denial, fear, anger, acceptance and transformation. It doesn't matter if you start at age 20 or at age 68, the obstacle course is the same for everybody. It is only by traveling that we learn the meaning of our journey is individualized. No two journeys are the same.

Each of us has an individual path. This doesn't mean we can't help each other— far from it. We are the most necessary supporters and validaters of one another. Nonetheless, the path we travel says sometimes on the healing trail we walk it alone, that is, according to who we are, what we have lived and what we are working on at the moment. Some of us will turn to alcohol to help us, others to drugs, still others to harmful relationships or self-mutilating behavior. Some of us, until we choose healthy ways to heal, will choose all the crutches we can find to stop the pain until the time we begin our healing. And even then, some of us will have setbacks and relapses until we finally accept and understand that we are the ones that reclaim and re-empower our own lives, and that our histories of SA are but the fodder for us to overcome obstacles, and be the women we are capable of being in our healthiest and most loving sense.

Our goal is one of self-possession. To be self-possessed is to be free and to know our own truth among all truths. Everyone has creative energies that live and breathe from deep within and seek expression that only each of us can give to self. No one person has a lock on truth nor the only key to freedom, and we are therefore then, our own best guides and healers.

* * * * * * * * *

"There are as many healing paths as there are survivors."

Strength

"Why does it seem I always have to be strong?

Everybody thinks we're strong, that we are the workhorses of the world, of humanity. Everybody thinks we should be able to handle these problems, and that they come with the territory of being women, and more specifically, women of color. When they show our pictures, it is always one in which we have a serious and impenetrable look in our eye. They show the straight-backed woman, her face implacable and unreadable except for what the viewer projects.

After years of such perception and reaction, is it no wonder we hide our true feelings so that after a while even we don't know what we feel? Even we become out of touch with our vulnerabilities and frailties, and of our need to be nurtured and taken care of at times, especially during our healing walk. Is it no wonder our elderly sisters save their smiles for the infants just entering the world?

We who are women of color and have journeyed on a path to heal don't always have to be strong; in fact, we can't always be strong. Our enslaved ancestors often cried themselves to sleep at night; our Chinese sisters wiped stubborn tears from their eyes when looking upon the never-ending trail of railroad tracks; and our Native American sisters stilled the beating of their rapidly coursing hearts as their children were stolen and incarcerated at so-called Christian schools. And all over the world, women of color have said at one time or another that they would lay their heads down and one day sleep in peace forever. And we who are healing today need not feel ashamed that we can not withstand the constant assault of memories that will not be abated unless we deal with them directly and ban them forever from our psyches. Greater strength is to be found in the heart that is tender and merciful, than the stiffening of a sister's head that won't turn for fear of what she will see and feel.

* * * * * * * * *

"Strong as I am, I am still entitled to nurturing from the Universe."

"What right do I have to take up space?"

There ought to be workshops where survivors can easily re-learn the tools, or just learn them, for self-esteem and appreciation. We learn by experience not to think well and highly of ourselves. Some of us develop blinders to the positive qualities of our beings. Not wanting to be "spotlighted" by others, we often downplay whatever strengths we have, lest we be recognized and focused upon by others. That might bring on the possibility of unwanted attention, attention we think might be dangerous and attention we think we can not handle. So we downplay our strengths and, like all muscles that are not exercised, they become weak.

Self-affirmations are a good way to re-inhabit that part of us that needs attention. They are a good way to bolster our egos. Affirmations come from self, and therefore, reinforce deeply that which is true and good about us. It really is okay to affirm ourselves in whatever strengths we have. It is okay to say, for instance, "I am a good person," "I have a right to be here," "My needs are important and taking care of them is healthy for me," without thinking we are selfish or hurting other people.

We want to do more than just survive— we want our lives to grow and thrive, like all natural living things. We have a right to be here as much as the trees and the stars, and we have the right to grow in all our splendor as the Most Creative Spirit has deemed it so. We are...therefore...We Be.

* * * * * * * * *

"I, too, am a child of the Universe."

"Is there a place to rest and lay my head?"

When we were children, we came to expect that our orderly world would be shaken in an instance by our perpetrator(s). When we woke in the morning, we knew anything could happen to disturb our safety. We knew we lived in an environment where, at any moment, despite our most fervent wishes and efforts, our lives could be disturbed by unwanted touches and actions that we had no control over and that we had to submit to. Some of us thought to do otherwise would mean to die, or that someone close to us would die and/or suffer the consequences of our refusal. Many of us spent our childhoods and youth avoiding the perpetrator(s) at all costs, often looking over our shoulders, and never relaxing for a minute no matter where we were.

When we became adults and could live the lives we thought we wanted and were free of the perpetrator(s), we brought our hyper-vigilance with us, a skill we no longer needed with such intensity nor constancy. We no longer knew how to relax in safe places with safe people. As a result of our histories, we carry an expectation that something bad, something terrible, is going to happen at any moment to us. We are careful not to be caught off guard like we were as children, so we stand guard as adults, even in our sleep. As the elders say, "Every eye aint shut." Even that of a child.

We don't have to do that anymore. We can choose our friends and people we wish to share our lives with; we can choose the environments of where we live and where we work. We work our healing program, taking risks to trust other healthy and safe people. We learn we do not always have to be on guard, and that moments of aloneness that are filled with anxiety can be replaced with a peacefulness we create.

* * * * * * * * *

"Unafraid and healing, I sleep in peace."

"Is there a way I can stop tapping my feet?"

Much as we may wish, push, demand, cajole, or try, we can not move our growth beyond its natural outcome. If this were so, every survivor would wake up one day and be healed. We would simply follow the rules to *healing-from-sexual-abuse-this-way* and go on with new lives.

But in our real world this is not the way it happens. We can not do anything until we are ready to do it. We can not look at our memories until the inner part of ourselves is ready to do that. We can not see that which has been hidden for so long and for good reason until our psyches and our lives are ready to do the work that must accompany such healing, no matter how often we think we are ready.

In truth, we can connect with the Spirit of Patience as we do our healing. We must grow a tolerance for the person we are and for the time it takes to become the person we want to be and can be. We have spent a lifetime protecting ourselves, protecting our inner children, and so the road to healing may at times slow down to a pace that makes us feel impatient. Generally, that is the place where much of our healing takes place. It produces the frustration, the angst, the rage, and the fear that we have spent a lifetime locking so that the space of vulnerability and openness to life will not be irrevocably destroyed.

Just as we survived our childhoods and the perpetrators, we can do this, too. The abuse is over; it is history, albeit, it is our personal history. Nonetheless, it is finished. For many of us, our healing is just starting. For others it is a journey we have traveled where we learn over and over again that healing can not be rushed, that nature has its own timetable. However, this time, in waiting, we know that we are awaiting the birth of another part of our lives. Like the flowers that bloom anew each spring, we too unfold and blossom in natural progression.

* * * * * * * * *

"I can be patient in the blooming of my own healing."

"Why not go after the things I want in life?"

To soar on high, we must let the desires of our hearts fly. This, of course, means that we are not about hurting people to get what we want (although some folks may be hurt in the process). It means that our goals for ourselves have meaning for us, and not to do them is to stifle our creative psyche in our healing process.

Some of us want to write, some to paint and draw, some to work with people, some to become gourmet cooks, police officers— choices in life expressing our creativity. All along, we may have received messages that we were not capable of being or accomplishing those things, and we took those pronouncements as if they were truths. But now that we are healing, we are hearing our inner voices saying, "I want to do this," and saying, "I can do this," and then we find ourselves at a loss as to how to get started; or we become so overwhelmed by our self-doubts and fears that we don't do anything.

No matter how old we are or where we are in our healing path, we can begin to make choices that we want, that come from our heart's desires, and see them become realities. Phyllis Wheatley was a slave girl when she began writing poetry; and the Delaney sisters were in their 80s when they published their first book. None of these women had easy lives. All of them, like all of us, had to overcome internal battles as well as external obstacles. If we really want something, we must believe we can do it and then go after it. To do otherwise is to die a little each day, and we haven't come this far in our lives to do that.

* * * * * * * * *

"On this day, I can take the steps to do the things I want to do."

"Will I ever change?"

Learned hopelessness and powerlessness are the bane of our healing journey. They are like hidden bear traps on the path we travel as we heal and make our lives anew. They are the roadblocks we encounter whenever we are on the edge of a breakthrough from old patterns to new ones that work for us and make our lives meaningful. Hopelessness and powerlessness are complicated forces we have internalized, and when we accept that it doesn't have to be that way, and that our lives do not have to be tyrannized by these old enemies, we are truly on the way to moving forward. Sometimes these energies are so learned that we forget the most salient fact of our existence: despite all odds of what may have been, we overcame them. They may come back and forth in our lives, but the truth is, we survived our SA histories to become the people we are today.

We are seekers of living truth. We want our lives to work, to be healthy, to bring us joy and love. Otherwise, we would not be putting ourselves through the grueling pace of examining the ways we stop ourselves from growing and living fully. We would not be going from one therapist to another seeking to rid ourselves of the residues of hopelessness and powerlessness: anxieties, depressions, phobias, and fears that interfere with the healthy functioning of our living. We would not be attending support groups or 12-step programs had we accepted hopelessness and powerlessness as ways of life. We would not be trying, despite the memories and images, to have relationships and jobs that have value to us. If we look closely, we will see that each day as we move forward in our lives, hopelessness turns to hope and powerlessness evolves into empowerment.

* * * * * * * * *

"Whenever I falter, I remember I have always climbed out of the abyss of despair."

"Who am I at this moment?"

Some of us have different parts of ourselves that operate for us at different times. Because of our SA histories, some of us totally cut ourselves off from the center of our beings and have these different parts take over daily aspects of our lives. When we were violated by our perpetrator(s), we found a way to psychically disappear so that we could continue functioning in other aspects of our lives. We may have been designated as "moody," or better yet, "crazy," because our behavior swung from one extreme to another; or we came across as not "being there." It was a very creative, defensible way to handle a life with pain from which, as children, we had no escape.

In our healing we begin to recognize and accept these parts of ourselves that we may have created, evolved into, or become. Some of them are still very helpful and useful as defenses and ways of being when we have to navigate in a world in which relationships are tenuous and scary. And some of them are not so healthy and get us into "trouble," as we slip off somewhere while another part of us deals with outside reality.

The good news is that we can access these parts over time. We do not always have to be in the dark about the parts of us that save us or act out for us. Further good news is that we can either accept them as separate parts of ourselves, or we can integrate them into ourselves. Either way they are a part of us that saved us at one time in our lives. Our healing recognizes that in the world of CSA anything can happen, usually on a negative scale. And our healing also recognizes that our soul creates a way for us to deal with such atrocities as children, and that in the future as adults, we will be, if we are willing, able to reclaim those parts whether we integrate them or accept them as parts of ourselves that need to be embraced.

* * * * * * * * *

"Regardless of what part I show the world, it is still me."

"How come I can't take care of everything and everybody?"

We who are women of color are not used to tending to our own wounds— everybody else's, but not ours. Many times money and time are the issues. We don't have the time in a life already packed with demands from work, community, school, family, and church. Or we simply don't have the money or the insurance to attend to our mental health, our emotional well-being. And we have a legacy that has said, "We can do this ourselves."

That was then and this is now. The world has changed tremendously and so have life expectancies and relationships. The lines of roles have been redrawn, and often the boundaries cross over. We who have CSA histories struggle immensely with boundaries, what is right and wrong, and to whom and what we "owe." We are often taught to give back to the community, to not be selfish, and to go that extra mile. Alongside our perceived responsibility, we pile on guilt because we are not everything to everybody; namely our bosses, our spouses, our children, our partners, our families, our churches, and communities.

We do little good when we are overloaded and have problems festering within our souls. At some point we may have to withdraw, taking stock of what needs attending to within ourselves. Unfinished business, specifically memories and flashbacks, now vie for our attention as much as the external needs of others. We can learn to put ourselves first, which is something that has been a virtual *no-no* from the moment we were conscious enough to make decisions and be a part of society. But the truth is we can only give as good as we've got. If we are hurting and not attending to that wound, we are as weak as a broke link in a chain. A whole self is much more effective than a broken-spirited soul, and it really is all right to take time to tend to ourselves.

* * * * * * * * *

"I do not have to be superwoman."

"What could I ever do that might make a difference?"

Change and growth are tricky measurements for progress in our lives. We may work on a problem for years thinking we have solved nothing, and then one day find ourselves in a situation where all the hard work we've done to overcome our problems is manifested in a single moment by the way we handle a problem or interact with another person.

Some changes are easily recognized. We have a problem with organization in our lives and we make efforts to straighten things out, and over a short period of time we are rewarded by smoother executions of our everyday living.

Healing from our personal histories may be a bit less manifested. We may go over the same ground, we may address the same issue, and still find ourselves responding to the same situation in the same way. We become frustrated and turn on ourselves, berating ourselves for not doing better, for not making more progress in a more timely manner than we would like.

Often, we don't begin our healing journey until after a lifetime of living. By the time we start to address the serious issues and residue of our CSA experience, we may be well set in patterns of behavior that, though they cause us pain in the present, have presented defenses that work to let us function on a daily level. But that is *not* "living."

Trying new behaviors and new actions that free us from old fears and anxieties is scary, and the self does not like fear and anxiety. But if we are to reclaim our lives, then we must take the risks that will enable us to move with the freedom we so greatly desire. And these risks need not be giant steps, need not be large changes in our behaviors. In fact, it is almost an axiom that we take small steps and recognize that small efforts often result in great changes...over time. Each day gives us an opportunity to take one small risk in any part of our lives— at work, at home, or just trying one new activity we have wanted to do.

* * * * * * * * *

"Each day presents an opportunity for me to make a difference in my life."

"Why do I feel as though all this healing stuff is making me crazy?"

When we first begin healing, everything seems to come at us in a rush, and it is an "in your-face" kind of experience. When our memories return we may feel we are bowled over by an experience we can't control. They seem to come unbidden and strike us at our most vulnerable and intimate moments. Sometimes the return of our memories turns our world upside down. And not just ours. If we have family, spouses, partners and children, they too are in for a bumpy ride.

There is an inner part of us that oversees our lives. It is the wisdom of this Inner Spirit that lets us know what is and is not possible to do in our lives. It is this inner spirit that prods us to take on new projects and goals, and that includes our healing. No woman begins healing until she is ready. No woman takes on the humongous job of encountering her CSA past without that go-ahead. We can say that we were propelled by inner forces and that we had no say so, but in truth, we take on nothing and do nothing until we are ready to do it. Otherwise, the fears, anxieties and phobias we have carried through life to protect us would not be there.

While our defenses have done us well to help us survive, we learn that the pain of having them is a greater cost to our freedom and living. Our defenses often interfere greatly with our relationships with our spouses, partners and children. They may limit us at our jobs and often constrict us in our everyday movements. We may be asking ourselves, "Am I crazy?" when we start to change and reject our old ways of being. For us, with our CSA histories, new experiences have often been fraught with pain and ugliness. It does not have to be that way now, and in fact, most of the time it is not. Changing often means we get a new set of references to view our world and, more than not, means we are introduced to a new freedom to be ourselves in ways we never allowed ourselves to dream.

* * * * * * * * *

"I have so much to gain when I rid myself of my old defenses."

April 1

CLATTER
My mind roars
banging thoughts
from unknown vessels
I think I'm spinning
out of control
and suddenly
Jesus speaks
 "Ssssh. Come walk with Me."
I close my eyes
and I am free

"Is there room for inspiration in my day-to-day living?"

Most of the time we are our own inspirations in life. Not that we don't get spiritual help or assistance from others in our lives, but basically we are the architects of the living structures and relationships that orbit around ourselves. We have celebrations and moments that mark our progression in life, but the bottom line is that we construct the everyday world we inhabit.

When we achieve our goals, it is because we have found the resources from within to accomplish the tasks we set out to do. We have somehow recognized our strengths, tamed our weaknesses, and trusted the inner voice that prods us ever-forward.

When we are stuck and in a big way, it is because we have lost touch with this process. It is not because we have lost the knowledge of how it works, but rather, we have somehow strayed off the path of knowing ourselves. Reaching such a place can sometimes plummet us into the depths of despair.

Nothing we have attained is ever lost to us. It's like riding a bike. No matter how long we have not ridden, when once we get back on we may warble off balance, but it's only for a few minutes.

When we find ourselves at a loss for direction or if our lives seem to abruptly come to a standstill, we need only to remember how we started in the first place. Perhaps it was an idea from inspiration. We decided to act on the idea and we began with a single step. The fact that we are in the here and now at this time would suggest we know how to tap into our inner strength and find the way back to our rightful healing path.

* * * * * * * * *

"We are our own inspirations."

Self infliction

April 3

"Am I a stand-in for the perpetrator when I self-injure myself?"

To be afflicted is to have the marauders come at us from the outside. To self-inflict is to let the despoilers make our bodies their homes. It is to allow them to inhabit the corridors of our minds, and it is to give the keys of our hospitality to an evil intruder of our own acquiescence.

Demons used to be the monsters of medieval times and early tribal days. Now they are the shadows of our own thoughts, sometimes major characters in our nightmares. They come now in deeper disguise as ravishers of hopes and dreams, leaving in their wake ghosts of self-destruction and personal inaction. They are tricksters of the soul constantly casting the self-doubt and unworthiness images we live by in our daily lives— helplessness, powerlessness, despair, and of course, cynicism.

If we were to die tomorrow, and if there were only one truth we gleamed while passing this way, then it ought to be that the human spirit can withstand practically anything. Contrary to our need to self-inflict, self-destroy, and self-destruct, there is a part of us that is absolutely indestructible, no matter how long it takes for us to discover this precious truth.

No more do we need to be part of external and internal assaults upon ourselves by our own hands. We need not continue to punish ourselves for once being children who were at the mercy of unmerciful caretakers or perpetrators. We need no longer continue to believe their lies, and as adults, be their stand-ins. The next time any one of us decides we need to self-inflict, we should look at the hand that carries the weapon for our seductive pain and ask, "Whose hand is this?"

* * * * * * * * *

"The Human Spirit is not milquetoast!"

"What have I done that makes me so unacceptable, even unto myself?"

Some days our thoughts go like this: What have I caused to make myself so unacceptable in my own eyes, and to be treated with disdain and held in self-contempt? I have not murdered anyone. I have not stolen anyone's soul— I couldn't even if I wanted to. So, why this utter self-rejection and this dismal, encompassing self-hatred?

We rage incessantly against ourselves as if we were personally at fault for the after-effects of our abuse. Though we are responsible for any changes we wish to make, we are not responsible for what causes us to have to make them.

What do we do and where do we go when we appropriate our own self-hatred? When we internalize such thinking and embrace such soul ugliness that we are affected for days on end? How do we get out of such a state of being?

There is nothing we have done to cause ourselves to self-revile in such manner. But what we have done is internalize the hatred and ugliness our perpetrators projected upon us while inflicting their vile deeds upon us. If we are to be totally self-accepting of ourselves and all our myriad faults, self-hatred is the one feeling we have to let go and give back to our abusers where it belongs. We are deserving of our self-love and no one can take that away from us; only we can willingly give it away.

* * * * * * * * *

"I embrace all aspects of my self-worth with love and compassion."

"What is this compulsion connected to my soul?"

We create because we have to. If we could walk away, our souls unscathed, our psyches totally intact, we wouldn't spend a minute lamenting about the time lost devoted to our personal endeavor. The soul hungers and craves self-expression, and that is cause for compelling action of any sort. We are not unlike the Creator who created us. We must do, we can not simply be, and we must constantly actualize what and who we are. If we do not create we will surely self-destruct. It is the nature of the human body, the nature of life, our life. Nothing stands still, not even the quiet breeze silencing its sound from the wind.

We are not talking gestation, for that is part of the process of all creativity, and that is when creativity is being set in motion. We who are women have a connection with creativity that can give birth unto life itself. For us to ignore its primal urgings in other aspects of our living is to summon the death keel of our soul, and is to condemn ourselves to a self-created hell.

To deny ourselves participation in wondrous acts of creativity is a matter of our own life and death. If we want to thrive, if we want to walk in harmony with the Universe and in peace with ourselves, then we must respond to our inner voices that prod us on to self-express the gifts and talents we are innately given. To do anything less is to stop the process of our own creativity, and if we do that, we shrivel and die.

* * * * * * * * *

"My deepest sense of self is the expression of my creativity."

"Why do the ghosts of my past seem more real than the people in my present?"

Much as we may yearn to, we can not change the past. And even though we say so to ourselves frequently, it does not cancel out our changing our present. Some of us try to change the past by constantly rescuing others from living their lives. We provide answers they haven't asked for, lay out scheming plans they haven't plotted, and generally run ourselves ragged trying to provide solutions that aren't needed for people who haven't requested such designs. Meantime, we are busy masking our own problems and denying the truth that it is we that need to be saved from and by ourselves.

However, we can not keep reaching back in time, thinking unless we change the past we can not go forward. We can only go forward when we accept our past and face it square on for a healing. It's true, we can replay in our mind's eyes that which happened and give it a new ending, one we would like. For some of us, that helps us move forward in our lives.

What also helps us heal is accepting what truly happened in all its painful, living color and truth. That is what lets us get on with the business of living in our present: attending to our lives now, loving the people in our lives now, performing the life work we choose for ourselves now, and living one day at a time, learning that each moment we face the past, we are living anew to the truths of our present and our healing.

* * * * * * * * *

"Healing my past lets me live more fully in my present."

"Does everybody hear those noises in the night?"

Flashbacks have a tendency to come out on their own. Sometimes they are fleeting and easily dismissed from our minds. Other times they are devastating and can be a catalyst for huge change in a painful area of our lives. Our loved one does something— a certain gesture, a certain movement that brings a buried remembrance, image or thought to our consciousness. It can happen in our most intimate love-making and, depending on the flashback, so goes the quality of our intimate moments. Sometimes the flashback is so strong that we are no longer acting in the present alone, but must deal with the intrusive past in the present. It is a horrific experience. To have memories of the past impinging on the present, bringing feelings of fear, revulsion, or total self-rejection as we remember not only our perpetrator, but also ourselves with the perpetrator while engaging in a most intimate act with our lover, is to be twisted by an agonizing internal turmoil.

If we are supported then we will have partners willing to travel with us at these moments. We will have a personal safety net as we deal with the issues we must in order to come out on the other side. Our inner battle is intense. Our adult self, with all her wisdom, needs to come into strength and courage at this time and remind us of who we are now. And she needs to remind us who our partners are— our lovers, not our perpetrators. And it may be, at the time of a flashback, that the child who still lives inside us needs to be reminded of who we are now— that what we are doing is safe and loving and what we want, and not a dirty deed that is threatening, harmful, or that we are being forced to go against our will.

Flashbacks bring a tall order for healing, and yet the fact that we are in an intimate relationship, that we are loved and want to love back and want to share in all the intimacies associated with such love, suggests this is a healing worthy of our pursuit.

* * * * * * * * *

"Flashbacks are a reminder of what I've overcome and that there is a wanting of a healing for me."

"How long can feeling this good last?"

When we are riding high, sometimes it is frightening. To actually get what we want is frightening. To do what we want to do and have that be okay with the ones who love us now can also be frightening. For some of us, even the smallest gesture of kindness and love was not part of our familial foundation. To be the one to receive it later in life is frightening. And it is to acknowledge a past that was bereft of such substance. This is not about blame. This is about acknowledging the truth of our lives. To have consistent goodness in our everyday lives is not something we grew up expecting. But when we are in charge of our lives, when we set goals and reach them, when we make our dreams come true, and when our visions and everyday lives are reflective of goodness more often than despair or depression, this is to have a changed life. It is to have consistent goodness as part of the wholeness of our beings.

Quiet as it's kept, one of the difficult paths of healing is to accept the goodness that comes our way. To take in goodness is to accept that we are worthy. To have an intimate relationship with another is to accept that we are lovable. And to have work that we enjoy is to say we are purposeful and fulfilled. This is quite a load for those of us who thought we would never get what we wanted, who thought no one could ever love a person like ourselves, and who once thought we wouldn't make it to see the next sunrise.

It is possible to live the lives we want, and goodness can become part of our everyday existence.

* * * * * * * * *

"I am entitled to all the goodness that comes my way."

"What is it to be free?"

Just one day I'd like to be free. Oh, Mother Spirit of us all...just this once I'd like to wake up to a morning full of freedom. I'd like to choose to do any activity and not say, *Oh, no. I can't. After all, I'm afraid to walk around...I might run into a cat.* Or, I'd like to say, *I think I'll go to the city and just walk around looking in the shops,* instead of thinking, *Oh, no. I can't. I'm afraid to ride the subway. Someone might hurt me.*

After my free day, I'd like to be with my beloved and make love if that's what we want to do, without thinking, *Can I handle this? Will the memories come back? Will there be intrusive thoughts? Will I hate myself and feel "dirty"?* Just this once I'd like to be free of all my fears. I'd like to go to a social event where there are other people and not worry and think, *What do they want from me? Do I look okay? Is my hair okay? Are they talking about me? Did I say something stupid?* Just this once I'd like to be free. I'd like to make a wish list and then the next day get everything I desire. I want to be happy, satisfied, and full of wonder and joy. Just for today, I'd like to be free and not run from myself and my fears. I'd like to be expectant and hopeful that the day is mine.

Just this once, for today, I'm not going to "work" on myself. I'm not going to put myself down for how I do something or don't do something. I'm not going to criticize myself for saying the wrong thing or acting the wrong way. And, most of all, I'm not going to listen to any of the voices in my head telling me what a "fuck up" I am.

Just this once and for today, I'm going to love myself as much as I want without any criticism of any kind from any part of me.

* * * * * * * * *

"Today, regardless of what I 'know', I will act as if I am free."

"Do I need my family on my healing journey?"

If we have partners and children, then our relationships with them are an integral part of our healing. During our healing, our families can either be one of our strongest sources of support or our most difficult obstacles in our movement for a healthier life. Healing, like each separate being, is particularly individualistic. Some of us who have children may find that they are welcome diversions and lifesavers when it comes to our healing. Our children may be a source of hope and inspiration, validating our own inner children. Our partners, if we have them, may also be strong, supportive people. Or not. We may find our partners to be the lifesaving force to our healing, providing the comfort and space we may need to let ourselves fully heal. Our partners may be the ones to bring us back to safe touch and safe love. Our partners may be the beckoning lighthouses in the hurricane storms as our emotions go thundering about us, and tidal waves come crashing down upon us. It may be the light that our partners shine that keeps us hopeful that all is not lost, that somewhere there is a steady port. Or not. Some of us may have partners just waiting for us to get better.

If our partners are with us on this healing journey, then all the better. If not, it is a sad state of personal affairs, and yet another path in our journey to be walked so that at least our partners are not hindrances to our healing. We can never do enough talking and honest communicating of where we are on this journey, even if it's only to say we can't talk or we hear that our partners can't be there for us. It is in dealing with the truth, whatever face is presented, that we make our most progressive steps.

* * * * * * * * *

"My family, along with my healing, is my priority."

"Why is waiting such a hard thing to do?"

Waiting is a fairly difficult space for many of us to inhabit. Some of us have spent so much time waiting for negative things to happen that we do not fare well now that life may be totally better for us. The imprint is such that we do not expect the uncertainty of life to bring us any good news. The few times it has were so overshadowed by the "struggle" that we failed to take in its message that good things can come from uncertainty. It is in times of uncertainty that we must continue on with the rest of our daily life activities, while the Universe takes care of that which we can not.

Learning how to be patient is a skill we all need. In fact, when we practice true patience, we then survive uncertainty with an inner calm and gracefulness. No amount of worrying and anxiety is going to change the fact that it will take two days or two weeks before we hear about a job we want; or before we hear whether we are going to get a raise; or before we hear from our significant other about whether what we said or did will change the world— our world.

The soul has the capacity to see us through whatever uncertainty we may be experiencing. We know that from past history or we would not be where we are today. We do not control the external world, only our busy, personal, internal world. If, for the moment, the uncertainty is too much to bear alone we can always call a friend, visit a friend, go for a walk, read a book, watch a show, or tackle one of those cleaning jobs we have been meaning to get to. We do not have to just sit and wait until something happens. We can wait with purpose, with knowingness. We can meditate, pray, or relax, allowing our minds to imagine positive visions of what we want in and for our lives.

* * * * * * * * *

"Waiting is my training ground for patience."

"Why do my feelings seem like sap glued to a tree?"

No matter how you look at it, being stuck is just no fun. The pushing and the pulling, the anger and the doubts, and the overwhelming frustration singe on the soul. Of course, it gets easier as we go along— grow along in our lives.

Taking on the task of getting unstuck generally means we have to confront something, a thing from our past protruding it's disquieting head into our present. We may have to confront a person or situation outside of ourselves— maybe it's an unruly neighbor whose noise keeps us awake at night or a co-worker whose actions interfere with our work. It may even be an issue with our partners that won't go away because we haven't honestly dealt with it. Many times, we haven't taken the risk to move things along and are stuck in old, familiar ways of acting.

It may be that the best way we can get unstuck is stop fighting it and let whatever we're afraid of happen, and then we will know what to do to get unstuck. Despite our fears of what may happen if we stop resisting being stuck in order for us to shift our healing, we have to chance going through the "stucknessed", (yes, sisters, it's okay to make up words!), until we get past it.

We have enough wisdom in life to know that nothing changes unless we initiate such change. We also have enough experience to know that if we try, such things work for the better simply because we tried...putting one foot in front of the other...like always.

* * * * * * * * *

"One step at a time...one day at a time."

"Why does my rage seem to have a life of its own?"

And what shall we do with our rage, our naked emotion that knows no boundaries, and that leaves no stone unturned? How shall we lasso it in and make it work for us? How do we not let it implode in us when we don't know what to do with it? How do we not let it immobilize others when we give it permission to reign, and we unleash it upon anybody who comes near our boundaries?

We sistas who have spent a lifetime stuffing our feelings down inside may seem drawn to this thing we call "rage" in the most unexpected moments. It seems to come from nowhere and has such power. Unleashed on its own, we are incapable of censoring what comes out of our mouths and we express how we feel— strongly and deeply. Our passions are aroused, and feelings we usually put to sleep, keep under wraps, or hide from ourselves are revealed to anyone crossing our paths.

The wonderful thing about rage is that it lets us know we are alive. In fact, its purposeful gauge is to let us know something is wrong; something is sorely amiss. Contrary to our popular belief, rage does not just spring upon us— it often gives little hints before making a full performance.

When we address the little hints— the nagging headache, the somersault stomach, or aching legs, for instance, then we put our rage in check. But, if we allow these feelings to drag on day after day, month after month and do nothing to heal them, then we in fact leave our sensibilities no choice but to one day go off and rage on! The choice, as always, is ours. Our passions are better put to use locating the source of our rage, working with it, and then directing the new energy toward advocating a cause or feeling we love, rather than distancing ourselves from the rest of our feelings and those we love.

* * * * * * * * *

"I am the Keeper of the Flame."

"What worthy thing could I possibly have to say?"

Quiet. A deep sister. Heavy. Still waters run deep. All words some of us have heard others use to describe us. Quiet and shy. A sweet sister. Nice and smooth to be around. Descriptions we perhaps cultivated lest anyone should learn the real truth— we didn't think anyone actually wanted to hear from us. We were, in fact, ashamed of who and what we were. We didn't know how not to blame ourselves. Of course, being quiet kept us from the maelstrom, kept us from being criticized, and most importantly, kept the anger and hatred directed away from us. No one wanted to hear our truth. At best we were a nuisance and at worst, a "family" problem, or the "problem child." We were the ones to bring the family shame by putting all the family's dirty laundry in the streets and the social agencies. No wonder they hated us. No wonder they turned away from us with our unlovable and unspeakable problems, bringing those dirty little secrets into the light; releasing the terrible knowledge we kept hidden just so everything would be all right, until even we couldn't stand the repulsion of the little secret that kept getting bigger and bigger with each new day, and bursting wide open without our permission.

The waters are not always still. Waters from the deep of the ocean can make its presence felt as its crashing tidal waves attack from its abyss; or the waters, free of its deepest rage, can soothingly caress the edge of the sand and stroke it with beams from the distant moon. We need not stay in silence anymore, nor fear what might we may say, think, or do.

We are our own freedom fighters, advocates, saviors, and rescuers, and a raging silence is a terrible thing to insist upon ourselves. If we are silent, let it be a conscious choice we think is necessary and not a silence because we are afraid of what might happen if we speak our minds.

* * * * * * * * *

"Silence is its own language."

"Is it possible to look in my mirror and not see my reflection?"

Ah, and when we are dispirited what shall we do? We think there is no place to go, nothing left to be said, and no one we can turn to for solace, comfort, and spiritual uplift. The heaviness that weighs on our chests seems unbearable, and the days ahead seem meaningless, null and void. Yet we continue to carry on our daily lives, seeing in the moment no end in sight. Perhaps that is the key..."for the moment." It is a bleak time for us. We are, in a word, inconsolable. There is nothing in particular that is wrong, but in a way, everything is.

It is in these times when we most want to give up on our dreams, our visions, our inner voices and inner children that we must reach deeper within than we ever have before, and not turn to the voice within that says, "It doesn't matter anyway."

There is a part of us, a place within our very souls, that is invincible, steadfast, and that can withstand any assault from wherever, and from whomever. This is the place we can return to in order to go into the world again. Make no mistake— we have withdrawn from the world to nurse our wounds, and it is in this very special place that we reclaim ourselves. It is from this place that our faith breathes steadily even though we may feel no hint of it. It is from here that our hope shimmers inwardly to dissipate the loss we so keenly feel. And, it is in this dwelling that our courage is fired to temper our daily challenges. Here, we make peace with ourselves so that we can keep on believing that each day is worthy of our presence and our participation. We persevere, *giving ourselves the gift of choice and hopeful possibilities,* and then we move in the world again, with the awareness that our Spirits continue supporting us as always.

* * * * * * * * *

"My soul knows its own way to healing; I just have to be willing to go there."

"What table is this?"

And then there are those of us, we who are women with restless souls, that will not be appeased nor quieted. We will not for another day have our truths silenced. We will speak even though others may not want to hear the words we say; we will sing with joy even though those around us would scoff at the melody of our happiness. We will take up our space righteously provided for us by the Universe. We may have many wants but our needs are few— a safe refuge from the outside, a lover to warm our nights, and a home to shield our children. Some food, as well, would be nice. It seems simple enough to ask for and to receive and yet...

We who are women with restless souls and a hunger for a life we have not yet tasted— we women who have only been teased by its emotional aromas and the magic of its sensual fragrances— we women with our restless souls and hearts of children and spirits that will not be denied— because we travel this journey of healing, have faced many challenges, overcome many obstacles, have risked many fears not of our making and because of these steps we are willing to walk are now sitting down to the full banquet of life's most scrumptious meal, saying *yes* to the joys of life itself— our life.

* * * * * * * * *

"Everyone deserves a nutritious meal at a bountiful table."

"And what shall I do with this day?"

What is the awesome power of neglect, this so-called benign abuse to all— children, lovers, even nature? A neglected seedling will still grow. Unlike the seed planted by the loving gardener, the neglected seed will sprout according to the whims of nature. It will take whatever it can get from the ground below and whatever the sky rains upon its thirsty sprouts. It will, if it can, survive. If not, it will simply die. But those that don't die have this great and awesome desire to survive which will not be stilled, stopped, or denied. And in the end, it may be as strong as or even stronger than the seedling that has received nurturance, and sustenance from its loving gardener.

We who have survived the vestiges of a neglectful upbringing are witnesses to the soul repairing itself from long-term aloneness. Our willingness to enter back into the human race by whatever means necessary and to love and be loved is truth triumphing over projected failure expectation. By virtue of searching to heal completely, by our constant journey to make the soul whole, we triumph over an empty past and fill it with what we so sorely missed— friends who love us, work worthy of our talents, and we have learned to nurture the dreams and visions of our hearts.

Any time we fall off this path of triumph, we need to only remember from whence we came and that we are lovable, worthy, and have a Divine Creator that sees fit to compensate she who is "less than" to become "more than". Each day, no matter the history of our past, is a new beginning. Each day we have the privilege and gift to shape our lives as we want them formed. It is why we are called "survivors".

* * * * * * * * *

"There is no greater gift than the life we live."

"Why does my body seem to ache in one place or another all the time?"

Many of us experience chronic physical pain— headaches that never go away, stomach aches that churn for days on end, bad feet that make our soles feel as if we are stepping barefoot on thumbtacks, arms and wrists that hurt with throbbing nerve pain, sinus problems that cause us to walk in mind fogs— the list is endless. Sometimes we simply suffer low-grade pain from all of the above at one time or another, thinking pain is a daily sustenance of life's offerings. It is not.

Our sisters that have traveled this path and moved on to another level of healing have learned that addressing emotional and mental issues tends to put us back in health modes that don't include daily, chronic, physical pain.

The headache that rages in our head is telling us that it can no longer be stuffed into a corner in our minds, and that its truth will find release either by our looking honestly at what the rage is, or by lodging inside our brain and continuously pushing against our heads. That burning in the center of our bodies is telling us that we can no longer stomach that which we have swallowed, and that either we look at it honestly or else it will burn a hole through the membrane linings as it tries to get out. All of our body pains are signals to us that all is not well, and though we may not have been able to address them properly as children, now that we are adults we can tend to them immediately.

It is possible to leave chronic pain behind. It is possible to heal from physical pain that has traveled with us from the past into our present daily lives. It is possible to now look at the reality of who we are and where we've been and to know that we can live in our bodies without pain or denial, and find relief.

* * * * * * * * *

"I can trust my body to signal steps in my healing."

"Can I heal the loss of my family or hope for their understanding?"

No amount of denial, fantasizing or pretending otherwise, and no amount of endless searching is ever going to fill the gap of "why?" Just when we think we have put this matter to rest, it raises and rears its ugly, two-fisted head again. We who are women of color and have a family history of sexual abuse as our personal legacy, and we who have been disowned from our families in one way or another because of it, have difficulty accepting being orphaned in such a manner and for such reasons. It is not unlike the person who loses an arm or a leg. We are still aware of the lost connection of family— the mother and father we once had.

Sometimes it is just an acknowledgment on our part. Yes, we know there is a loss, but it is not the paramount issue of our lives. But sometimes, we feel it more acutely than at other times, and the ache for something we can not feel anymore begins to grind on our brains and eat at our hearts.

Regardless of the circumstances, the *whys* and the *hows* of it, we feel the acute loss of what we thought we had— a mother, father, and perhaps some brothers and sisters. And if we have not lost them by their absence in our lives, some of us have lost them by the lack of emotional ties; the ties that bind are bound no more.

We deal with this loss as we do most of the losses in our lives that have meaning for us. We grieve in our way and soothe the souls of our "orphaned children."

* * * * * * * * *

"I grieve my inner child with understanding tears and self-love."

"When will these old feelings of mine leave me for good?"

Every now and then we are still touched by the clinging despair and depression that a legacy of childhood abuse will leave behind. Make no mistake that those of us who have survived such personal wickedness have made tremendous gains and progress in our lives. We may be going along with our daily lives where nothing has changed, and it may seem that suddenly the energy and zeal we have for living is rudely replaced by a void of nothingness. Nothing makes sense, nothing has meaning, and nothing could make any good come out of what we have and who we are. We find ourselves wondering if getting out of bed is such a good idea. During this time, facing another day seems unbearable. We try to make meaning, logic, and understanding of it all. We try.

We may not get the support we need during these times. We don't understand it, so how can our loved ones understand it? What to do? Ride it out? Fight it out? Negotiate? (I'll get up and do one chore and then go back to bed.)

If we were to seriously mother ourselves, we would simply say, "Don't worry, it's just temporary. Eventually it'll be better and I'll feel better. It's okay to be where I am." Sometimes our healing is a matter of accepting where we are without thinking it will last for days on end or overturn our lives. It's only for a little while. A bad day or a few bad days doesn't mean we are running away from ourselves or failing to heal. It's just a setback; it's just a bad day that happens to everybody regardless of personal histories of childhood abuse or otherwise.

* * * * * * * * *

*"Even though afraid and looking over our shoulders,
we see there is nothing to run from anymore."*

"Where can I go when the next thing that happens plucks my last nerve?"

Going deep inside. Away from everyone. Away to a place where no one can touch me. Sometimes it's like that. Nothing else works. When there is no one and no place to go, inside is the last and only refuge. When we run out of options, our souls provide the refuge.

We are not all the same and so it should come as no surprise that as many as there are of us, there are as many lifestyles and ways of living. To be sure, there are rules so we can live in harmony, or at least with some order. But the other side of the coin is that the way of life is defined as much as by the numbers of us that live.

Our souls are much wiser than what we perceive ourselves to be in our everyday living. Our souls are what keep us connected to the "bigger" picture of life. Our souls are the ones that provide the answers when we think we have run out of answers. Sometimes it means going into the deepest parts of ourselves. Sometimes it means withdrawing from the noise, and hasting all around us to listen to our wise, inner voices. Sometimes it means seeking that place inside that no one has access to except us.

* * * * * * * * *

*"Isn't it wonderful, that consistently, when all else fails,
the answer lies within ourselves?"*

"Why is it that I do everything I can to heal and still not much seems to change?"

It doesn't take much for some of us to be thoroughly discouraged. One navigates life through learning and doing. For many of us, early experiences taught us that nothing we did and nothing we learned was going to change the outcome of the day. So thoroughly did we learn this lesson that when things did change, we attributed it to something else, like fate or other people, not choices we willingly and gladly made. After all, no one willingly and gladly wants to change their caretakers into monsters or human rejecters of themselves.

And now, here we are at a turning point in our lives. We have a chance and opportunity to do what we want and we are resigned that it can not be done. Doesn't matter what it is— could be a decision to go back to school, choose a new career, move to another state, enter a committed relationship— and we find ourselves not making a decision to move at all, neither forward nor backwards. As if we could stand still while all around us the world goes marching on.

Well, there is a simple truth— no one can change our lives, live our lives, and make our decisions for us, except us. In the void or the vacuum where we choose not to do anything, others will make decisions about their lives and that, in turn, will affect our lives.

We are neither children nor helpless victims now. We are survivors, grown women, and even if our inner children clamor that things are not different, we know that not to be true. If we still have doubts that all our hard work to heal our lives has changed nothing, we can always check with our friends or our sisters further in the path of healing who are most honest and supportive in helping us.

* * * * * * * * *

"Looking around at my sisters, I know that I can do that which my heart desires."

Disconnected   **April 23**

"Why do I feel like I'm cut off from not only the outside world, but myself?"

There are times we feel unconnected to anything or anybody. On days like this, it feels as if we are adrift or literally just floating from one space to another, from one person to another, and when our task is done we are floating again until something from the external world or someone from outside of ourselves makes contact with us. We are momentarily engaged and then we float off again.

It is not the worst place to be, this floating space. But sooner or later we must come back into ourselves, must re-inhabit the body we are escaping from and the thoughts we wish to avoid. Sometimes our minds simply want time off from the constant thought-battering of insecurities, doubts, fears, and anxieties about ourselves. Our inner selves may be the captains of our ships, but even our inner ships can suffer a mutiny.

We need to connect again with people who care about and support us. We need to connect again with the part of us that knows that we are temporarily lost and disconnected from our innermost selves. We must ask ourselves, "What do I need to do to bring myself back into balance?"

Like any situation that we may try to avoid, it's a good idea to do something positive. We can make our next action be something we "want" to do, something we "like" to do. Or, we can call someone we like. We can get in touch with one of our inner children and ask them what they would like to do that's fun or pleasant. Our healing is not always about working on our problems and issues related to our SA. Healing is also about having fun and joy in our lives, and that means finding activities that will provide us such opportunities for ourselves and with those who care about and support us.

* * * * * * * * *

"Time out has its place and so does re-connection to others, and especially myself."

"What shall I do when I don't know what to do?"

The world has plans, schemes, and machinations all set in motion and moving along on a schedule all its own. And we are tired and anxious and frightened all at the same time. We work and we strive and we plot and we plan, not unlike the world; but unlike the world, we can not go on indefinitely without nourishment and time out.

Sometimes we want so much to be like those folks who always seem to have it together— their houses are spotless, their children mannerly, their partners love them, they progress yearly at their jobs, and they always seem to be at peace with the world, with ready smiles on their faces. There seems to be no problem that gets them down, no troubles they can not surmount, no foibles in their lives they can not untangle.

Sometimes when life seems to swirl about us and we find we are grasping at everything while holding on for dear life, it is helpful to remember that the "very hairs on our heads are numbered." In a world that seems beyond our comprehension, it would help to remember that we have a Higher Self, a Divine Power that acts when we can not. It is also helpful to know that we have only one life to live, and that is ours.

* * * * * * * * *

"Only I can live my life."

Staying   **April 25**

"How will I know whether to stay or leave a relationship?"

We are at times the most restless spirits in the Universe and know the place of leaving very well. Often we do so because we don't know how to stay because, in our eyes, once again, someone or something has failed us and our expectations. And while all of it may be true or none of it whatsoever, leaving does nothing to change our worlds. We do.

Sometimes leaving is the best thing in the world for everybody involved. Nothing good can come of a relationship that has dragged on too long simply because we didn't know what we would do once we left. Those of us with backgrounds of abuse have learned that leaving can be the only answer, especially since the perpetrators didn't think they were doing anything wrong. But what happens when we are in relationships and we aren't getting what we want, but our partners are open to change and want to find a way to live together as much as we do...and still we feel the pulling to leave? When is it right to stay amid the compromises and promises?

Nothing of beauty grows without labor and pain. Even the plants have to withstand turbulent weather and natural chaos. Leaving because we don't know what else to do only produces another situation where, at some point in time, we will have to come to the same precipice of decision making. If we are in relationships where we love our partners, spouses, lovers and they love us and are willing to make the changes needed to be made, are willing to show up and honors us and our relationship, then we have an opportunity to stay and give ourselves the *gift* of having a loving relationship, and one we are surely deserving of.

* * * * * * * * *

"We are who we are no matter where we go."

"Is there a Divine Creator in my small scheme of life?"

Spirituality, like sex, like love, like driving...is such a personal thing. Our viewpoints, our belief systems for why we are here, at this time and on this planet, are very personal perspectives indeed.

Being here, alive on this day and in this world, is probably one of the greatest mysteries of life, if not, the greatest mystery of all. Can any of us really think that it all ends when we die? The hunger inside of us to do more, have more, be more than what we are today...the hunger that causes us to create...the hunger that causes us to crave and have love...all must come from some Primordial Creator.

When we are faced with our daily living— be it our jobs, our relationships, or our everyday routines, and when we are confronted by profound problems, some of our own making and others simply tossed at us to deal with, such as rape, incest, battery and/or assault— we must have an inner strength to withstand such confrontations. If we do not, then our very first order of business is to find and build a viewpoint, a vision if you will, of how we meet and deal with the outer world.

Sometimes we may join a spiritual group to share these personal beliefs we have in common. Other times, we may choose to walk our path of spiritual belief in solitary travel. Whatever we decide, it is our souls acknowledging that we have a Higher Power within our grasp, a Spirit that dwells within, walking with us even if invisible to our eyes, sharing our daily lives and helping us to learn why we are here at this time and in this space of the Universe, and living an existence we call our lives.

* * * * * * * * *

"We do not walk alone in this mystery we call life."

"What do I need to do to get focused?"

There are days when we are rolling with the rhythm of the world. It's doing its thing, we are doing ours, and we are in harmony. Problems are not overwhelming. We soothe the aches of our children, assuage the egos of our loved ones, take care of our inner world, and feel pretty good about ourselves because all is going well. And then suddenly it all stops and we are momentarily stunned by our inability to get back on track, by our inability to focus our lens for clarity of what is actually happening in our lives.

Our thinking seems scattered at these times. It's like we have a pack of marbles in a suede bag and suddenly the tie becomes loose and the marbles are falling out of our hands, dropping on the floor, bouncing here and there, and some even getting stuck in corners.

Feeling temporarily scattered is not the end of the world. We come from backgrounds of sexual abuse and may have difficulty with distinguishing scatteredness from disassociation or end-of-the-world dramas. Being scattered sometimes simply means we are overloaded and need to regroup. Being scattered means scooping everything up and resettling, and sometimes simply means we need to "get a grip." It doesn't mean we've made a step backward or fallen off the edge. It just means we're part of the everyday world of life.

* * * * * * * * *

"Overload.. Regroup now!"

"When will there be a time we can all walk in peace?"

We are not the world's trash can. We may have decided, for whatever our reasons, that it simply is not worth the time or energy to engage in the bullshit shenanigans of others. We may have decided as part of our life plan not to engage in fights and debates about anything unless it has a direct result on us. Some of us may have decided that peace at all costs is the way to go. There is enough war going on this planet to make everybody happy who wants such things, and we have decided we will not participate in violence on any level, maybe even to the point of giving up our *right* to self-protect.

Yet we all know of situations where someone else will take the opposite viewpoint— everything is fodder and use for debate. These folks are so argumentative that they take the opposite side no matter what, even if it's against something they believe in! Fine for all that, but then somewhere along the line we become their targets.

It could be anywhere— in a work situation, a community meeting, or at a family gathering. Someone there likes to pick fights, likes to instigate group dissent and decides to focus in on us. If we are survivors of family incest, we may well have been the family scapegoat. And, as such, the tacit permission to pick on us was exercised regularly until we were able to be independent and move out.

While in the present time, we may often choose not to engage, it is not good to allow ourselves to be other people's superfund landfill. We are not the dumping ground of the world or our families. There comes a time when we must stand up for ourselves for all to see. For one thing, it's not good to allow another person to hold the rest of the world at fault for *their* problems; and two, it's not good for us to be their targets. Others need to know that if they don't have boundaries, we do.

* * * * * * * *

"Regardless of the situation, I no longer accept the role of victim."

"Will my need ever be filled?"

We who are mothers take a lot of hits for the ills of the world. And for that matter, so do our mothers take a lot of hits for what's ill in our world. No one's done a study, but more wars have been fought for lack of mother-love. When one has an in-built, embedded sense of security about one's place in life, wars are easily avoided. A sense of certainty that says, "This is where I belong," comes from our experience of being loved, and of course, our earliest experiences come from mother-love. It is being nestled and protected in the arms of one glad of our existence that eventually gives rise to the ideal healthy woman maneuvering around in the world of adulthood. It is in the imprint of such love that we go forward to take our place in the world.

But what happens when we don't have such experiences of security, when we don't have the imprint of mother-love? What happens when we crave and hunger for the insatiable need of the mother-love we didn't get? Or can't remember?

We mother ourselves. We learn how to love ourselves as mothers— unconditionally and with total appreciation for the simple fact that we are alive and that, in truth, we are lovable. We somehow dig deep and reach into our psyches where our most primordial memories are of love and comfort, and we grow the necessary ways needed to mother ourselves. We grow the arms to hold us, we create a space to contain us, and we create a place where no matter what happens with us, internally and externally, there is a refuge to which we can return...again and again for as often and as long as necessary to feel at home in this place we call our world.

* * * * * * * * *

"We are mother of self."

"Is there a difference between depression and sadness?"

Sadness is at times self-sympathy. It comes without judgment or castigation. It comes without "what ifs" or "only ifs." It is a state of being that asks for nothing and holds nothing against anything or anybody.

Sadness can be recognition of a state of affairs. Ours. Unlike depression, sadness does not immobilize us. And unlike anger, it looks for no target. Sadness belongs to us, is a part of us. It is recognition of how things are— not what we would like them to be. It is pain received and acknowledged. It is quiet reflection so we can go back into the world, functioning as we would like to. It is the feeling that reminds us that we are part of the human race, that we have dreams we want to see fulfilled, and that we can be and are the ones to do the fulfilling. It is the insight of knowing things do not have to be as difficult as they sometimes appear. It is the hindsight of knowing that we will do better next time.

Sadness is the sweet tears of a long journey. It is the reluctance to say good-bye when we know we have to move on. It is the feeling that moves in harmony with the rest of world in recognition of our human condition and how we are part of the bigger picture. It is the blanket we give ourselves to comfort from the cold night. It is part of our woman legacy that leads to the door of hope for a better day. And it is in recognition of who we are, what we are not, what we have done, what we have not done, that all is not in waste, that nothing lasts forever, that everything has its own time, and that the words *always* and *never* are not actions, but just words.

* * * * * * * * *

"It is okay for my sadness to be self-sympathy or empathy for others."

May 1

LITTLE TOUCHES

Little touches
have big consequences
and are best accepted
with a wary eye
a keen mind
intuition
and training
in self-defense

"Will my partner support me on my healing journey?"

Next to the healing process itself, healing from CSA without partners that are supportive of the work we have to do is devastating to most of us. Few are the survivors that can compartmentalize non-support in their living situation with a partner. We do have choices, even in this situation, but they may be choices we do not want to make.

While we are healing, we are changing. And when we change, it means that our partners may change their behavior and expectations of us and the relationship as well. Without the support of our partners in an active, ongoing relationship, the healing process becomes murky and more complicated than if we were single and living alone.

* * * * * * * * *

"Supportive partner or not, I still must heal."

"Is being true to myself as good as it gets?"

Every now and then our healing takes a step forward to another level, moving onward to higher ground. Sometimes when we are in the thick of it, it does not seem that we are making changes, only letting out pent-up feelings and thoughts we have never expressed before. Then, we may find ourselves at another level where we are confused and unsure of what is going on in our lives; we do not know if we are coming or going, only that the pain is abating a bit, and that everything is not as intense as it used to be.

But there are times, and for some of us, even days, when we come into our health, and of the possibilities that could happen in our lives. We come out of the maze of our healing work and begin to enjoy the fruits of our labor. Why else seek healing except to experience and have a more fruitful and joyous life? Why else put ourselves through the trauma of lancing wounds unless we thought we could heal the injury and become whole? For healing is about wholeness and balance, and a sense of well-being in the world we live. Healing is about healthy self-gratification and about growing and changing so that our lives are happy and joyous, and we are fulfilled with ourselves and with our loved ones. Healing is about finding our spot, our place, and our nature in life. Healing is about living in the present without the past ghosts and monsters having a premium spot in our daily living. Healing is about saying *yes* to the creative forces that flow through our very beings, asking for expression that only we can give it.

Our CSA histories do much to blot out the expression of our true selves. In healing we see who we really are, and no one and nothing can take away our authentic selves.

* * * * * * * * *

"Authenticity equals 'be true to yourself even around others'."

"How can I get professional help when it's so damn expensive?"

Many survivors would seek professional help if they could afford it. Therapy allows us to explore the "whys" of the things we do that we don't understand. A therapist is a helpful guide as we risk telling our stories and then trying new behaviors to find solutions to old problems.

Many survivors have found that friends and loved ones don't want to hear our stories. The idea that an adult would sexually assault, rape, molest and violate a helpless child is revolting and repulsive to hear for a lot of people. And yet, in order to heal we need to share our stories with someone who is willing to listen and be witness to what we have to say happened to us.

Some of us can not leave our homes because we are afraid of what might happen to us when we step out the door. Others of us avoid employment opportunities because we fear we are incapable of performing the duties and responsibilities even though the truth is we qualify for such job positions. Some of us fear to enter into intimate relationships because we are afraid of the trust needed to be close with another person.

It is a vicious cycle because we need money to pay for professional help and yet numbers of us are living in poverty or have low-incomes or have no insurance and can not afford the help we need. At the same time, our fears, anxieties, phobias and other defenses that have become part of our daily living do not allow us to make or attain the funds we need to pay for professional help, and therefore travel the healing journey on our own with varying results.

Some of us are fortunate and can get help through local rape crisis centers where an allocated number of sessions are free. Sometimes that is enough to help us find a way to afford a therapist to help us on our journey of healing. It is not a sign of weakness to seek professional help. In fact, it is a sign of strength and another path for our healing.

* * * * * * * * *

"Healing is my priority and I will find a way to do it."

"Are there other people who feel like me?"

No one knows exactly what makes one person different than another, but the history of our CSA is as individual as our DNA genetic code. Who's to say why, if two people share a traumatic experience, one person seems to be a high achiever and the other seems to be falling all over herself no matter where she goes, for everyone to see?

Some of us are overachievers and excel at everything we do. We do well in school, at the office, on the home front with our partners and children, and no one is the wiser of the inner turmoil we experience on a daily basis. If we seem to lose it once a month, it will be chalked up to PMS. But if we do not deal with the inner voices we hear telling us of the real feelings and thoughts we have, that once a month will turn into twice a month until it hits almost on a daily basis. We may start to see the house that Jill built come tumbling down, brick by brick.

Others of us are underachievers and we excel at nothing except perhaps putting ourselves down. We do not do well in school, on the job, or on the home front. We argue with everybody, including ourselves. We can see nothing right with ourselves, only anything and everything that's wrong with us.

Then there are others of us that are simply "out there." We can not make contact with anybody, and sometimes not even ourselves. Except like a small bird that has flown the coop, we fly around intermittently and taking a rest, precariously balance on the wire.

Our personal histories may manifest differently to the outside world, but we have shared as a group the distrust, the betrayal, the inner struggle, the little voices that eat at us like termites and tear and wear us down; all from which we seek to heal so that we might live harmonious lives as we are intended by the Divine Oversoul of Life.

* * * * * * * * *

"Though my path may be different from others, I do not walk alone."

"Is there an end in sight to this road I'm traveling on?"

Wouldn't it be great if during our healing we could shelve our feelings for a few days or a few weeks and get back to them when we feel stronger, better, or more up to dealing with them? Wouldn't it be great if we had the option to schedule dealing with our issues at a time that would work for us instead of when they came up? The thing about healing sometimes is that it is so inconvenient. Many of us have projects from our jobs that need our full attention. Some of us have projects we have committed ourselves to in our communities or our churches. Others of us have one or more children that need every free moment of attention we can muster, and healing at these times just seems so impractical all the way around.

Dealing with issues on our own schedules is wishful thinking on our parts, because we know that's not how it works. Once we begin to look at our lives— at the abuse and its effect upon us and our loved ones— there is no turning back, and our healing is not based on our external timetable. In fact, it may be the external world that has kicked off our healing. Something happens on the job that triggers our memories; a child of ours may come to the age when we were first molested; or we get married. For that matter, we may already have been in therapy and we "stumble" across a forgotten incident as we pursue other issues.

Whether we are in the beginning of our healing journey or in the thick of it, we may feel that it is never going to end, and that we are stuck with feelings that are painful and disturbing. But the truth is nothing lasts forever, and when we grow, we let go of so many things that are no longer necessary or useful to us in our lives, especially our fears, anxieties, and phobias. When we are in doubt about the length of our journey, we can check in with our friends, loved ones, and support resources.

* * * * * * * * *

"Should I lose my way, my Higher Self knows the path and leads me ever-forward."

"And why would I celebrate her?"

Mother's Day. Do we recognize it or deny it? Many of us healing from CSA, incest, or rape by a family member may have strong, ambivalent feelings about celebrating a day that recognizes and honors our mothers. Some of us are real clear, though. Either we do recognize and celebrate it without any misgivings, or we have second thoughts because Mom was "there" and/or she didn't know what was going on, or it's another day like any other— that indeed, we would be better off not acknowledging a day in which the person we honor causes us pain, disappoints us, or exists only as someone we thought we once knew, but who no longer is considered "Mother" in our hearts.

Few are the people who would argue there exists a bond stronger than mother and infant, but many of us walk the two-edged sword of mother-love, mother-wound. She was "there," but she wasn't. She knew about the abuse and/or ignored. We told her about it and she didn't do anything to stop it or to save us. And yet, when she could, when she was strong enough to rise to the occasion, she stepped in and in some cases totally removed us, and the family, from the tyrant of our abuse. She may have even asked for our forgiveness for not doing something sooner or not doing anything at all. And we may feel that if we forgive her we are betraying our truth and ourselves.

We are not betraying ourselves when we choose to celebrate the woman who mothered us through life if that is what we want to do. It's simply saying, "I love you in spite of all that has happened and I want to celebrate that love with and for you." We are not denying our past histories, but rather, we are embracing a relationship which survived an ugliness in the family that none wished had happened, nor were powerful enough to stop. Even if the sword is sharp at times, it doesn't change the fact that this is the woman who raised us, and in her way, did the best she could. We celebrate those times that she was "there," whenever she could be, and however many times that might have been.

* * * * * * * * *

"If we have no mother to celebrate, then let us celebrate the mother in ourselves."

"How can I stop internalizing thoughts that do not belong to me?"

We survivors of CSA often blame ourselves for the assault, rape or molestation. And even after many years when we recognize that we were only children at the time, subject to the whims of adults around us, we still blame ourselves to the point where sometimes we say, "I wish I'd never been born." Sometimes blame is not so obvious, and we pick and chip at ourselves, saying things like, "I really screwed up," "I should've fought back," "I shouldn't have been so sexy or flirtatious even if I was only two years old." We continue to carry the guilt and the blame into our adulthoods, punishing ourselves for a crime we did not commit, but in truth, were its victims.

Sometimes if we looked forward to spending time with the perp, or if there was a hint of pleasure that our bodies reacted to, we really took the blame for the abuse, saying it was our fault because of our feelings for that person, forgetting that the majority of children are filled with good thoughts and feelings for the adults that spend time with them.

Sometimes we don't take care of ourselves, seek the treatment we need, or heal from the emotional scars, because we think we should be punished. We feel that our problems and fears are the Universe's way of punishing us for what happened.

Of course, none of it is true. Children are not responsible for the actions of adults no matter what the relationship to the child. When abuse happens, it is never the child's fault. One of our biggest steps in healing is to see how little power we had as children, and to give up the self-blame. When we let go of that self-blame and responsibility, we free up our energy to heal our minds and our souls. When we are consciously aware that we have forgiven ourselves for being children who were helpless and powerless, then we can begin to see our way to the wholeheartedness of our healing.

* * * * * * * * *

"The shame belongs to the perpetrator, not me."

"Will I ever find my way back to my soul?"

There is a point in our healing when we seem to wake up, where we look around at the world as if we are seeing it for the first time...as if seeing ourselves for the first time as who we really are. It is almost as if we come home to ourselves.

This is not about a rude awakening. This is about looking in wonderment at what the world has to offer...for real...and our relationship to it...for real. It is about looking at our reality.

As survivors we spend a lifetime, and a young one at that, honing our defense skills, hiding, so to speak, until we're so good at it that we end up not only hiding from the world but from the very essence of who we are. In order to live our daily lives, some of us spent a lifetime not being ourselves, denying who we were to ourselves and to the world. Time passes. We no longer have to do that. We may end up hiding for a very long time unnecessarily. We are so cautious about who we let see us and who we are willing to let into our lives. And then we begin this healing commitment, this healing journey. And we become aware, sometimes excruciatingly, painfully aware that there are whole sides to ourselves that we do not know, and that we have become afraid of knowing because we have had to hide so much just to be, just to move around, sometimes just to breathe and stay alive.

A homecoming sometimes presents itself in awe. A soul coming home is awesome.

* * * * * * * * *

*"And when she had shed the tears she did not know she carried,
her soul grew light within."*

"Why do my walls I built for protection now seem like prison bars?"

At some point in our lives, we actually become free of major obstacles resulting from our past, individual histories. Those phobias we thought would always be with us, we have vanquished from our realities. Those fears which could stop us from taking a first step towards anything— work, family, relationships— we have soundly defeated. If these old, internal enemies come around, we know how to dispel any power they may have had in directing our lives. We know how to re-empower ourselves by letting them go and recognizing them for what they are— external thoughts we no longer internalize.

One of the things we may find happening to us is that when these walls come down and we have the freedom to rebuild, we may not know how to use the tools before us, or even what those tools are. For so long in our lives it seemed we were without choices, but as we grow in our healing we realize we have numerous choices. And with these new insights, some of us then fall into a poverty of thinking that says we still don't know how to make choices for ourselves.

It would appear that not only do we have to heal our souls, we must also heal our brains...that is, our way of thinking. Just as many of us grew fearful of feeling, many of us grew fearful of thinking, of trusting our own thoughts to make the right choices for ourselves, of the ability to choose the right lover, the right job, the right place to live, or the right friends. Sometimes we made choices that were too little to solve our problems and sometimes we made choices that were too big, trying to solve everything in one day.

During these times it helps to return to some of the adages of 12-Step programs with sayings such as "Keep it simple," "One step at a time," and "One day at a time." Sometimes in taking down the walls of our defenses and rebuilding our lives, it is not necessary to rebuild new walls, but rather, strengthen the foundation of our new truths. Such steps on the path of our healing call for different ways of thinking, which of course starts with one idea at a time.

* * * * * * * * *

"All new ideas begin with a single thought."

"And where does it go?"

A lot of us are familiar with the old fairytale of "Rumpelstilskin," the gnome who slept for twenty years. It may seem to some of us that in our healing journey when we recover memories we thought were forgotten, it feels as if we slept through our lives numerous times.

It is no news that survivors of child abuse have difficulty with setting goals and following through to the completion of such goals in a timely manner. Childhood, where time seemed to stretch forever, for some of us became a reference point for not moving forward. Sometimes, we still act as if we are on childhood time and we move through our lives in tempo with our inner childhood clocks.

Sometimes as a result of our CSA histories, procrastination becomes a regular pattern in our lifestyles. We put off completing tasks and goals as long as we can because we have learned that the future may bring us untold and unmanageable trouble. Others of us become obsessive because everything has to get done and be perfect, or we'll suffer unbearable consequences. As a result, our timeline for goals that we set for ourselves becomes distorted in our adult lives, and it may be that nothing gets done as scheduled and on time.

Learning to live in present time in an adult mindset can be one of our challenges in healing. Realistically planning goals we can carry out is how we keep ourselves in balance. We know that when we go outside the present time, we run into trouble. We know that going outside of present time causes worrying and unnecessary anxiety. Dealing with the here-and-now as opposed to obsessing about the problems of tomorrow is one of the ways we know "where times goes" and also that we are healing.

* * * * * * * * *

"Our healing is the present."

"What does it mean to be free?"

There's something about the nature of summer that brings us feelings and thoughts of freedom. The warmth of new days allows plans for doing activities on the outside. We can go out of our shelters, shed heavy clothing, and do more things. We have more movement, more time, and our days are longer.

Some of us do not want that freedom and do not welcome the breath of summer's light. Some of us are frightened because in the blaring light of freedom we may see just how chained we are to beliefs and actions that we inhabit during the winter.

Freedom means we can be what we want and do what we will. Freedom also means we have the actual opportunity to set goals and accomplish them...or fail. Freedom means we can take a chance because we are no longer locked up, for whatever reason, by others or ourselves.

When slaves in America were emancipated, many were overwhelmed by suddenly having barriers and boundaries removed from their paths. After leaving the plantations where they had been previously enslaved, understandably, many returned to these places because they were unprepared psychologically and socially to be the determiners of their own fates. But some were determined not to be turned away; some reached down deep within and were committed, regardless of the obstacles placed before them, to make use of their freedom to enhance their lives and those of their loved ones.

Despite our fears and misgivings, many of us have worked long and hard for this summer of freedom from our fears and our beliefs. We have toiled continuously to bring balance to our lives, and to live the full lives we have dreamed. Like all the seasons, we must move onward with each new year and with each new task completed. And because we are human beings endowed with this need, our souls rise fervently to the beckoning call for our life of freedom.

* * * * * * * * *

"With each step of my healing I am free to choose to do what I want."

"Do I need a crisis to get myself functioning?"

It may seem unreasonable at first that we have to tell ourselves over and over again that we really are okay, but the truth is that is what we have to do. We may have lived lives where we were told over and over again that we were simply "wrong"— wrong for living, wrong for wanting to be safe, wrong for wanting to do the activities *we wanted* to do, wrong for wanting to validate the very lives we were given so that when the time came, we could live the lives we wanted, and wrong for wanting to be the women we wanted for ourselves. When it all came true we found ourselves in askance, "What else?" "What's wrong with this picture?" "What's wrong with me?"

When we are doing the things we are supposed to do, when we are living the lives we have made for ourselves and it still feels wrong, when we feel as if our lives are *wrong*, it's probably a good indicator that things are "right," and that we are proceeding as we should. Probably more than anything, one of the challenges we must face and need to accept is that life does not need to be full of crises and problems to get from point A to point B. When we accept that our lives do not always have to be in crisis, we are able to see life as something that is full of challenges and excitement instead of only obstacles and problems.

* * * * * * * * *

*"Sometimes the kaleidoscope of life that appears chaotic
needs a keen eye to see the emergence of the true pattern."*

"Was ever there a wound like this before?"

Death is sometimes welcomed by survivors. Sometimes it seems like an option to a painful life that many of us are living. In fact, many survivors of CSA feel as if some part of them is gone forever because of the abuse and it is not uncommon to hear some of us say, "I feel like a part of me died back then." Sadly, some survivors commit suicide in childhood as a result of sexual abuse.

Regardless of whether one is a survivor there are times we welcome death, particularly of a loved one who has a life-threatening illness and is suffering because there is no treatment available. Evenso, we are never prepared for its impact upon our lives. As survivors we experience something similar, especially if it is incest and by a family member we have daily contact with. Once we have been sexually assaulted by a family member we realize that anything can happen in life including the death of our family life as we once knew it. We learn that nothing is certain, that in one moment our life can be turned upside down for the worse, and maybe it would be better if we were dead. We will never again have the family we had before the incest. We may, in our healing, have to come to terms with the psychological impact that we killed a part of ourselves so that we could continue to survive in an insecure, unsafe and assaultive environment

Like the death of a loved, we don't get to say when or how long we may mourn the death of our childhood. We have to live with it and like all mourners grieve that loss so we can come back into health and participate fully in life. That road is a tough one to travel, but not impossible.

.

* * * * * * * * *

"Loss of innocence and childhood happens to everyone;
how we make peace with it is up to us."

"And who would have thought I'd come to this place?"

When we delve into our healing, even totally committed, it can seem that it may never happen. We fear that the bad times will never be over, that the struggles in our relationships will always be there, and our memories are as if it all just happened yesterday. Sometimes on our healing journeys, we may even want to kick ourselves, literally, for opening the proverbial Pandora's Box which holds good and bad news.. We ask ourselves, "Why did I do this?" "Why couldn't I have left this alone?"

We know nothing lasts forever in this world. Just as the good times of the past leave us with a longing and yearning to have those times repeated again, the bad times, unresolved and unfinished business, can leave behind a powerful pull to look at the memories from our past. Thankfully, and in spite of its pull, we want to say good-bye and good riddance to all the garbage that became a part of our lives.

Over time, we gradually notice that we are no longer our worst enemies, that our lives are in fact fulfilling and, sometimes even joyful beyond what we could have wished for ourselves. Finally, we are living our lives more in balance than out of balance. We see that our lives are healthier, that our relationships with our friends and/or loved ones are better, that our work lives are what we want, that we are pursuing dreams we only wished for ourselves, never actually believing that we could live the lives we wanted. Seldom does this triumph come noisily and suddenly. And all of it is a matter of hard work stealthily done on our part, not giving up on ourselves when we felt we couldn't go one step further, and taking risks we were uncertain would lead to our healing.

It's not often we get to give ourselves a satisfactory pat on the back, and not often we get to welcome back that part of ourselves we thought was lost to us. It is gratifying to know that if we are patient and trusting of our Higher Selves, this is possible for any and all of us. We need only look at others to see that the path has been paved and that it is open to us all.

* * * * * * * * *

"And we are all of us Blessed."

"Why can't I fill up?"

Sometimes we seem to get our lives together. We seem to get a reprieve from the aftermath and residue of our sexual abuse histories and we get to coast a little bit on an even keel, sometimes actually enjoying ourselves.

And then sometimes life is more than just a struggle. There are obstacles we still must overcome that we thought we already had overcome. Sometimes we just can't seem to fill up. We feel that nothing is enough, that nothing we can think of will fill the cup, will soothe the restlessness that we can not seem to contain while we fervently search for anything that will give a hint as to where our energy can go and move us through to the next phase.

During times when we have these wants that can not be filled, perhaps it is best we stop struggling and just stay, sitting with the feelings that come from knowing that the cavern has no bottom, the cup will never be filled, and the craving will not be soothed at the moment we want it to. Sometimes we just have to sit and wait and listen to what inside of us *can* take care of us, and in a Zen-like manner acknowledge to ourselves that which causes us so much wrestling with our spirits will only be quelled when we stop struggling against that which will not be quelled.

* * * * * * * * *

"I am the me I do not know."

"When will the pain end?"

It is, every now and then, a matter of the unbearable pain of being. No matter what we say and what we think, it seems as if, for the moment we can not rid ourselves of the everyday constant of mental stress and emotional pain. For some of us it is low grade, takes a tremendous amount of patience and faith on our part, and we seem to move at a snail's pace, if that, in our healing. For others, it is a sudden glimpse of the feeling of unbearableness and we are compelled to fill all the empty spaces and moments so that we never have to acknowledge the depth of the pain. We jump in full speed ahead and walls and fears be damned.

We can not stand guard 24-7. At some point, we stand face-to-face with the pain. In the world of healing, there just is no getting around it, and there is no escaping the reality of what we are feeling and where it is coming from. The only way to heal the pain is to go through it. We seek to make ourselves whole and that means acknowledging all our parts and memories that come to us for self-recognition and a healing only the Spirit, with our cooperation, can give.

During this time we need not give up hope. As adults we will never be helpless like we were as children. Even when the memories come back and we experience that which we ruthlessly banished from our child reality, we can always remind ourselves that we survived it, that it all happened in the past, and that today we are healing. By directly looking it in the face and feeling the feelings that arise, we are securing ourselves in the knowledge that we survived it all. Now. Our healing can continue. Again.

* * * * * * * * *

"It is not magic, but truth that heals-- even when it hurts."

"How can I help them in a world so different than mine?"

Our young female children are hurting and lacking in love not only from society, but also by our families and communities. Of course, not all our female children are unloved. But, there is a sizable number that seems to be growing each day that find themselves wanting in the way of parental love and community connection. It is an alarming realization that now, more than ever, teenage girls are experiencing battering from their boyfriends. Such liaisons serve to point out to us that there is much work to be done in rehabilitating our communities and families, for we know that children most often mimic the behaviors of those adults closest to them.

We who are women of color and of African descent know only too well the vulnerabilities we face as part of our legacy in this society. We know that society sees us as Black before it sees us as the same as others. Because of the embedded racism within the psyches of our society, we know that when we have problems, society sees those issues and concerns as "Black" problems or the "Black problem." Childhood incest and molestation affects all people in our society, but when experienced by Blacks it is considered to be a "Black problem."

We shouldn't be surprised that no one takes the sexual abuse and incest of Black children as seriously as other racial and ethnic groups. But just because society doesn't take seriously the problem of sexual abuse and incest in our communities, that is no reason for us to turn away in helplessness or shame from those who live it the worst— our children.

Those of us who have healed must reach out to sisters and brothers who are, on a daily basis, living in an environment of neglect and sexual abuse. As children we were alone with our problems, and as adults we have the choice to help others not be alone and to reach out to them. Even one smile from a stranger can, if just for one moment, give hope to a child trapped in a world of silence and fear.

* * * * * * * * *

"I have traveled too far in my journey to doubt that I can make a difference in the life a child."

"What do they mean by the 'Courage to change'?"

I am no longer the woman I was before walking my healing journey. There are times I forget the frightened woman I was now that I'm the free woman I am. Free to go where I want, free to be with the people I want, free to pursue the career I want, and free to wake up in the morning and be free of all the fears and obstacles I've overcome in the past.

And yet, sometimes, like now, I am afraid of the person I've become. I've taken off all the raiments from the past, and on my bed lay my new clothes— clothes I'm not even sure which part of me has picked out. Each day is a discovery of the new me, and sometimes that is very scary. I have an inner strength now that no one can touch or destroy. I *know* this. And yet there are times I am still afraid and anxious and yes, sometimes even panicky. It seems and feels crazy because they are, after all, only my feelings. Sometimes I wish I had my old fears back, my disassociations, my obstacles that would stop me from doing what I wanted to do, my phobias and walls I built to keep others out and me locked in.

Now I turn to Courage to be the me I truly am. Sometimes I do not like what I see. I am different than before my recovery. But I am learning what "the courage to be" is. I am learning to accept my newly-healing self with all my new fears and new situations. Wherefore I didn't care about things or people, I do now. It takes courage to feel again, to allow another person to see me for who I really am, and trust that I've chosen wisely in friends and lovers. It takes courage to trust that in showing myself, they will not intentionally hurt me or betray my trust or shatter my newly found ability to love again.

I look in the mirror, searching for scars no longer visible, yet I remember still their placements upon my face. Bravely, I meet my reflecting eyes and with the newest of feelings, and more than a little courage, I like the me I see.

* * * * * * * * *

"I have traveled too many paths in my journey to forget how far I've come."

"Why do I always feel I need to jump-start my life?"

She had already chosen in her mind the kind of car she wanted. It had to be brand new. Frequently, as she passed various car lots she would make a note of a car she liked and continue to her destination. Finally, she decided, on what car she wanted and the next day she went to the car lot and picked out her car. It was perfect— shiny, smooth, her favorite color, purple; it was compact but not tiny, and had all the accessories. Taking the key from the salesperson, she turned the key over, revved the engine gently and then heard it click off and the motor stop. Turning to the salesperson, she simply looked in askance. The salesperson shrugged and said, "Try it again." She tried the ignition again, and sure enough the motor kicked in and continued its hum as she smoothly, comfortably, and coolly drove her new car home.

Sometimes it's like that for us. In order to get going we may think we need a jump-start. We may think we need to look under the hood, tinker with a few things, or even have the engine rebuilt before it can run again. But most times, we just need to try again. When we think everything is just right and fixed and we are ready to go, we may find we can not start. We begin the checklist. Did I do this? Should I do this? Would I be better off doing this? We try everything we can think of that might get us started, trying to figure out what's wrong when everything about us says all the working parts are there. We could make our lives a little easier if, instead of trying this, that, and the other, we simply do nothing more than try the first step over again.

Just like the woman who turned the ignition key a second time instead of making extra work for herself by looking under the hood, we can simplify our lives, too. Everything that doesn't start right away doesn't have to be a big deal. We can take it easy and simply try again. Nine times out of ten, that's all it takes to get where we're going.

* * * * * * * * *

"There are days made just for driving with the wind."

Her body was bruised so badly that you could see the blues and reds turn purple a mile away. Drunk with last night's pain, she stumbled up her steps into her apartment. Cursing as her arm hit the cabinet where a bottle of whiskey waited patiently for her trembling fingers, she poured a shot of promised numbness, thanking the burn it brought to her stomach and then, in the presence of the empty room she said, "Fuck 'em." She sat down at her kitchen table, closed her eyes, and thought back to the night before, playing the *should've, would've, could've* game.

She thanked whomever it was that "ran" life that at the end she couldn't feel a thing, and prayed the man would just get up, leave, and take his slobbering tears with him. Who would've thought her prayers would be answered with a cop car and loud banging on the door and him leaving in handcuffs screaming at her to get him out of jail if she knew what was good for her.

She was impervious to the questioning, poking, and prodding of the personnel at the hospital the police had taken her to. She mostly remembered flashes of the night and was stunned by the fact that it didn't even hurt when he hit her. With each punch to her head, she listened to herself think, "This should hurt. How come it doesn't?" Too tired to fight him off, she went limp as he raped her. Then he began crying to her about what a terrible man he was and how he didn't mean to hurt, and then asked if she would forgive him.

When she left the hospital, she could see strangers shaking their heads, passing knowing looks, passing judgment on her as if they knew who she was or what had happened. Moving through her home, she locked every door and window, and got into bed with a butcher's knife. Drifting off to sleep, she vowed to herself that if anybody ever attempted to do what he had done the night before to her again, she wouldn't be the one going to the hospital after it was all over.

* * * * * * * * *

"We may encounter many obstacles before we seek a healing."

"How shall I reclaim that which was taken a long time ago?

We should not be surprised that one of our most difficult challenges to confront and champion is the reclamation of our personal strength and power, and our ability to exert it to further our growth and achieve the goals we set for ourselves. For many of us, the first time we exerted our personal power by setting boundaries and calling "foul," ended in disastrous results— certainly not the scenarios we had figured for outcomes with our child minds. Those of us who thought we could do so would tell the truth, and thought that in truth-telling the problems would be fixed and disappear. It is the desperate wish of every child who is being sexually assaulted, raped, abused, molested, or incested that she is believed by those adults to whom she tells her story. We survivors know better.

Our survival was intricately bound with our mental development, and for children life has no gray areas, no philosophical theories to explain their predicament. For children life is about good and evil, fair and unfair, wrong and right, and those boundaries are taught to us very early and clearly, especially the one that socializes us to always tell the truth.

If as children we were neither heard nor believed, as adults we can now rectify this injustice and in doing so, reclaim that which was stolen from us and return it to its rightful place: back into our souls. No one has the right to hurt anyone, especially a child. And all of us have the right to heal. It is our birthright and legacy as children of the Universe.

* * * * * * * * *

*"Reclaiming that which can only belong to me
is my inherent right as a child of the Universe."*

"Just how resilient are we as children?"

"I just want to put this behind me," he said. His matter-of-fact tone and directness belied the fact that he was just seven years old. He could have been 30, 40 or even 50 years old the way he was handling probably one of the biggest turning points of his life. He comforted his mother, telling her not to cry. He was decisive when he said he'd be ready to do the interview in a few days, just not the next day. He would talk with the police and the child workers and just "put it all behind him" so he could "get on" with his life.

Enough had already been taken from him. What good could come of grilling him, even if ever so gently with all our skills? Maybe, contrary to what we already knew, he would be one of those who would forget and not be bothered anymore with it. After all, men even more than women, are socialized to skillfully bury and/or dismiss so many of their feelings. Maybe this wouldn't be the life experience that would push him over the edge later in his life, like generating a new drug addict or alcoholic or teen prostitute.

But then again, maybe he would be one of those time bombs, burying it all and later in adulthood exploding, and some future lover, spouse, or innocent by-stander would pay the price of a long-forgotten, depraved adult's crime.

Better to push, even if gently, to help him confront it all as soon as possible. Better to risk emotional fears, words, and actions we do not want to hear from the lips of a child survivor, so this heinous assault won't be the reason for future failures or defeats. Times are changing and our children do not have to suffer in silence as they did in the past. Now we must be brave enough to help them face their fears as we, too, face ours. Child molestation, rape, incest, and abuse of all kinds are still happening, and it's on our watch.

* * * * * * * * *

"As long as a candle flickers inside our souls,
it is never too late to be a seeker of truth."

"How many forms of betrayal are there for our children? Let us count the ways."

He is stunningly beautiful. At first, people want to call him a pretty boy. For lack of words and knowledge, they will revert to clichés and say he is "effeminate." His posture, whether standing, sitting, or however waiting, is angry and wounded. If you can withstand his stare and look deeper, you will see the wounding that needs a "laying on of the hands," a healing of the heart.

He didn't want to be here. For a small spate of time he gives up much of his protection and tells us, if resentful and angry, a story we can barely hear. He speaks softly, and we are not sure we can hear what he has to say. Something clicks. He relaxes. He feels safe. He believes the possibilities of action we have given him will help him.

In the end we don't. We can't. His stories give us no hard evidence. It's too late. His perpetrator, his father, has already been visited by the police. He knows his son is with us at this very moment. When he gets home the father will interrogate the son and no mercy will be proffered. If he is lucky, this young boy-man will survive the night. If he is smart, he will run away as soon as he gets the chance, before he has to go home and find a safe haven of his own, where even we can not find or touch him.

We have made promises we can not keep. We have no "hard evidence" that his father rapes him occasionally except as the young boy-man tells us. We are legally as powerless and helpless as he is. Only he was smart enough to know it in the beginning and yet so tired and wishful that when he came upon our kindness and care, he let his guard down.

None of us will sleep well tonight. None of us should. And neither will he. His father is not the only criminal in his life.

* * * * * * * * *

"We can never stop closing our eyes until all our children are safe."

"Can we put them back, piece by piece?"

I heard her bones creak, belying her young age of 20. Actually, I was wrong. As the nurse proceeded with the exam, I heard the bones crack one by one. Sometimes it seemed so loud that surely they were splintering off and slamming through her skin, showing no blood or bone at all.

I try to look into her eyes but she will not look at me. She will not look at anybody. I try to maintain my gaze but the room is spinning. I think I can not breathe. Words I would say to her I say to myself: "Breathe. Breathe. Remember where you are. You are in a hospital."

I shake my head and focus again. I will myself to meet her eyes. I will myself to continue the beginning of the healing process. I tell her it is over, we are in a hospital, and if she wants she can hold my hand as she goes through this necessary exam.

I say all these things as I cover her with newly-heated blankets in hopes that they will alleviate the brittle cold that seems to engulf us both. I do not say that this act will in any way cover the terror that she has experienced for the last two days. Nor is this the time to tell her that even though she can not imagine it, should she choose, that even as battered and assaulted as she is, there is a healing to be had for her when she is ready.

With the exam over, she closes her eyes and appears to drift into sleep, and I whisper to her that I will stay with her until it is time to go home. For the moment, that seems to be enough for her fingers to release their grip from my numbly-squeezed fingers.

* * * * * * * * *

"There are broken bones and wounded souls;
both are healed by want, need and time."

"What's love or sex got to do with anything anyway?

One aspect of our sexuality is discovering who we are in relation to a person we wish to be intimate with. Our experiences strongly determine how our internal wiring may be set for quite a while in our lives. Depending on our experiences, we may find that our wiring has been twisted or broken and may need re-wiring; that is, as we heal we need to weigh current experiential knowledge against past mindsets.

Part of our healing is separating mixed messages. Though we may know as children that it is wrong for a parent or another family member to choose us for sexual involvement, we are incapable at the time of separating what they are doing from what we are. If we found ourselves trapped in such an abusive situation, we may have faulted what happened as a direct result of our existence, i.e., incest is bad, therefore I am bad, and these feelings are bad. It may be extremely difficult to erase such teachings from our minds. Later, when we are adults and enter into intimate relationships, we have to deal with the vestiges of these experiences. We may leave lovers behind because we can not separate such thinking. We may lose hope that we can ever have a healthy, mature, intimate relationship. We may think, *If it weren't for this one thing...* we would be flying with another person at our side.

The truth is, regardless of our CSA histories with incest from a family member or being raped, we would still have to deal with intimacy issues. That is the nature of relationships— being close, takings risks, and dealing with matters of trust regarding our hearts and dreams.

For survivors, our challenge is to separate what was then, from what is now. It is a difficult challenge, but not an insurmountable one. We deserve to love and be loved. The choice and work is ours.

* * * * * * * * *

"The ghosts of our past can be banished to our past."

"What's so great about love"?

It's not news that some of us have given up on love. Evenso, there's room for hope. If we have given up on love, it means that at some point in our lives, we knew what love was or at least we have some idea of what we think is genuine love.

Some say love is devoid of pain...maybe. After all, it's love that triumphs, which means there must be a struggle of some kind so maybe love is not devoid of pain. Maybe love is the great healer. No life is devoid of pain. We see suffering in our lives and in others' lives. Sometimes we see it in the faces of our children, such as those who are born with life disabilities or who are suffering from a traumatic life experience and we weren't there to help them. Other times we see it when something we do causes our children pain, such as a split-up with a lover or a spouse, or in a moment's haste when we turn our own anger indiscriminately on them.

Sometimes we see pain when we look in the mirror and are momentarily caught off guard by our reflections. Perhaps we see a hardness in our eyes that we hadn't recognized before, or maybe all we see is a dullness that we don't think belongs to us. We can become so dismayed that we can not continue to stare back into our own eyes. All is not lost.

We know how to recognize love. We see it when our children have been hurt and we soothe the pain by our own wisdom or by a simple caressing touch. We see it in our loved one's faces when in one moment they are dejected over an important factor in their lives and they turn to us, and some word we speak or some gesture we express restores a momentary loss of faith in themselves.

And we see love in ourselves as we find ways to make ourselves whole again, doing things and trying new ways to bring our lives back into balance, regardless of how painful it may be to look at, or how many times we tried before, refusing to accept loss as the victor. Otherwise, why would we be here at this moment, traveling our healing path?

* * * * * * * * *

"All healing is the gift from the Spirit of Love."

"How can I love now?"

There is no power greater than love. It is the gift that Deity gives to us all, and for some of us to *not* know our power is oftentimes a greater belief in our lives.

When we are angry at our beloved, is it more anger that heals the rift? When we are frightened of something or someone, is it more fear that eases our senses? Fear on top of fear to end all fear? Can we be frightened into a sane life? And when we are distrustful of one another, is it more distrust that renews our trust?

Love comes not by itself. It is tremendously fueled by faith— in ourselves, and the world we live in. We women who seek to heal the distortions left from an experience of sexual abuse will find that healing comes full circle back to love. Such love is what was damaged; such love filled with incredible innocence and unwavering trust in those we love is what we seek to reclaim. And reclamation such as this requires our having faith that love is our birthright and that *no one* has the right to take it away, especially with our acquiescence.

We run into trouble when we forget that we are more than just "women." We are women with souls. We are greater than that which we can only see. It is a fallacy to believe that this is only where we are from, this planet earth. We *know* on some level that we have a Divine Home somewhere. And that is why we ask for more than a humdrum life; that is why we ask to be wholly complete. We are driven by a Divine Presence within ourselves and we crave such connection to that kinship which often reveals itself in the Spirit of Love.

* * * * * * * * *

"Love is the treasure we all seek."

"What would it be like to live without my fears?"

We may have acquired certain phobias to help ourselves defend against the real fears in our lives: feelings and realities. The reality of being trapped and powerless may be too much for a child's mind to handle and so to function, we place the real fears of our life situation on substitute objects: fear of heights, fear of being in small, enclosed places; fear of open places, fear of certain animals such as spiders, cats, dogs, or birds.

The real object of our fear is displaced. How is it possible that the ones that love us can forget and strike out against us in a moment of violence? Their violence. Some of us may remember experiences being in the park with a trusted family member and suddenly adult hands start invading intimate parts of our bodies and we are told not to scream or not to tell or it will be worse the next time. With many of the assaults, we were frantically searching though our minds and asking, "What'd I do? What's happening?

When we are adults and have no further use for our phobias, when we have moved on and attended to those reasons for our phobias and worked them out, we may find that the phobias no longer have power. Suddenly, we see the object of our fear and the feelings don't come anymore: the panic, the dread, the anxiety, the confused thinking— all of it is gone. We now have energy to do other things, to focus our minds and lives on matters other than our old, intimate enemies. And we are at a loss.

Living a life in the shadow of fear and casting that fear off so the power is no longer there presents us with the new challenge of looking at life differently, going to places previously closed off to us, and trying new activities because now these fears are no longer with us. Just as it took time for these fears to develop into full-blown phobias, it will also take time for us to reclaim the lost freedom of our lives. Let us be as patient with ourselves in adjusting to our newfound freedom as we were in accepting and learning to live with our all-encompassing fears.

* * * * * * * * *

"There are places in my heart waiting for me to come home."

"Wonder when we'll finish the battles of war at home?"

Today I shall fly a flag of peace for:
    Brave souls that fought
    Brave souls that died
    Brave souls that died believing in freedom
    Brave souls that died because they didn't see the hit coming
    Brave souls that died because they couldn't fight anymore
    Brave souls embodied in children who deserved so much better

    And then I shall say a prayer that:
    Prays for no more war
    Prays that we might sleep with both eyes closed
    Prays the littlest and the smallest fear no more, especially in their sleep
    Prays the hungry eat
    Prays the homeless find a welcome hearth of their own
    Prays that everyone go to sleep and awake in the morning,
    forgetting they were supposed to fight

    And when I wake I shall have a life that shall be brand new. For I believe that if I can imagine the worst, surely I can imagine the best. And why not, just for once, trust that life is good and the worst of any situation has a solution? And if it is not, then I shall say a prayer for the brave souls we are in spite of our many lives that live a war in which we have not chosen and still we choose to "fight the good fight."
    Amen.

* * * * * * * *

"For those who believe, there is
untold power in prayers liberated from our hearts."

"What is this thing called power?"

Breaking the legacy of powerlessness is another one of our great challenges. Maneuvering through the world from a position of strength and power is to embody the "I am" in all its facets. It is to embrace who we are holistically. The secret of our empowerment is to accept ourselves totally. We may have weaknesses, but that doesn't make us "weak." We may have strengths, many of them, but that doesn't necessarily make us "strong." But, being able to recognize our weaknesses and being able to utilize our strengths to get what we want and need is to grab hold of our power within.

There is no shame in recognizing what we can not do. In fact, it is that process that allows us to do the doable. If we want an intimate relationship, free of the fears and defenses we have accumulated throughout the years, it is the recognition of our weaknesses that enable us to build our strengths. If we can not trust because we are fearful our partners will hurt us, it is in traveling such a fear that we dispel it so we can take the steps to trust again.

A number of us are great sprint runners. We see danger and say, "Uh oh. I'm outa here." Works when there's real danger. But in truth, we go on about our daily lives, and most of the time the day ends without external danger and so our signals are no longer useful. But it is the learned fear response that once worked for us as children and no longer does as adults that becomes our "weakness." It is the recognition of such bogus fear that is our strength. It impels us to move forward. And many of us are courageous enough to take the step to move into an area that may be uncomfortable for a short while, knowing from ours sisters around us that such steps lead us to a path of empowerment. And life is like that, is it not? Circle after circle we return, time and again to the core of our souls. That is our power.

* * * * * * * * *

*"Our core, our center, our life force is
where our strength and our healing begins and ends."*

June 1

HOLD ME TIGHT
Hold me tight
and I will
never let you go

"How come, 'No one's going to hurt me' doesn't always work?"

Despite the fact that we are survivors of incest, sexual assault or abuse or rape; and regardless of the fact that we may have long-term histories of anxiety attacks, panic attacks, depression, or PTSD, we women of color still have the image of being strong thrust upon us until even we believe the double-edged sword of such strength. Well, yes, we are strong. *However*, we are just as vulnerable in our beings as we are strong. Even an oak tree chips and has scars from hurricanes, tornadoes, insects, and dry rot.

We have been told we are strong so often that when we are falling to pieces even we can't believe it, not even temporarily; and as a consequence, we take the least care of ourselves than any other being in our care. We even treat the dog better than we treat ourselves, making sure the animal gets fed and gets its basic needs taken care of, talking to it in soothing tones while our own feelings go unchecked.

Our feelings are as important as anyone else's and any other living thing. We deserve to take care of ourselves, to look out for ourselves, to honor whatever feelings we may be having without the harsh judgments we have collected over the years. We have a right and are entitled to whatever feelings may inhabit our bodies and our minds. And we have the right to turn them into positive actions, nurture ourselves and take sustenance from the free gifts that indwell us: the gifts of grace, love, and beauty.

* * * * * * * * *

"Today I will remember I am a child of the Universe."

"What is this deep darkness inhabiting my mind, body and spirit?"

The edge of despair, where we sometimes stand and fall into what seems to be a bottomless pit, could hardly be said to be a blessing. And yet, there is something positive to be said about it. One of the important truths of a trying time of despair is that we *can* come away with the knowingness that we are feeling human beings, women with deep feeling souls, and when our world goes awry we have an inner temperature to gauge our feelings that, if not assessed properly, will come to a boiling point.

We *are* feeling human beings. We are born with these feelings to not only navigate in a world of trouble, but also in a Universe that provides joy and happiness. We often don't realize this when we are stuck in a rut that seems to have room only for havoc and chaos in our personal worlds.

When we let a situation get so bad that it appears uncontrollable and we feel we are responsible for the mess, the only thing left to do is to forgive ourselves and go back to the beginning and start over. Every new morning gives us not only yesterday's unsolved problems, but also another chance to work with the Universe in harmony to find our solutions. We just have to give ourselves the permission and say to ourselves, "Okay, I'll start again."

* * * * * * * * *

*"In spite of my own destructive impulses,
my Power within is ever-willing to show me the Way."*

"Will there come a time when men and women are at peace with one another?"

Rare is the woman who has not in one way or another been sexually assaulted, abused or harassed in our society. Talk to a woman long enough and she can tell you tales of disrespect and contempt she has experienced simply because she is a woman. There are less dangerous and threatening times as these, but no one, no child, no elderly person, no disabled person, is going to be able to travel our streets in personal safety, without threat to their being until women are respected, loved, and free on this planet.

We are a young world. Civilization has evolved screaming from our barbaric pasts. There is so much love to cultivate, and we women have done great things on this planet to make each era and generation a little bit more loving, even in the midst of seemingly endless violence and war. The establishment of a loving and safe world can only be done with a helping hand from each one of us.

As we invent new and healthier ways of living, the planet will change and the foundation will abide. It is by our painful experiences that we unfold compassionate and truthful ways of living. It is our ultimate triumph here to look back in honor to the ways we meet the world, and on our terms.

* * * * * * * * *

"I am an integral part in the healing of this world."

"What are my signs before I go spiraling down to the bottom of the pit?"

The abyss of psyche pain is a darkness all its own, and like no other we experience. All at once, our bodies can ache all over, our minds have no escape, and our hearts are heavy with self-doubt and self-rejection. We don't love ourselves at such moments, and we don't think anyone could possibly love us with our faults and driven ways. This is where a number of us think we have come to the end of the road. We think, *"What difference would it make if the world were to lose another woman by her own hands?"* Stop. Our loved ones would miss us dearly, and our kindred sisters would be devastated by the loss of another one of us because of the perceived, overwhelming obstacles of a single hour or day.

We all know this particular road. In fact, all of us have rejected such urges at one time or another; they are tempestuous demons either of our own making, or they are thrown upon us as we make our way through daily living.

We survive this by making a safe space in our minds that is absolutely unassailable for our moments of darkness. It is possible and we can do it. And for just a little while, until we find another person to share our pain or find a way out on our own, we can have a safe inner haven while we trust our creative soul-knowing power to lead us as we walk this path, for however long it takes.

* * * * * * * * *

*"When pain seems like the only thing I know,
it is up to me to change it."*

"What's all this stuff about 'inner children' have to do with me?"

We who are women of color often scoff at the idea of the "inner child" and meeting and taking care of her needs. We are so busy with the daily practicalities of life that such an endeavor seems like an indulgence or luxury. After all, we have all those "isms" to take care of— racism, sexism, ageism; you know, the isms. But long before present-day pop psychology and the recovery movements came along, the Master called Jesus, planted such a seed. Unless we start living in the present and addressing our daily, spiritual, and emotional needs, we shall never have the love we so longingly want and deserve. Such a life is rich with love and forgiveness and unconditional acceptance of everyone, regardless of their status as seen by society. Everyone is on equal footing and is of equal value in this Kingdom of God, and it really doesn't matter if you aren't a "believer." The concept alone lets such beauty and truth stand on its own. Children come into our world full of goodness and love, crying only when their basic needs are not met.

Children need other people and do not survive in isolation. To aide in our being to experience happiness as adult women, it helps to sometimes remember what it was like when we were happy as little children, so that we might find that "inner child" in ourselves again. There is much joy and happiness we can learn from her again.

* * * * * * * * *

"Today I will take time to get to know my inner child."

"I know my addiction causes me pain, so why don't I stop?"

Though we all have different addictions, we have in common an addiction to one thing or another. Cigarettes, hard drugs, over-the-counter drugs, TV, alcohol, food, caffeine, other people, candy, whatever. We can go overboard with all of them in our consumptuous living. Sometimes there is so little joy and satisfaction in our lives that it seems only fair that we should have some kind of addiction, even if it means killing ourselves in the process. And what a high we get, what a great way to get out of the feckless lives we live, and it doesn't matter if the joy is short-lived. Like the addicts we are, we rationalize that the addiction is worth the momentary happiness.

It's not. We all have to come down, and when we do, we are sick emotionally or physically, and often both at the same time. And underneath all these addictions live unmet feelings, unwanted feelings, and scary feelings. We kid ourselves that everything's okay and that we have it all together as we go about our daily tasks and business. It takes a lot of sobering self-love, commitment and action to get help so we can say and *know*, "This is me, and I have as much right to be on this earth as the trees and the stars and the sky, and this is where I stand, free of my addictions."

* * * * * * * * *

"I can be courageous and give up my addictions."

"What shame am I carrying that I self-mutilate?"

Few are the women, perhaps women of color with even fewer numbers, who are willing to admit one of our darkest and deepest shames— self-mutilation. No one knows that in secret we may bang our heads, or cut our stomachs, or take a knife and scar a leg. What would they say around the family table in our absence if they were to find out? What would they think about us on the job if they were to know? And if we have children, would someone try and take them away from us?

We self-mutilate out of pure desperation. Getting an answer from something, even if it's our own pain, is better than no answer at all. Being heard by the wall is better than not being heard at all. And causing ourselves to bleed will tell us we are alive when we believe there is no one in our lives to validate this hurting and simple truth.

Some of us have been deeply wounded by the circumstances in our childhoods and adolescent lives, and without self-pity. But with righteous indignation, this is our particular truth; and though we have lived to tell it, we often don't. Instead, we erroneously take it out on ourselves, secreting the silence that binds us to a past full of lies not of our own making. We are no longer victims. We women have survived these atrocities. We have stories to tell and stories to be heard. If our sisters do not want to hear it, who will?

* * * * * * * * *

*"I am no longer a child and alone. There are
sisters who are willing to hear and hold my story."*

"How will we get rid of the permeating violence in our lives?"

We are all so shell-shocked and weary-worn by the everyday violence in our lives. We have come to expect horrendous stories of violence as the rule, not the exception.

We could eradicate violence if we would simply stop hitting our children. Imagine a society raising a generation of children that had never been hit, a society that would have to learn how to live without raising their hands to strike another person. The majority of us think such a goal would be impossible. Many of us live by the Old Testament, "Spare the rod and spoil the child," but anyone who has raised an arm to a child, knows the child is at a serious disadvantage.

If we are to teach children to find solutions to their problems without hitting another person, we must do that by modeling our own behavior. And yes, children know how to push us to the edge of our limits and sanity. But, if *we* can not set by our example another way of living, then the violence will continue from one end of the scale to the other— from domestic violence to planetary violence. In order to create a better world, we have to create a home life void of hitting, slapping, and beating. It can be taxing and tough to come up with discipline and consequences that do not including hitting as punishment, but it is possible as a number of families are consciously raising their children in such a manner.

* * * * * * * * *

*"Perhaps if I understood the true nature of my anger or rage
I would not hit my child at all."*

"Even Jesus sent the apostles out two by two."

No one makes us feel better than a sister on common ground. Yes, there are those of us who have close men friends. This is not about that. This is about friendship in the arms of sisters. We have a way of listening and extending to one another that only women know how to do. We nurture. It is another part of our biological DNA, so let's not negate such a positive characteristic in the name of egalitarian rights. Yes, it's true that men nurture, but in men's ways. We women communicate quite effectively in vast and innumerable ways. Looks can be more communicative than words, and a "Hmph!" said in a certain way says a lot more than a book chapter could hope to express. Of course, "Girrrrrrl," goes a long way and always has. And one hand gesture can tell a whole story. Then there's that intuitive skill we've had since Eve. Let's embrace that, too. It pays to be able to read a room full of people just by scanning the energy. Enjoy it. Such a skill is a gift, a characteristic we can develop and own.

But most of all, it's about letting our hair down with each other, propping our feet up, and kicking it for hours talking about nothing and everything under the sun. And it's more than a comforting thought to know that no matter what goes on in our inner worlds we always have our friends who accept us for exactly who we are— sometimes more so than we do ourselves.

* * * * * * * * *

"My journey has been made lighter by the good company of a friend."

"How could this have happened to me?"

Those of us who have been raped are often caught unawares. Doesn't matter if it's a stranger or intimate lover. It's not like we don't know it happens in the world. We hear about it every day. We just never expect it when it happens to us. Don't touch us when it's over. Don't come near us, for everyone's' intentions and motivations are suspect.

There's no way to assess when the damages will be fixed. Some of us recover "shortly." Some of us never recover. And many of us walk a fine line of fragile trust and an ever-conscious knowledge of possible betrayal by any one. If we are lucky, it will become a nightmare we wish never to dream again. It will lose its hold on us and we will be able to move forward in our lives without a hint of its presence, and its nefarious powers stripped away.

We are empowered by reclaiming, however we can, what was stolen and taken from us, what was so dreadfully violated. It is not about sex, don'cha know? It is about entering a life force, ours, without invitation, without permission by our souls. Rapists know this, even if unconsciously. It is why they rape. But no act, no evil, is ever unmet by the ultimate hands of justice and the ministry of mercy. It may go unanswered momentarily, but the truth wills out. It is the saving grace from the Divine Creator, especially when someone steals the essence of beauty from another soul meant to share the goodness of the Universe. It is something we can remind ourselves of as we heal.

* * * * * * * * *

"I can heal from even this dreadful crime to violate my body and my soul."

"Where is this thirst coming from?"

We are human beings endowed with a spiritual heritage.

Is it odd that the bearers of life have a built-in need to quench the thirst that hungers for the joy of life? For those of us who think we should choose to shut down, are we not be hankered after by some part of our personality so that our soul does not die?

The desire to survive any given situation is by design. The need to achieve and to triumph over our challenges is also part of our human heritage. It must be. We all have it. Were it not for this, we would never feel that aching need that clamors for more that sometimes leads us to disastrous relationships or projects we made a mess of. It allows us to continue loving when we know everything tells us the odds are against it, or to keep on truckin' even when it seems we are spiraling down and going to "hell in a hand-basket." It is the nature of spirit embodied in all human beings. What we do with it is up to us.

* * * * * * * * *

"The Spirit does not rest until it connects with the soul."

"How many hits is one too many?"

When is once one too many times? The first time. Abuse gone unchecked only escalates. That is a given. That is something we can depend on happening in life. No one is going to stop this except for us. We can go to as many agencies as possible, getting the help for ourselves, but the bottom line is that we say when enough is enough. The first time is enough.

Ever notice how the batterer only hits those he knows he can get away with hitting? Doesn't hit his boss, not the stranger on the street, not the neighbor next door. The consequences are too great. But he seems to think that it is okay (and has gotten the go-ahead from society) to hit his partner. Luckily, some of us have said no more; the cycle has to be stopped.

Violence on any level is unacceptable at any time whether verbally, emotionally, or physically; and when accepted in any form, it does damage to us spiritually, and ultimately wounds, and sometimes, in fact, destroys the soul. There are safe houses, friends, and families willing to help sisters who want to choose a better and safer life. All it takes is for us to say, "No more." just once.

* * * * * * * * *

*"I am not at war. I have a right to live peacefully,
especially in my own house."*

"How did I get here again?"

Set backs can work twofold. First, they can remind us of how incredibly vulnerable we are to the hidden workings of our abuse history. That is a set back at its worst. On the other hand, if we can still ourselves for just a moment in the midst of an old storm, we can steady ourselves, weather the cold storm, and come out ahead. After all, we've been here before. We know what we have to do to get out. And yet it is incredibly painful to be in a space we thought we had conquered.

The thing about set backs is that they raise those feelings of self-blame, such as, "It was my fault," or the deepest cut of all, "I'm not worthy to live because something is so terribly wrong with me." It's the she-monster raising her head again, twisting our necks around to look back at events we had no control over then. The good news is that we have control now. We can change because (1) we are no longer children and powerless and (2) because we want to, and have the ability to do so, and (3) we are healing. One set back, two set backs, however many doesn't matter. We have the wonderful ability every day to make changes in our lives.

We are good inside. Set backs do not make us bad people, no matter whose eyes are on us. We have the right to make as many mistakes as necessary to come out at the other end of the tunnel and step out into the light waiting for us.

* * * * * * * * *

*"I've been down this path before.
I know every twist and turn intimately."*

"How do I overcome this one?"

There comes a time when we lose our most cherished dreams. Despite everything we try to do, we may end up watching everything we've worked so hard for go up in a cloud of gray and choking smoke. And nothing can make the pain go away. We who are women steel ourselves against such insidious assaults. If it's not our jobs or our children, then it's our love lives, sliding on a slick, wet highway, outrageously out of control.

We can put on the brakes, look around, survey the debris, and then begin slowly back on the super highway of life. We may need a short respite from the stresses of the world. We may need to take a road where we can replenish our souls in ways we haven't tended to them before.

Starting all over may be doable, but it isn't easy. We may need to let that withdrawal skill work for us in a positive way, renewing ourselves in meditation and communication with our Higher Power. Such communion surpasses all explanation of life's complexities, and nothing is stronger than the Spirit within. And we may begin again, renewed, refreshed, and with a clearer vision of where we are going next on this path we call life.

* * * * * * * * *

"Even amongst the fallen debris, my Spirit stands."

"Can I remember to be gentle with myself when my self-doubts begin?"

Sometimes we get stuck on specifics and start to doubt ourselves. Like, we can't remember the times of a particular abuse even though we remember the temperature of the day. Or maybe we remember the way the perp smelled, but not what he was wearing. It starts to snowball. And because we can not remember a lot of the little things, we start doubting if the abuse really happened.

The abuse happened and many of us know who the abuser was and when it happened. Somewhere along the way, in the midst of our innocent childhoods, someone who we trusted came along and forever changed the courses of our lives either with a single, solitary, horrendous act, or in many of our instances, lots of horrendous acts over a spread of time.

It really doesn't matter if we don't remember all the specifics of the act. It really doesn't matter if all we remember is that we were abused and assaulted at some point in our lives. And though the perpetrators may never be brought to justice, we can have justice. We know the truth and we are the jury to our lives. We are the judges to our living, and we can give justice to the way we live our lives.

* * * * * * * * *

*"This is not a case of mistaken identity
and I am not the perpetrator."*

"Can I believe what I remember?"

It's a tricky violation. When we are first violated, particularly by a trusted person, some of our first thoughts are, *This can't be happening* or *I don't believe this.* In the midst of the violation of our deepest selves, while we are being attacked, we are in a state of disbelief. Is it any wonder then, that later when we are fully capable of handling the experience, we may have some doubts, and that our new nemesis, clever as they are with their new weapon, "false memory syndrome," seek to exploit such a defense?

It is like rape. Numerous women file charges and take the criminal to court on rape charges and sometimes get convictions. But it is when one woman recants that the media pounces on such a case, and the wheels of justice begin to dismantle the truth of the real victims. One recantation does not make false rape for all time.

"What is truth?" asked Pontius Pilate, the greatest coward of all responsibility. You see, sisters, we must not let ourselves become confused by fact. Fact is not necessarily truth.

The truth is that for the overwhelming majority of us our memories are returning, and what we remember *did happen* to us. The truth is that in our discovery, many of our lives have improved, our relationships have gotten better, and the nightmares and the fears are disappearing. A lie would not do that for us; it would not effect lasting growth or beauty. A lie or falsehood does not beget healing. Healing from the memories begets the truth.

* * * * * * * * *

*"Trusting my truth no matter that I stand alone
is better than believing the lies of others."*

"When will my cup runneth over?"

We women who have children and who walk our path of healing may travel a twisted path through a forest with trails of brittle branches and hidden rocks. If we are overwhelmed by our experiences or feelings we can not always give ourselves the undivided attention we need. We have jobs to go to, as many of us are sole supporters; and even if we have partners, our income is heavily depended upon.

And oh, the literal price we pay may be heftier than we thought. Counseling and therapy can be costly. Sometimes the healing work we need to do calls for professional help, which means dealing with people that charge fees. We are constantly juggling our budgets to meet the many necessary expenses, which at times we may question if professional therapy is not a luxury. This juggling becomes a constant balancing act in our lives.

It is comforting to know that others have walked the very same path of this journey, and they are healing. It is difficult but not impossible. We have navigated other painful journeys and walked into the open space of freedom. We can continue do it as long as we need to.

* * * * * * * * *

"The Universe is abundant and generous even unto my needs."

"Why is it that as soon as I get money I feel like I have to get rid of it?"

It is no secret that we survivors have a hellish time managing our money. This medium of exchange, often tied into our self-value system, plays havoc with the best of us.

The wonderful thing about a new day is we can always start over. Never giving up hope on ourselves is a mantra we ought to hold, like those awful mantras we were given such as, "Don't tell," or "It's our secret," or "Give me a kiss and I'll give you a dollar."

We are not the children we once were, and our inner children need us so much to straighten up the awful lies we were told and to replace them with the beauty of truth. We can heal and handle our financial matters in a healthy way. It takes time and commitment, but we can heal. Money is neutral. It has no life of its own except what we give it. To re-empower ourselves we need to redefine our notions of what money means to each of us.

* * * * * * * * *

"I can take care of my money to take care of myself."

"Is there no end to this madness of mine?"

How do we honor where we are and where we've been when our world looks so bleak sometimes? How do we not curse ourselves out? How do we stop putting ourselves down? How do we inhabit our bodies so that it feels like a home with a welcome mat at the door? If we are loyal to others (and many of us are) can we extend that same loyalty to ourselves? If we put others before us can we do the same for our inner children? If we value the lives of others can we not purpose that same sense of worth to ourselves? Can we give ourselves the respect and dignity we so deserve? How do we do for ourselves what we so willingly do for others?

Many of us are in the helping field or service field giving and giving, and *always* making ourselves last. Why? Yes, it is part of our heritage and socialization as women to do that. After all, many of us are mothers and know that children's needs often come before ours. But even so, we can only give as good as we've got. If we do not get enough rest, enough recreation, enough love and support, we in turn will not be able to go the extra mile our loved ones may need; we will not be able to see the need to have fun when we are constantly working; and we will not be able to give them the love and support we so painfully deny ourselves, because we will have stretched so far that we will supersede the point of diminishing returns!

* * * * * * * * *

"The more I value myself, the more I value others in my life."

Headaches June 21

"Why does my head seem to hurt all the time?"

We women are famous for our headaches, and with good reason. We get a lot of them. In fact, it's not unusual that some of us have headaches every day. Some of us think that's the way it's supposed to be. It is not. When we were children we had to hold everything in. There wasn't anyone to tell and if we did, who would believe us? Painful as it was, our headaches saved us from full consciousness of what was going on. It would be hard to concentrate on what really happened if, instead, we were concentrating on a pain in our heads that wouldn't go away. On the other hand, it is one of the natural outcomes for holding so much feeling in check. But it's a defense and a habit hard to unlearn.

A raging headache in our adulthood is a wake up call. Something needs fixing— balance to our inner lives, a loose thread on the job, or unfinished business with our partners or children, just to name a few. If we don't attend to the rage, we can be sure the rage will attend to us.

We can learn new ways to handle old feelings. We don't have to stuff ourselves now. We don't have to hold anything in. We can express ourselves whether through direct contact, writing, drawing, breaking plates, ripping phone books, whatever. Just as long as we're expressing and not stuffing, because stuffing overflows and when it rises to the top, it looks for expression. If we don't do it, our bodies will.

* * * * * * * * *

"I feel best when my expression matches my feelings."

"How could you leave me this way?"

Nothing's quite as alarming as the signs that the people in our primary relationships— our spouses, our significant others, our key intimates, our partners— can not travel any of our healing journey with us, can not join us anywhere in our recovery, and are only waiting for us to get "better." Some of us can live with this. Most of us can not. We have had too many important people not "show up," and the lack of an appearance by our partners only adds salt to an already too-acrid wound.

Mostly it is sad. We are brokenhearted over it. We can not believe the one person we truly love can not be here for us now. It is overwhelming for us and unthinkable for them. They are in denial. They wish this had never happened to us and so they act as if it didn't happen, leaving us to handle the crises that arise in our healing by ourselves.

We can rage at their abandonment, but it does nothing to alleviate the pain of our broken hearts caused by the unexpected defection of a loved one. We just didn't expect them to bail out like all the others.

We handle this love loss as we do all of our losses— by going through it. We can't run from it— it will follow us, and we can't hide. But we can stand brave and honest and true to ourselves, grieve our losses and know that like much of everything else, we will survive this new, unwanted pain.

* * * * * * * * *

"I must honor the hurt caused by the loss of belief in me by my loved one."

"Why should I honor him?"

We do not need to offer excuses for a day which we do not wish to celebrate for whatever our reasons, whatever the holiday. But perhaps no celebration is more tongue-in-cheek than that of "Father's Day." It's enough to make many of us puke. It stirs feelings of rage and unfairness. It causes grief. It makes a mockery of our histories. It is one of the biggest lies of our lives, celebrating the acts of a man whose main achievement in our lives was a distortion and a perversion of our childhoods.

It takes a lot of healing to rid ourselves of the bitterness of our experiences. Sometimes we get to do it "right" if we have children and they have a father who is completely trustworthy and loving. Then, vicariously, we can see what a childhood would have been without an abusive father. We can see how they cherish their dad, how they relax into him, how their wholehearted trust is returned in love and honor.

Sometimes our distrust of our fathers is not that clear cut. For some of us it's a gray area. Asking ourselves, "Should I or shouldn't I give him a Father's Day card?" can send us into turmoil for weeks. Others have forgiven and moved on, and such a matter is not an issue.

Though we share the day in common, it is a matter of individual choice whether to celebrate it or not. Whatever choice we make, let it be the healing one.

* * * * * * * * *

"Not all fathers deserve to be honored and it's up to me whether I celebrate mine."

"Is this a necessary thing for me to do?"

We who are women of color have been admonished to honor the family no matter what else goes on in our lives. We've been taught that having a family is a guarantee to never having to be put "outdoors." We've been taught to not air our dirty laundry in public, that family business is nobody's business but our own. We are asked to not embarrass our racial communities because "it's just one more thing 'they' can use against us, just another racist ploy."

Regardless of the age of when we do break the silence that a father or a brother, or an uncle, or a cousin or a grandfather has sexually assaulted us the reactions vary, but few are the mothers that can wholeheartedly support us with this news. Seldom can she take in what we are saying. They don't want to believe it any more than we want to know that a man we are supposed to be able to trust is untrustworthy; in fact, he causes us grievous pain. And once we have laid the problem in our mothers' laps, there's no telling what fireworks will explode.

Sometimes we must be prepared that such a revelation may send us "outdoors." We are told in a variety of ways that we are not welcome in our homes anymore. When we make a decision to disclose or to confront, we need to remember that sometimes in reclaiming the truth we may very well be cutting off people we still want in our lives, and that it may not be possible to continue those relationships. We may need to create new families, starting with ourselves.

* * * * * * * * *

"The truth is freeing, even if it means I may have to stand alone."

"Why is it that something that appears simple is only seemingly so?"

We may never know just how much spontaneity and innocence was stolen from our lives. For those of us who have survived sexual abuse, sometimes nothing about sex comes easy for us. It seems no matter how much healing we do, nothing ever seems right. We are angry, and rightfully so.

Many of us experience a rude awakening. We are in touch with our sexual feelings, but not in touch with the repercussions of our abuse until we involve ourselves in a relationship, and then...bam! We are suddenly halted to a screech, as what we want to do and what we can do conflict. We are sometimes haunted by flashbacks and intrusive memories that cause us to reject our present lovers and our participation in one of nature's finest gifts to human beings— intimacy on all levels.

We have learned to be wary and distrustful of this most wondrous act of coupling, and with good reason. But it leaves us in a most painful quandary. If we say *yes* to our feelings, we may have to confront memories we so carefully buried out of our consciousness. But such confrontation of intrusive memories is part of the package that we commit to make in order to heal. We may not always believe it, but we will know that in time, even the past will no longer have power to take away what we so much desire in our present lives. With healing, no one and nothing can take away what is ours; no one can stop us from being who we truly are without our permission.

* * * * * * * * *

"I am a sensual and sexual being, and that is good."

Self-Possession **June 26**

"How long does it take to repossess a soul?"

I took possession of my life last night. I realized it today. I stretched back into myself and in a moment's time, fully mine, I claimed what was rightfully mine, a gift that could be precious only from me— a gift that was stolen, taken and purposefully hidden from me. I took back a force that was all but depleted from my skin, and that hung on like a skeleton wrongfully placed outside my body. And in the same quiet, cunning way it was stolen from me, I crept back on the last leg of a fantastic journey, and crawled through mine fields not of my own making. Yet a part of me, thinking I had no more fuel left and losing sight of where I was headed, found a reservoir of strength that never seemed to end no matter how weak I became. And as long as I took one breath at a time, day-by-day, I could go on to the next moment. I could even rest without loosening my grip on what seemed only a tenuous thread holding my life and me together.

Once, I thought my indomitable spirit would triumph with exploding stars and loud, thunderous applause with lightning from the skies. Instead it came peacefully, like the presence of an ethereal touch by my angel, and I knew what I had, what I had been born with, was mine. No one and no circumstance could ever fully steal me away as long as I have one breath left to take in and let go from the boundaries of my soul.

* * * * * * * * *

*"In the final analysis, that which is inherently mine
can only be taken or stolen temporarily."*

"Just how long is all this going to take?"

Wouldn't it be grand if we just had one fell swooping experience to knock this abuse experience out of our lives once and for all? How much would we be willing to pay if we could be guaranteed that the next 24 hours may be hell— ten times infinitely worse than birth labor, but when we're through, we will never have to deal with this issue again? Would we sell all we own? Would we beg, borrow, or steal? Would we work overtime daily so that we could cover all the expenses?

It's wishful thinking at its grandest. Sisters, the road to healing is cumulative. It happens daily, sometimes consciously, and other times we are totally unaware of what our Higher Power may have in store for us on a spiritual level that we have yet to tap. It is a mixture of conscious effort, dreams recalled and not, a mingling with others, our support people and loved ones, and the faithful trust of a child that the Universe unfolds and has a place for us as well.

Some of us do have spontaneous awakenings, not unlike Paul of Tarsus on the road to Damascus. But they are the exception. Most of us are the rule. In order to "get" the truth we have to know it and live it. Self-inspection and re-inhabiting is a slow process. We are, after all, evolutionary beings. Few people "arrive"; most of us are on a non-ending journey that holds wonders we have not even yet dreamed.

* * * * * * * * *

"I am a child of God and every journey I have undertaken
is accounted for and blessed."

"Has spontaneous combustion created anything but chaos?"

Is it possible to heal without Divine Creator-knowingness? If I do everything right and still don't believe in a Divine Creator, will my life be blessed? If I can't have a life as good as one who believes in a Creator, then what's all that talk about free will?

We do not all believe that there is a Creator. Numbers of us do believe in a Deity of one faith or another, for many of us were saved by a faith that sustained us throughout our abusive childhoods. When no one else was there, the Divine Creator was, as well as all Her celestial helpers. Many of these helpers took us somewhere else when the abuse was taking place. We have maintained these relationships with our unseen helpers, and our lives manifest our connections. But what of our sisters who don't believe in a Creator of any sort, of any Higher Power? Some of us were abused in the name of this very Creator; some of us were manipulated and maimed by these charlatans dressed in the Creator's clothing.

We are often given the choice at different stages in our lives to accept or reject that there is a Divine Power working throughout the Universe and in our lives. We are no longer children, and we have the power to see through deception. The only certainty we have is our very own experience. Few believers regret that they do so. But there are many who wonder why it took so long to drink from this fountain of grace.

* * * * * * * * *

"Nothing is stronger than a belief system; mine should meet my needs in healing."

"When will I come home to myself?"

Up until now, I've been running, looking over my shoulder, and hearing a fearful, inside voice saying, "Run, Babe, Run." But today, in yet another gentle and moving revelation, I was given back a part of myself that had been lost on a day I can still see clearly in my mind's eyes. The winter was moving out with a slow breeze from a March wind over the old, red barn, and yet it was warm enough for me to sit down on the roof and feel its warmth through tar-papered patching. In resignation, I looked out over the horizon and felt my freedom being taken away from me, slipping away on the last of a purple sky, on the wisps of the tails of an unformed cloud, and taking my feelings with it.

And when it was clear to me that the best of me was gone and all that was left was a yearning in my body, empty of a sweet and tender part of my soul, I took off running in any direction I could. I kept running until I couldn't run anymore, until the aches in my legs caused my stomach to cramp, the veins in my head to throb, and my blood ragefully coursed through my tremulous body. And when I felt the static jolts of the stopping of my heart, I choked it down and kept running. It seemed I ran forever.

And then today, for the first time, I heard the clearest of all my voices, purposefully and soulfully telling me, "Stop running." And for the first time in my life, as I stand in tune with the Universe, I have tears of joy for me and who I am.

* * * * * * * * *

"My soul came home as quietly as it left."

Child's Play

"Why can't every child have a childhood?"

We who are women of color tolerate horrific things without breaking the rhythm of the blinking of our eyelashes. Given the sometimes seemingly unending chaos, we are often world-weary witnesses, and we know that at times it really doesn't matter what we say in a situation, the only thing that can make a difference is a matter of time— time and distance. But when it comes to our children, we are not afforded the luxury to wax and wane profound thoughts, waiting for time and fate to do their jobs. We have to care for our children's fears more than they do, for we are the ones entrusted with their total well-being.

We can no longer deny the unrelenting and persistent reality that our children are unsafe from not only strangers, but even some of us. They are the easiest of prey and they have every right to expect that the places where they live, play, and learn will offer them protection, freedom, and security.

We must make predators know that facing us has greater risks than the thrill of terrifying and preying upon our children. Our children deserve their proverbial place in the sun, especially in their childhood years, and it is only right that they look to us to make sure they have it. Every child, whether ours or not, deserves a childhood free of stalkers, predators, rapists, murderers, and perpetrators of childhood sexual assault.

If we know of someone, a stranger hanging around our kids and neighborhoods, a family relative, sibling, partner— even ourselves, we must be brave enough to get help and intervention. We must never be silent, idle, and inactive witnesses to the knowing destruction of any kind of abuse to our children who share the world with us and depend on us to provide them a world of safety.

*Dedicated to Sherrice Iverson, Girl X, Christina Williams
and Danydia Betty-Jacqueline Thompson © 4/21/98*

* * * * * * * * *

"It takes a village to raise a child."
                    ...An African Proverb

July 1

CHILDREN GIFTS

These gifts
we call our children
we ought to treasure
more
than we know
and more
than we do

"How do I handle this sorrow in my heart?"

It wasn't that she couldn't accept that the situation had gone bad, that all the clichés of love and war had become a reality for her and that the relationship was over,. What was most painful, most excruciating was that it was daily and constantly reflected in her face, upon her awakening, throughout her day, and the last thing her mind saw before she fell asleep.

And now, it of course was raising the dead, or at least a few ghosts who haunted her during the day and invaded her dreams at night. She awoke crying in the mornings, frustrated that her refuge had now become a land of hidden symbols nagging at some truth she had long forgotten, and refused to leave her alone.

Still, she marveled at the part of her that seemed to look at it all with a disconnected compassion, a knowingness that right around the corner what she was looking for would be there. She took comfort in the fact that despite all her fears, her hope had not withered in the face of this latest loss. She looked upon herself as almost a new person, secure in the knowledge that of all the strengths she had, tenuous as it might seem to her at times, her faith had not left with her illusions and denials, but instead seemed to point to a new clarity to see things as they were and made her more determined on her path of a righteous healing.

She knew that the things she thought she couldn't do, she could; and the part of her she thought would not show up for her was no longer something she needed to question. In fact, the only thing left to question was what other choices she missed when she felt she had run out of options. Some of her dreams, along with her heart, may have been broken, but never, never, never her soul and her spirit. Some things were simply immovable and unshakable, and for all of that she was grateful to an Loving Creator that provided such kind compensation.

* * * * * * * * *

"Sometimes our darkness moments are ones of enlightenment."

"How did they go on living?"

It was the music that always got her through. But she wished she could tell all of kindred sisters how much she loved them, how brave they were, how courageous they were, how her heart filled with love when her eyes rested upon them, and the pride that flowed through her veins when she thought of all they'd overcome. They rose every day, holding their tongues and moving about their lives with their secret freedom.

No one told their stories, and when finally critical mass arose out of the collective breaking of silence within the community of women, the survivors— the "Comfort Women" joined their sisters; and, aside from disbelief from their families that these horrors happened to their relatives, perhaps the hardest to take was the disbelief that the survivors could actually speak of it, could give voice to it, and could indeed say "No" to the taboo of breaking the silence.

She wanted to tell them all before they went to their graves that there was no shame that was theirs, that the blame was not theirs to carry, and that the pain would be gladly shared. It would be a burden of love, if that; and at least in her eyes, if no one else's including their own, they were her heroes, and there really wasn't anything at all to forgive.

She put the music away. She also put the book and her notes away as well. She made a note to tell them that she got it— she really got it. She understood that we must be our own reasons for living, that we can not live for only those we love because they will surely leave us eventually by powers beyond our control as in "dust to dust". When that happens, we will have to come up with reasons for living even if it means going through all the vicissitudes of our lives and waiting patiently and living fully until we are "ashes to ashes" and that isn't our call.

* * * * * * * * *

"That which may seem unspeakable is only waiting for the ear willing to hear."

-184-

"Can independence be part of my vision?"

There comes a point in our lives, when we actually become free of major obstacles to our healing, resulting in a new independence to living our lives. Being adult and self-actualizing one's own life calls for taking those risks that we have been so busy protecting ourselves from by steadily building defenses that can withstand any perceived assault from others or by self.

Many of us have been independent for a long time and yet do not feelingly and knowingly accept it. Sometimes the reality of being independent scares us so much that we refuse to make decisions that would manifest the fruits of independence in our lives. We remain in relationships that are toxic to us, in jobs and careers that poison our emotional balance, and keep even our most deep-seated desires hidden from our self-acknowledgment, lest we be compelled to actually change the whole structure of our lives.

Those of us who are actively healing our lives, walking whatever roads we must to enrich and change our present so that our lives do work for us, learn that we must risk experiencing what we fear in order to have a chance for our own happiness. Some of us can not even envision a "happy" life. Some of us are content (and understandably so) to be able to awaken to another day free of our past perpetrators or any thoughts of the experience(s), however it may have affected our lives.

Our commitment to our healing means that we are in a constant state of becoming the women we are and of expressing our Divine-given, innate abilities. No one ever becomes independent by a simple decree of, "I am independent." It takes time learning to trust one's own voice and one's own self to know that where we are at any given moment is where we need to be in order to live our own independent life.

* * * * * * * * *

*"My path of independence leads me to self-creative
decisions enhancing my life and happiness."*

"How come the distance can not be seen for how close it really is?"

The first day she woke up on her honeymoon, the birds greeted her with a song that sounded like it carried a message of goodness just for her. She thought their song was a metaphor for her marriage— that it had a beginning, a middle and a natural end. She thought wrong. The breakup of her marriage hit her with the impact of a car careening off the highway towards a brick barrier as the driver realizes the brakes don't work and the car is going 80 miles per hour.

She could cry now for what she could not do then. She could see how fragile she was even if to the world she presented an aura of self-sufficiency and independence. Too, she could see how her biting words and sarcastic witticisms only served to mask a vulnerability she would not touch for years. Maybe if she'd known then, she might have done things differently, or not done some things at all. Maybe.

At first, she would wake up and frantically call out his name while simultaneously realizing they had divorced and she was alone in her bed. As she moved on through those early months, she realized our understandings do not always come when we want them to. The saying, "Would it that it were." is the longing of all dreamers and the hindsight of those who are wise. It was during this time that she frequently wept in frustration for that which she could not change.

Still. Despite it all and her inclination towards depression, she woke up every morning and agreed to get on with the business of living, just because she woke up. Most days it was for the practical reasons. She had to make a living. And some days, even with some frequency that she had not expected, she woke up because she wanted to, because she still wanted to live and do the things her heart longed for. Some days, the future did not seem so hard and far away, and the possibilities for happiness were more than a notion. Such possibilities were potentials she knew she could actually make real. And she had friends, family and loved ones who still cared about her. It was her marriage that was over and not her life.

* * * * * * * * *

"We do not always find what we want in our own time,
but truth will out, we will find that which we seek in time."

"How come I let some of the littlest things about others bother me?"

It's never the annoying person at work that comes up to you out of the blue and starts acting in a weird manner, like yelling at you as if you were their child. That's easy. You can either defend yourself by asking them if they've lost their mind, or you can act as the sane one and ask them if they'd like to talk in a more conducive manner to someone else.

The ones that really get under your skin, the ones that really throw you off kilter for a while, the ones that really send you for a loop and actually hurt your feelings, are those closest to you. Now here's an old one, "You only hurt the ones you love."

When that zinger comes from a friend or a loved one that you've misjudged, for whatever the reason, it may weigh on your mind over and over, almost obsessively for an hour or so, until you figure it out. It's a reactionary survivor's defense, *"Someone I love says I've offended them so I must have done something wrong."* It's a frequent thought pattern: When something goes wrong in a relationship, nine times out of ten, the first thing we survivors do is blame ourselves.

But here's the thing. Some people we involve ourselves with in relationships are toxic people and we don't understand just how poisonous they are until the relationship starts unfolding. Oftentimes it's really not about us, and rather than dragging our minds through the muck of ill-gotten memory tapes, we can take the opportunity to shift the thinking in our mindsets, that everything is our fault. Sometimes life and people are the way they are because that is simply the way life is. It's not about us all the time. It's just life.

* * * * * * * * *

"Sometimes it's okay to just let things be."

"When will we come up with a T-shirt?"

T-shirts seem to be the personal expression of whatever we're thinking or feeling on a particular day. We don one on that says how we feel about peace, war, love, or any kind of political expression. We wear them proudly when they speak of our personal commitments such as saving some threatened animal or some rainforest. We wear them to let the world know who we are in the world of sports, or that our family's had a reunion. And we wear them to let the world know of our survival of medical wounds, and wars. That is, except for the survivors of incest, rape, and CSA.

You don't see many of those. Well, there are a few that say in bold letters: "Speak out against sexual violence," or "It shouldn't hurt to be a family," or even "Don't be quiet"; but you won't find one that says, "I survived incest," or "I survived CSA more than once," or "I survived rape with gun pointed at my head and I am healing." Nope. Nothing like that. It's not like the survivors of alcohol or drugs whose shirts may say, "I'm a survivor and 3 years sober," or like cancer survivors, "I won the relay and outran death and am in total remission." Nope. Nothing like that at all.

We need warriors to continue to break this silence. We need to be brave and courageous and wear our T-shirts that say, "I survived CSA and have reclaimed my soul." But we would really have to be brave, wouldn't we? It's hard enough to finally bring the societal taboo into the light, breaking our silences and recognizing it for what it is: a hideous and most destructive criminal disease.

We've won the most important battle against these types of crime. One day, we will proudly wear the t-shirts we want, recognizing we have truly done nothing of shame and have indeed survived a nightmare that, while one can awaken from it, lasts many, many moons.

* * * * * * * * *

*"Letting others know our experiences
is one of the most healing things we can do."*

"I am strong, but why do I feel so beaten?"

She came home feeling as if she had been given a left-and-right full twisting punch to the stomach by a Grandmaster. She felt numb from the pain that she had just learned. It wasn't that her world had ended or that her life as she knew it was over. It was about the fact that she had been struggling and sacrificing and doing without for such a long time, and a debt she owed had finally been paid off. Or so she thought. And then today, as she began making plans that would widen her circle of life, she was told, "No, you owe more." "More" meant two more months of going without; it meant running out of money within two days of a payday, and the next 13 days would be about how to survive without money and get the things she needed: medicines, food, classes, gas to get to work and get around, and of course, the trip back home to where those who knew her also knew her heart, and little was left to be explained or argued about.

She wanted to retreat. Wanted to get in bed and not get back up again for days. She wanted to sleep and dream of places and people where she was loved and wanted. She wanted to wake up and have peace. She wanted to believe she could do this with a minimum of her brain feeling like it was on fire.

Others had gone before her. In truth, this was neither an infant path nor an unknown journey. She wasn't ready for it. But truth be told, it was here. She was a warrior— survivor of all. She was part of that kindred group that could go through it and come out with some healing wounds and reminding scars. It was her destiny. Warriors did not give in and did not give up. But they did cry. Later, when no one could see how much it hurt, she would cry. She would no longer rail against her fortunes of life or the fortuities of eternal plans. She would fight to the end. She would not go out in defeat. She was a warrior. She was a survivor and that said, she could go through anything and like the sun, rise again in the morning.

* * * * * * * * *

Even warriors stumble and fall
on their journey for that is the Way.

"How could this little thing cause so much hurt?"

Deep inside, but close to her mind and heart, she felt an emptiness she couldn't seem to get rid of. Oh, she knew the causes. Hell, she knew the root causes. But they didn't seem to help alleviate the pain that stayed with her and wouldn't go away.

This was not Healing 101. She'd been traveling a long time on this path. There was little left that could surprise or throw her off balance. And yet, she couldn't shake the pit in her stomach. She couldn't connect it to a thought that would say, "That's it!" and then it would dissipate, as it would do whenever the wound was discovered and healed.

No, this one seemed to walk with her for a while and only taunt her at her perplexity while dismissing her pain. There was no getting around this pain of existence in an otherwise-fulfilling life she had rebuilt, reclaimed, and recovered. This one was interfering with her renewing.

She thought, *Perhaps I'll never get the answer to this one, but I know I can't stay here.* One thing she did know, she did learn, was the saying, "You gotta go through it." Simple and tough as that.

That day she went through it, not counting the days ahead that it might come back. She let herself feel the pain, emptiness, and turmoil inside of her. She cried and teared throughout the day. She did things even though her stomach kept telling her not to, or it would rev up more pain. She did it because it was the thing to do, not the "right thing" or not because she "had" to. She did it because it was the Way. It was dealing with what the day brought; and though in retrospect it may have seemed small, even a small enemy can be quite powerful. And since the enemy dwelled within her and since she was on the healing path itself, she was more powerful than the enemy within. It was an old enemy, but she was an older survivor. She would prevail over this obstacle, just as she had all the others.

* * * * * * * * *

"The enemy throughout is not as powerful as the champion within."

"Is it possible to have one night where I don't have nightmares?"

Let us place nightmares right up there with flashbacks and unwanted memories. Our nightmares come of their own accord and leave only when we awaken scared, shaken and disoriented as if the dream had actually happened. We feel the hard beating of our hearts, the aloneness of the late night hour, and the vigilance that says we can not go back to sleep until we wait for the morning sun to rise. And there's nothing worse than a hangover from a nightmare that continues sporadically throughout the day, interfering with our concentration on our tasks. As long as the nightmare is continually playing throughout our heads and we are lacking sleep as well, we are not fully there for the purpose of that day, whether work, school, or loved ones. In actuality and over time, we do have the power to change our nightmares.

Here's something guaranteed to work: The next time we have a nightmare, when we awaken, we use our imaginations of how we would have wanted the dream to end. For instance, is someone chasing you in your dream and you can't scream for help? If so, imagine that in the next nightmare chase, you scream as loud as you can and all your friends come to help you; or that suddenly you become larger than the monster in your dream and you can do anything you want to it and do so, or you can remove yourself from its presence. At least three times each night for one week before you go to sleep and also immediately after you awaken from a nightmare, imagine the scenario of what you want to happen in that dream.

Some may scoff at this exercise, but it has been tried before and works for many of us. Like any new activity, it takes practice, but after a few nights we should be able to see the difference in our dreams, and we should be able to get a better night's sleep. The monsters aren't always the winners. Sometimes we get the monsters and they don't come back again.

* * * * * * * * *

"I am in charge of my life and of my dreams."

"Why is this so hard?"

Sometimes our healing is a matter of "nose to the grindstone," a matter of going up a steep hill, knowing if we stop we could roll right back down to where we started from. Going up a hill, we feel all parts of our bodies being called into action, calling on muscles we have not used in a long time, and so we feel the stress of such new and necessary action. We feel the strain on our leg muscles, the ache in our thigh muscles. We feel the pressure on our chests and we feel the harder beating of our hearts. It is all an indication that we are using parts of our bodies we haven't used in a long time to accomplish our new goals.

Our healing/feeling journey is sometimes like that as well. As we address our issues and seek to exercise new behaviors, we may find ourselves being called upon to use inner resources we haven't used in a long time. Our new feelings arise, and because they are new, it is unknown to us that we can handle this new burden, this new task. We can. We can be so afraid of our feelings that as we let ourselves feel, we start running as if we are being invaded by new combatants. We are not. We are simply receiving feelings that are finally coming home because we have invited them back into our bodies.

It is only scary because they seem so unfamiliar. They disrupt the usual way, the hidden feelings we have kept deep in ourselves. New feelings stimulate new thoughts and the unknown, and as survivors the unknown has usually brought us fear, so we keep this at bay as much as possible.

As survivors in healing, we know it is not possible to keep feelings away. Once we have tapped into our lost selves, we know our healing is dependent upon our embracing the feelings and truly making them ours. We women, endowed with many shades and hues, know that to reclaim our centeredness, our connection with the Universe, is to reclaim the selves we have hidden from for so long; and to embrace them is to embrace our health and to embrace our lives.

* * * * * * * * *

"Healing can be grindstone work...no ifs, ands, or buts about it!"

"Why am I always anxious when I want to do something for me?"

It can start off with something as simple as a flicker of doubt in our minds with thoughts such as *"What if I can't?"*, *"What if I don't?"* or *"What if I shouldn't?"*— something along those lines where what we want to attempt to do is stopped before the idea even gets out of our heads. Our most powerful enemy is the voice within us that says, "I can't."

Doesn't matter. We could come up with a thousand and one reasons why we can't do something, all of them rational at the time of their presentation, and some even justified. Just ask a child of about seven or eight years old. They can give one million reasons why they didn't put their shoes in the closet or why they left the milk on the table. Or ask them to find something right in front of their faces, and because they don't expect to see it, they don't.

Sometimes we carry that same thinking into our adulthood. Maybe it's because no one ever showed us how to get beyond the "I can't," and we only learned "I can" fleetingly, and when we had to. Ask women giving birth whether it's possible to export 10 to 14 pounds of new life through a vaginal canal, and they might snicker at first, then roll their eyes at the prospect, knowing only too well that if they had to, they could, or else they'd die trying.

Our dreams and wants are like that. Sometimes if we don't just push away the "I can't," and trust ourselves to our inner visions, we will surely die for lack of trying, the signature of our own hands at our own inner death. Some things stay simple. We just have to try. Our anxieties could vanish if, instead of worrying, fretting, or crying, and in the Spirit of Faith, we risk it all, taking our fears with us and saying, "I can."

* * * * * * * * *

"Anxiety is but another form of the She-monster
in one of her more elaborate costumes."

"To whom are they talking?"

Disassociation, as an identity disorder, has received a lot of attention recently. Apparently, there has never been a time in history when so many people have said as a group, "What are you talking about?" or "I don't remember any of this."

Disassociation is one of the more creative defenses survivors have been able to utilize to survive our histories. It allows for the normally-present self, the ego, to step away from a dangerous and painful situation and to observe it as an "other." Many times it allows for no memory of the experience until a person is able to handle the experience. Sometimes, it can allow for a way of life where different "parts," and for some folks different "personalities," come forth to handle everyday life. While this is a handy mechanism for survival when there is no escape, it can be treacherous when all things are equal and we are no longer subjected to abuse. It can be dysfunctional when we are adults and have to function in a working world, in a community, and/or in our families as responsible people.

Everybody disassociates on some level— from the mild daydreaming of being totally in our own heads to the splitting of different personalities that retain memory of what is going on in a specific event. There is help for those of us who have chosen disassociation as a defense to navigate in the world. We can learn to use it to our benefit. We can learn who our different parts are, how they come out, and what issues cause them to come forth, so that we can continue healing. Some of us may choose to integrate the different parts, while there are those of us who wish to have the parts remain individual and still helpful to us in a more present and cognizant way. The choice, as always, is up to us.

* * * * * * * * *

"All aspects of myself can be healed."

"When I feel lonely why is it difficult for me to call a friend?"

There is nothing so lonely as when we feel there isn't anybody we can talk to, go to, and rest into, taking comfort in the fact that others care about our lives and whether we live or die. Our past has effectively taught us how to turn away from others, more so when we need them most. The cruel irony here is that most of the people we know would gladly lend a listening ear if we picked up the phone or went to visit them. We are the harshest judges of who we are, the unmoving adjudicators of our own lives.

We are not hopeless. No matter how bad it gets, it can never be equivalent to the pain we suffered as children. Therefore, it is imperative that we remember we are in charge now. We are the ones who call the shots for change in our own lives. It is the day-to-day decisions we make that shape and form our daily lives. It is not easy, but it is doable. If we would choose to be less lonely then we have to take the risks we so wisely in the past chose not to. But this is not the past. We are older, wiser, and more powerful. We have friends and people who love us now and who want only the best for us. It is up to us. Now. It's not easy and we don't always believe it, but the rewards are greater than the risks.

* * * * * * * * *

"I need to remember that my friends and loved ones care for me deeply."

"Who am I now?"

She woke up somewhat groggily and looked to the other side of the bed noting her boyfriend had left her a note. It said, "It happened again and last night was it. I'm outa here." She began feeling panicky as she walked over to the closet, opened the door and saw that his small section was empty and thought, "No tears this time." Suddenly, she slid down the closet doorway and with resignation thought, "Not again."

"Not again" meant one of her insiders had gotten triggered and without her choice, or so it seemed to her, acted without her permission or knowledge. She didn't know where she went during those times and she was glad it was mostly short-lived. But short-lived or not, it created havoc in her love life.

Whatever part this was of her, it was mostly an angry and rageful part. Her therapist had diagnosed her with Dissociative Identity Disorder (DID), apparently because her mind had a way of separating parts of her life and there were two or three parts inside her that held different sections of her life during the time she was sexually abused as a child. These parts were different from the part of her that lived her everyday routine such as work where she seemed to be an upbeat manager and never got angry.

She knew what her boyfriend meant when he said it was the "last time", because her angry part had come out a few times before between them. One minute they had been holding hands and the next minute she had slapped him. Apparently he must've leaned over her a certain way, a way that reminded her of the long-time sexual abuser in her childhood. This was one of the triggers, and true to form her other part came out and took care of what she perceived as a dangerous situation. She only knew it was true because she saw her hand print on his reddened cheek the time it had happened before this last time. His face held a mixture of anger, pain, hurt and frustration when he confronted her about what she had done.

Well, at least this time she wasn't in denial. She was now ready to get to know this part that others kept telling her about herself.

* * * * * * * * *

"Whether one or many, knowing one's self is a major part of the healing journey."

"How come we are never prepared for the unexpected?"

A 14-year-old girl went to bed one night. She did the usual things. She took her shower, read a chapter in her book. She kissed her mother and father good night. She climbed into bed, set her alarm clock, and slept the dream of a child.

The next morning, each time she looked in the mirror she cried. Her eyes were puffed terribly against her pretty, brown skin, and as she slid to the floor crying hysterically but in silence, she wondered if something weren't terribly wrong with her. She thought she was the worst girl in the world, and most of all, she really believed she'd done something wrong while she was sleeping. She might have thrown her covers off and exposed a leg, or worse, her vagina, as she slept unaware of the temptation she posed to anyone who chanced to come into her room. But then again, she didn't know she was being watched except by her guardian angel, who apparently wasn't doing much guarding at all that night. Or maybe, like her mother said, she suggested it with the way she moved and walked down the hall as she headed off to bed. Whatever the reason, it was obviously her fault.

She went to class that day and the days thereafter. And she would wonder, *Why?* No matter how she looked at it, no matter what answers came up, none ever satisfied the question of *Why?* She couldn't fathom how her life, in one act, was forever changed, all her family relationships were changed, and that in one moment she went from loving daughter to suspicious trespasser to those she loved.

We who are survivors and adults know that there is no reasonable answer to a child's "Why?" We only know that in time, she will be free to make peace with the question of "Why?" and with herself. And in the end, that will have to suffice the "Why?".

* * * * * * * * *

"The question 'Why?' is infinite; justice and mercy are of this earth."

"What am I waiting for?"

The waiting is endless, and the emptiness longer than the days of winter. If she sits and waits here, nothing bad can happen to her. If she sits and waits, maybe someone who loves her will come along and take her with them. But only if she sits and waits. If she moves and does different things, surely trouble will come her way.

Waiting is one of nature's greatest teachers. She learns, from day to night and night to morning, to wait until it is safe. She learns not to reach forth, lest she feel the slap of a hand. She learns not to move her legs, lest she run and knock something over, and then she'd be knocked over. She learns to wait as chaos abounds all around her; and she and knows, from lessons already learned, that to wait means she could become invisible to everybody, and herself, too. She could go to the corner of her mind and wait until her mother came to take her home, and then everything would be okay.

She sits alone at her kitchen table. Years have gone by, and following all the rules and waiting according to protocols, every time she thinks she might go out on her own, she is amazed that the day will go by and still all she does is wait. She can not even cry because, of course, she is waiting.

Every now and then, she forgets she's not supposed to wait, and takes off on a joyous adventure until she hears the voice that says, "Sit down and wait." But for some reason, she starts to listen to the voices of adventure and they begin to haunt her later days. She begins struggling with waiting and moving. One morning, sitting alone at her kitchen table as usual, she gets up, looks out the window, and since nothing ever happened while she waited, she opens the door and walks outside.

* * * * * * * * *

"Waiting can help me know when to move forward in my journey."

"I wonder if men wish they could cry as much as they wanted to?"

And what of the men? What of our brothers who have suffered silently with us and amongst themselves? What of these males who can not risk telling the world their awful, awful secret? Who understands their fears and tears? Who will hold them at night while they weep? If they weep?

Who will protect them, and us, from their unanswered rage?

Once, a young, fatherless adolescent boy was molested, raped and threatened by a family friend and trusted member of the community that if he told someone about what happened, his perpetrator would tell all the people the boy knew that the boy was a homosexual. Later that night, the boy agreed to meet the perpetrator at the perp's house. The boy's fear of being thought of as homosexual was greater than his fear of being raped...again. Even later during this same evening, the young, fatherless adolescent boy was arrested for the murder of his perpetrator. At the age of 15 he was tried and convicted of murder. Imagine that. Fatherless, sexually assaulted and raped, and then convicted of murder— all before the age of 16. Who will hold him when he weeps at night? If he weeps?

Wouldn't it be great to see a TV commercial by a professional male athlete, strong and buff, telling boys that if they've been sexually assaulted and/or raped to call an 800 number? Wouldn't that be something? Wouldn't it be better than reading that a 15-year-old boy was convicted of murder because he killed a man who raped and sodomized him, and threatened to tell the world he was homosexual? Wouldn't that be something?

* * * * * * * * *

"I looked over at a man crying and saw his hurts were as great as mine."

"Are we not more the same than we are different?"

We who are women deal with differences all the time. We are constantly reminded that we are not of the male species. Like so, the various races are constantly reminded, on a daily basis, that they are not like the media-dominated White mainstream culture.

We are a competitive society, and discrimination is a part of our everyday thinking processes. It is how we make decisions. We weigh in both the good and the bad, and make our final thoughts for the best outcome of any prospect. We seem to run into the most trouble when we apply such thinking processes to our personal relationships.

Our first encounter with anyone sets such thinking into process, as we immediately take in what the other person looks like. Innocent children have no problem with different people and almost, without fail, accept them exactly for who they are. It is only later that they start discriminating in their play with others that some are too fat, too skinny, speak funny, don't talk the same, too black or too white. By the time they start formal schooling, these value judgments are well into place. We all know how cruel children can be on the playground. Some of us know firsthand, like when one of our children comes home brokenhearted because the other kids won't play with her because she's "too ugly." Some of us know this from our own personal experience when we were the objects of such rejection.

We who are women know there is no good reason to exclude another person from anything, and racism does that. It teaches us to exclude another from our lives based on the color of their skin.

But we do not have to be part of the exclusion process. More and more, as we accept ourselves for who we are and where we've been, as we begin to accept in ourselves in all our forms, we are able to accept others in theirs. Self-love and self-acceptance promote acceptance of others. It is simply the way of the Universe.

* * * * * * * * *

*"Today I will remember that it is by the act of inclusion
that I and my communities heal."*

"Is it possible to for more days like these?"

There are days made simply for marveling— a day of exhilaration and full of promises met, a day when we and the Universe are in tune with each other. Of course, it is not so much that the Universe changes, as it is that we actually feel our important part in relationship to it and others. As consistent and as predictable as the Universe is, it is the flaming, constant chaos and craziness in our personal worlds that cause the breach of such daily wonderment. After all, the sun rises every day, the sky lights up with stars even when, in the darkness, we can not see them. When we are in a state of grace, all of this is possible to see. When we lose connection to grace and become consumed by the petty and necessary disruptions in our lives, then daily living becomes laborious, and our visions become shady and distorted.

To keep our days of marvel, we simply have to step back and remember who we really are. We are integral parts of the Universe, and even more importantly, we are integral to the people in our lives. Our journey here is really so intense that we indeed short-change ourselves when we try to go it alone with unnecessary detours of our own making. We are more than simply the physical bodies we inhabit, and we have the proof of a wondrous natural environment, along with a host of other individuals, to prove it so.

* * * * * * * * *

*"It's a simple truth that no matter what I do or don't do,
the sun rises each and every morning!"*

"Where'd that saying 'a bad hair day' come from?"

Misogyny, Chauvinism and White Supremacy (MCWS) seem to be, at times, like the AIDS disease— constantly mutating. Every time we seem to have a handle on it, or even a glimmer of immunizing ourselves from it, another strain appears to present another life-threatening situation. MCWS is a devastating disease that causes alarming pain to a Black woman's life, especially when it comes to our hair. There is no such thing as "normal" when it comes to the perception we Black women have of our hair. There is no such thing as rejection of objective reality, because our reality and our legacy has never been objective since our ancestors were stolen to America.

We are even laughed at by our men, rejected for our naturalness. And when we try to accommodate the standards they desire, which are so very foreign to us, we are still made fun of for being what we are not.

For Black women who have hair deemed acceptable and desirable by White culture, even then we can not take pleasure in our natural genetics; for we are made to feel that such hair stems from White genetics, and not from our ancestors.

In the planet community, we are made fun of constantly, no matter what Continent we live on. Our hair is rejected, hair that is so much a part of culture, so much a part of being and feeling like a woman.

Here's what the media and societal standards are today: A woman with a head full of hair. Straight hair. Long hair. Blond hair. Blow-in-the-wind, shiny hair. Hair many of us do not have and yet the hair we have is condemned by the outside world, or even by some of the lovers in our world.

We carry a shame for which we have no reason to be ashamed of only if we accept being that which we are not. We are survivors and if we are accepting of who we are, at the end of the day, that's all that really matters.

* * * * * * * * *

"Hair is the crown on my head to wear as I want to."

"I used to love the summer, didn't I?"

She loved the summer. No school, endless days of fun and "What should we do now?" That is, until the last summer of "What should we do now?" He did it. She could just as easily trace back her dread of summer as readily as she could recall up the night it happened— a night after a softball team game and on the brink of teen-dom, as she was still running after fireflies watching them glow in the cup of her hands, and then letting them fly away again.

Perhaps it was her fault, anyway. Maybe the fireflies didn't like her catching them any more than she liked him sneaking up on her and clutching her from behind, his hands grabbing newly growing breasts she learned to hate. But she was a quick learner, and just like the fireflies, she ran off at the slightest release of his grip. She ran to the back of the yard where other adults would be and she would be safe, temporarily, until his next run. Eventually she would have to run no more and would fly away just like the fireflies.

Reclaiming her love of summer is just as important as reclaiming all of the other things and feelings she lost while trying to survive this family stalker. We survivors are used to giving in to the "easy" stuff. We minimize, compromise, and tell ourselves we don't care, because in the larger scheme of things, having survived sexual assault, rape, and/or constant molestation of one sort or another we think that struggling with something that isn't forcing itself upon us just isn't worth it.

The truth is, all aspects of our lives that were stolen and/or lost to us, whether as a defense or because they are tainted with triggering events, are worth recovering, even the enjoyment of a season of a year. We may have to practice at going back out and enjoying the summer nights, until we remember again how alive we felt before we lost the love and expectation of a part of nature, and a part of ourselves.

* * * * * * * * *

*"A lost love of a season can be found again
as all things are possible when we are healing."*

"Whoever came up with the idea that a person could be infallible?"

Pope John Paul II died recently. Of course, they had a big funeral and everybody came, religious and secular. Hell, there were so many priests there, they could've done an Interpol investigation and rounded up a lot of sex predators parading around as priests. There wasn't much of a chance of that happening, and so the burial ceremony went on as planned. What was most noticeable about all the visitors, dignitaries, and members of the church that participated in the final mass, the final Eucharist to this religious leader, was the lack of women of equal status to the men of authority in the church.

Until women throughout the world are equal to men in decision-making power and are eligible for any position a man holds, the road to peace will remain just that— a road, and one which many can travel.

Perhaps we survivors notice these things more acutely than others and are more offended by them than others. Our senses of what is and what is not just find their reference point in our survival of being overpowered by another, and it inflames our senses of justice and mercy.

We do not have to be witnesses to the powerful vs. the powerless in such grand standards as the funeral of the Pope. We are witness to such things in our everyday lives. Children continue to need protection from pedophiles; women remain in need of safe houses from abusive spouses or partners; victims of rape need those who know to say, "This is the way," and men who are survivors need to spread the word more about their own healing from sexual abuse. We who are healing must not forget that we are some of the best healers when it comes to survival, and we can act on that knowledge to help change injustice to justice whenever the opportunity arises.

* * * * * * * * *

"We survivors are also healers."

"Even though they see it, why can't they believe it?"

People in denial do not want to believe a perpetrator can be a husband, wife, mother, father, brother, sister, uncle, aunt, cousin, or family friend. The perp could also be a celebrity, a sports hero, a rabbi, a priest, a minister, an imam, a teacher, coach or a childcare worker. People don't want to believe that these chameleon citizens, these heinous human beings masquerading as family, friends, pillars of the community, philanthropists, and entrusted caregivers *are who they really are:* pedophiles that can, will and do commit sexual atrocities upon our children.

Such atrocities include, but are not limited to: grabbing and fondling a child when they are certain other adults are not around to interfere, molesting a child secretively in the presence of other adults, sneaking into children's bedrooms at night and raping them vaginally and/or anally; performing or having the child perform cunnilingus and/or fellatio; tying them down, or chaining their necks, wrists and ankles; and of course, other unspeakable acts meant to hurt and inflict humiliation. Some of these happen only once. Sometimes they happen frequently throughout an entire childhood.

Sometimes these molestations, sexual assaults, and abuses occur in the most horrific ways unimaginable, leaving behind a trail of blood and other bodily fluids, as well as a future fraught with neurosis, psychosis, or survivors just leaving their minds for some unknown time. And then sometimes it happens gradually. The perp gains the trust of the victim and tells them it's okay to *"do it,"* taking their time until their victim acquiesces and thinks such behavior between adult and child is natural, and their innocence is forever lost.

It is a good thing that truth, no matter how long it takes, will not be silenced, and neither will all the voices and truths of survivors.

* * * * * * * * * *

"The truth will not be silenced no matter how long it takes to be heard."

"When will this free-for-all end?"

Every now and then, maybe because of the weather or the time of day the sun was setting she would remember a time when a college friend invited her over for the weekend, ostensibly to spend time in the city and to meet her friend's family.

Color, in our survivor's book, was just that— color. While she knew of the in-fighting, the lines drawn in the sand, the quips, cruel remarks on different shading and hair texture, she had never quite come upon an experience such as this.

It wasn't as if she had asked to come over. Her friend asked her if she wanted to spend the weekend along with another mutual friend at her mother's house. Since she was from out of state, the opportunity for a home-cooked meal was not to be passed.

There was no way she could have anticipated such a weekend. Most of what she remembered was that for two days, the only meals they had at the house were toast and spaghetti— toast was one night, and the other night, they had a saucer of spaghetti. And it wasn't like they had money to spend at restaurants. They were in the work-study program, except for the host friend.

What she remembered of her friend's mother was the back of her body as she walked away after they had all been introduced upon their arrival. They never saw her again during the visit, or even when her friend graduated.

It was simply a matter of skin vs. skin. Her friend's mother, while clearly African American, was fair of skin; "blue-veined," we'd say. And her hair was straight without need of a hot comb. Clearly, her daughter's friends did not meet the color test. Both of them were brown-skinned, shades of toasted brown and bark wood trees. Her daughter apparently was oblivious to her family's inhospitality and her no-longer-to-be future friends. It was yet another lesson of "less than" our survivor would learn on her path of healing.

* * * * * * * * *

"I shall not tolerate abuse on any level nor in any arena in my life."

"Why was she invited over?"

Sitting by herself in a room full of people she had met a few hours earlier, she couldn't imagine why her friend had invited her to come to a party and then disappear. Perhaps her friend did not know what was offensive or rude or what it was like to be treated as if you were invisible in a place where you were supposed to be welcome. But the survivor knew, and felt a deep sadness for a loss she could not explain to herself. And afterward, the survivor would sometimes wonder what her friend had to endure to get to a place where she thought such treatment was to be extended to those she called "friend".

On the other hand, she was proud of herself, this survivor. She realized that day what was and wasn't acceptable to her anymore in terms of how she was treated by her friends. Just because somebody said something didn't mean they meant it; and just because they said you were their friend didn't mean they were, indeed, your friend.

Before, she would have just dismissed the disrespect she had been shown as something people did, and the next time she saw them she would act like nothing had happened. But she was no longer pretending to others, and more importantly, no longer pretending that these things didn't matter to her. How she was treated by others was very important and respect for her was a big part of that treatment.

This healing of hers, sure to have its pluses and minuses, delivered a plus from that day. She'd learned a truth and felt good about the decision she had made. No guilt. No second-guessing herself. No pretending just so she could have a friend. She wasn't afraid to listen to her mind anymore. It was definitely a plus day.

* * * * * * * * *

*"When the red flag goes up, it doesn't always mean
that there's something wrong with me."*

"Will I always feel sad"?

It does seem that for many survivors, our sexual assault becomes our reference point for all future behavior and feelings. When we begin our healing, it may become difficult to sort out what feelings *are* and *are not* related to the violation of our bodies and the ensuing emotions we experience thereafter.

Depression and grief are natural states of being for anybody given a set of circumstances that bring up such feelings. Not being able to obtain goals we set for ourselves or failing at something may cause temporary depression. The break-up of an intimate relationship or experiencing the death of a loved one can cause a period of grief.

However, sadness is quite distinct from grief and depression. Sadness is a response to a given situation in the present, not a leftover, unfinished piece of business stoked in the stoves of depression and grief. And most sadness is a mood that passes in response to the present situation. Sadness does not linger for weeks on end like depression. Sadness does not keep us isolated from our friends over long periods of time.

If we watch healthy toddlers for a day, we will notice that they experience a variety of emotions all day long. One minute they're enthralled with their own discovery that they can put two bricks together, and the next minute they're crying that the bricks came apart.

When we are healing, we are not unlike the toddlers. We may wake up with feelings of happiness or sadness, but the events of the day help us sort out these feelings so that they do not linger on. That is, like the toddler, we find resolution in turning our attention to another situation as the day rolls on.

We may not at first think that the return of such emotions is a sign of our healing, but so it goes: A healthy life will express healthy feelings, be they happy or sad ones. The fact that we may experience sadness is not a sign of a set back, but rather, the steps we take on our healing journey.

* * * * * * * * *

"How long the day, how deep the sorrow."

"How much does it take to know and live our truths?"

The molecules in her soft, beiged-toned face suddenly coagulated all at once, and contorted the features of a sweet-looking young girl into a mask of trapped fear. "What did he say?", she thought. Just as quickly, the cells embedded in the skin around her mouth and eyes dropped the frozen fear, and morphed into a hardened masked that would last for the next 40 years of her life.

"Do that again," he said.

And immediately, she stopped all rhythmic moving in her walk, slumped her shoulders, and set her eyes fixedly upon nothing in front of her.

How could she know such power would be so devastating to all she loved and held dear? How was she to know the balance was shifted, and finally, there could be no doubt that her childhood was over? It all happened so quickly. And later, more was to come, and the durations were so painful, so surreal; it was as if it weren't happening to her at all. What this large man was doing to her made no sense at all to her 11-year-old mind. And while he performed what he wanted to a body growing strong, but still that of a child, her mind locked on not so much the pain, but a mantra of, *"This shouldn't be happening to me."* And this is how she survived his hands for the next three years of sexually violating acts.

Later, when she began her healing, she would know that this was the beginning of locking up all her softness, and that not only had her heart come to harden, but all the cells in her body held the key that would unlock that hardness. She didn't know, so she couldn't say, "Give it back. It's precious. It's mine." And for a very, very long time, she lived a stiffness in her body and soul that she could not feel.

Many years later, as she moved in lightness, as she moved in a path where she often stumbled, and just as often picked herself up again, she learned she had been detoured for decades, three to be exact. It wasn't until she found the path beyond the detours and the beginning steps of her healing, that her softness returned, and the rhythm of her insides became part of her walk and her talk again.

* * * * * * * * *

"Sometimes encouragement is the gift we give another who is traveling the treacherous path we have already walked."

"How will I know I've been healed?"

The knowingness of being healed and of healing comes to us all in different forms and different stages. Life is full of books; it's full of adventures lived and told, filled with stories from the varied individuals that walk this earth. Sometimes life is like a library. When you finish one book, there are hundreds of thousands more to read.

Our healing can come in layers, and we can eventually reach the core of our sexual histories and abuse. What we choose to do with that knowledge is up to us. How we choose to live and be after we've explored those issues is up to us. It is true for many, that healing from sexual abuse seems to be a continuing, life-long journey. But that continuum is made up of many, many things. Sometimes our healing is at a peak; sometimes it is on a downward trend; and other times it is at a plateau.

Sometimes the nature of our healing is exploring the feelings of pain, shame, anger, fear, rage, and anxiety; other times, our lives are filled with new feelings of love, joy, happiness, and trust. In the beginning, the experiencing of these feelings can be akin to a toddler's— sometimes we are filled with anger and rage, and we have temper tantrums we don't understand seemingly over nothing; other times we can switch modes and see that life is full of new and fun discoveries.

We will know when we are healed. When our memories are no longer the paramount issues in our minds; when our intimate relationships are not threatened with extinction, but rather, loving support; and when we believe in ourselves with more conviction than anyone else on the planet, then it will be a day to take another book out of the library, and begin another new journey of our lives.

.

* * * * * * * * *

"It is the self that decides the Omega and Alpha of its healing."

"Why is it so hard for me? So easy for me?"

Wherever we are in healing, we are always family to those traveling this path with us. None of us heal alone. That is a given fact. We may heal at different paces, but no one does it alone. Anyone who thinks so is kidding herself.

When we attempt to judge and compare ourselves to others on the healing journey with us, we do a disservice to ourselves while also dishonoring ourselves and our personal experiences. One can not compare the value of the experience of someone who is severely disabled and has suffered the worst of humanity's sexual abuse to that of one who is not disabled and has suffered a similar experience. We are who we are. We just don't have to travel the journey alone.

Each of us will choose what it means to be healed. Some of us will see our CSA experience as a distant nightmare or memory, forgetting that it happened, and remembering only when we are reminded by something we see, or someone who discloses that such a thing has happened to her. Others will experience what will seem like a long continuum of healing, delving into the thick of their healing, courageously facing their unspoken and protected truths as they seek to balance the core of their being.

As we continue to grow beyond our sexual abuse histories and reclaim that which we lost or had taken from us, our core being becomes stronger and we begin to see live our lives not only from the perspective of one who has been sexually abused, but rather someone with new skills and new experiences, and the yesterdays of our fears have been transformed into new challenges of our todays.

* * * * * * * * *

"Every healing journey is unique and individual and so am I."

"What does this thing mean— to be healed?"

Fear: an unpleasant emotion caused by exposure to danger, expectation of pain, etc. a) state of alarm. b). danger; likelihood of something unwelcome. c) apprehension; an uneasy expectation of the worst; be apprehensive about.[8]

Panic: sudden uncontrollable fear or alarm. a) infectious apprehension or fright esp. in commercial dealings. b) panic button: a button (often imaginary) for summing help in an emergency.

Anxiety: the state of being anxious. a) concern about an imminent danger, difficulty. b) nervous disorder characterized by a state of excessive uneasiness.

Terror: extreme fear. a) a person or thing that causes terror. b) the use of organized intimidation; terrorism. **Terrorize**: to fill with terror.

We survivors are frequently challenged to overcome deeply embedded imprints of fear, anxiety, panic, and terrorism we live daily. If we are to heal, we must replace fear with love, anxiety with peace, panic with trust, and terrorism with unshakeable courage. The journey of healing is long and often laborious but its blessings are many and a healing can be had if we are willing to make the journey.

---

[8] All definitions from: Oxford English Reference Dictionary: Revised Second Edition. 2003

* * * * * * * * * *

"I am the defining moment of my life."

August 1

CRUELTY

I used to think
you were difficult
now I know
you are cruel

"Why can't I remember when we lost touch?"

How much time do you have? How could we possibly explain the family loss we experience? And who would listen anyway?

It doesn't happen all at once. It happens over time and space. It gives a little here, and tears a little here. It rips part of a seam and then breaks a rift in the fabric. Pretty soon, one string unravels and another untwirls. The cloth is rent in several places and disintegrates sometimes just from a touch. Then suddenly, the family seems like a pile of rags from a once-favored dress.

Unlike families lost in one fell swoop, many survivor families may remain physically intact for a very long time, some for a lifetime. A lifetime of existence and no contact is sometimes worse than death, worse than losing loved ones in a tragic accident where only one family member remains. At least in death there is a marker, a headstone to the dead acknowledging their existence and implying relationships. Some survivors have families that imply relationship when, in truth, such connections are dead.

Survivors, even like some non-survivors, must learn to forge new family relationships. The world is full of people who will be surrogate mothers, fathers, sisters, brothers— even grandmothers and grandfathers.

Death of any kind causes anger, grief, and sadness. It may be harder to pinpoint at times when survivor's families are still in existence but, offer no substantial contact. For some, the best thing to do is to acknowledge the loss of the love of the family member or the whole family including if the perpetrator is a family member. Betrayal of love via incest and child molestation can be as deadly as any other illness that takes the life of a human being. And as always, the survivor must decide for herself just who must be mourned, who the grief is for, and then she must take care of herself as only she can do.

* * * * * * * * *

"We are entitled to grieve the loss of any and all family members we wish to mourn."

"Can I be a good parent?"

Children, our sons and daughters of whatever age, are the seedlings of the flowers of our dreams. It is hard not to interfere with their natural growth, expressions and dreams even if the roads we've traveled are similar.

Survivors seem to do double-time and double-work when it comes to raising a family, forever questioning whether we are doing right by our children, or if what we do is not somehow contaminated by the vestiges, remnant imprints and feelings we experience from our CSA histories.

Some of us are over-protectors. Sometimes we question— non-stop— whether we are doing the right thing. We seem to ask innocuous questions of our offspring, who sometimes patiently, but mostly impatiently, give us short answers to questions that cause us worry. Many of us know the signs of discomfort, of worry, and anxiety a child may be experiencing, but not know the reason why. Growing up, everyone experiences these feelings as they seek to find their way and to fit in with their peers, or seek their independence from us, as they should. But many of us don't want to make the ultimate mistake of missing a red flag, of missing a sign that says, "There is more to this than meets the eye; this is a sign of serious trouble"

Nonetheless, water doesn't boil while you're watching, and flowers don't bloom under the scrutiny of the naked eye. Everything comes to fruition according the Universe's plans, and our children are no exception.

No matter how much we want to and how much we try, we can not live their lives for them, even from an emotional distance. We truly must let go, let them fly, and let them experience life on their own, and on their terms. This is how we healed. And this is how they must walk through the world if they are to be free and to be truly themselves. Difficult as it may be, it is one of the most loving things we can do for them.

* * * * * * * * *

"A good and loving parent makes mistakes and admits them."

"How can something get so hot?"

Her days were hot and unbearable in the August heat. In some places an egg could be fried on the sidewalk, if eggs were still fried. Her nights were sweaty and dreamless, and when she awoke, sometimes her eyes were filled with tears. One night she cried deeply in her sleep and woke feeling relieved, if not spent. Her sadness remained throughout the days and despair continued to starve her hopes whenever the thought of change occurred as a real possibility for her.

Would the heat never end? Could the summer pass quickly by as if it hadn't happened at all? She was used to waiting time out, and that was what she needed. And aside from wishing that she could be someone else, she only wanted for the summer to be over, and didn't even know why.

The truth is that she doesn't have to be sad and waiting all the time. There are so many resources now for help. She is tired and wants help. Even in her sadness she can reach out and call a help hotline, and they will assist her in getting the help she needs.

The best thing that has happened from the 20th Century into the 21st Century is the growth of organizations, grassroots and otherwise, that are spreading the word that help and healing are available if any one wants it.

We survivors who are traveling the healing path have a tremendous amount of compassion, and many times can perceive another in distress. We, too, can take risks and check-in with our sisters and ask, "Are you okay? Is there anything I can do?" And if it seems too risky an intervention, we can give them an 800 number for a general crisis line. Sometimes we must stop on our path and make sure that some of those traveling behind us don't get lost, or stumble and fall off the well-footed pathways of healing.

* * * * * * * * *

"There are so many ways we can help one another."

"How often should we eat of this fruit?"

Bittersweet fruits – the taste of pleasantness and deliciousness engulfing one's taste buds, immediately replaced with a feeling of wishing to spit it out and simultaneously wishing you could retain that first bite that was ever so sweet, although it made promises it did not keep.

And yes, surviving CSA can be quite like that for a temporary time, a time one can not measure until it has passed. The sex act seems to forever become attached to seeking that delicious feeling, and yet when finished, a loathing and rejection of the act and our involvement can ruin the wonderfulness of the feelings spreading through our bodies..

How do we resolve the yin and yang of our sexual healing? To heal the wounded part of our sexuality, we often must revisit those feelings from our memories that make us turn away from the sexually intimate and loving part of ourselves yearning to be expressed without feeling as if we've done something terribly and shamefully wrong.

The truth is if it were something wrong, it would not be the way to recreate the human race. It would not be the whole choice of nature to recreate itself by such a sexual act of one being intercoursing with another being. If we were not meant to engage in sexual intimacy, there would not be this inbuilt sexual drive that is inhabits every human being.

Like any other part of ourselves that might be wounded, we approach this part of our healing with respect and with a plan to treat the wound for as long as it takes to heal All healing takes patience. All healing takes an intervention of some sort by self to fix the wound. And then bittersweet would be more a memory than an experience we continue to have and hopefully replaced with that deep satisfaction of completion when being sexually intimate with our lovers or spouses.

* * * * * * * * *

"We are all part of something bigger than ourselves,
even if we do not understand why or how."

"How shall I stop from dwelling in the past and worrying about the future?"

The pain is unbearable these days. I open my eyes and it all comes at once. I sleep as much as I can, but still I can not escape its awakening reality. I don't know how I missed this lesson with my eyes wide open, with vulnerabilities covered from all angles. Still, I took a fall I'd not conceived, and here I am.

The sadness invades my heart, fights my mind for control and its iffy as to who's winning. And I am not good company to anyone. Even my compromises are not enough for this round. Whatever shall I do?

I shall do as I have done since this journey began. I shall take the day that has been offered me and do with it the best I can. Sometimes my best is not good enough, and other times my best brings me a gift I'd not even imagined— a remembered touch, a gentle smile, a loving hug, or just kind words spoken from friend or stranger.

I can not imagine ever choosing this path for myself, this particular lesson for this particular life. I can not imagine saying, "Yes" if someone asked, "If you could do it all again and not change a thing, would you?" Not change a thing? Surely, my answer would be "No."

But I am here now having walked this path of life and healing, and that is all I know. And the only other thing I know is to keep on trusting that this is the way for me, this is the journey I chose at sometime in some life of mine, and this is the journey that will lead me to a triumphant destination.

* * * * * * * * *

"We do not always know why we say 'yes' to life; but to do otherwise is unimaginable."

"When will it be over?"

Washing the dishes, she felt his presence before he brushed her neck gently and softly with his fingertips. She shuddered and threw the glass she was washing against the side of the sink. She swirled around, forcefully pushed against him, and then watched in horror as her boyfriend stumbled back and fell against the handle of the refrigerator. And then she slid down the sink cupboards to the floor and began quietly crying, as scene after scene began flashing across her mind like a digital slideshow— all the times the perpetrator had come up behind her and violated her in any way he felt so called upon to do. Like the time he spun her around, grabbed a breast, and as she pulled back, he smacked her until the ringing in her ears made her think her head would explode. Or the time she turned away from the sink, happy the dishes were done, only to find that he had silently crept up and positioned himself so that he stood in front of her, legs slightly parted and arms akimbo, and a ugly smirk playing at his lips as his hands reached for her chin, and he roughly stuck his tongue down her throat.

Her boyfriend softly called her name and began telling her that he wanted to sit next to her and asked her if it was okay and she said, "Yes." He did. Then he told her he was going to take her hand and hold it in his. And he did. He told her he was going to gently pull her next to him so she could cry on his shoulders. And he did

And they sat like that until she could open her eyes free of tears, and she could see the beauty of the evening falling as a last lone sunbeam came through the window and she could hear the beating of both their hearts. She smiled wryly as her body relaxed into his. Her eyes began to tear again as she tried to say she was sorry. She heard him say, "Shhhh," as he pulled her even closer. And they sat like that long into the night.

And that was the kind of day she had. She wondered how many more of them she could survive; and she also wondered if ever a day would come when she could relax into her boyfriend's arms without a battle for her soul happening first.

* * * * * * * * *

"Battles are won only if we fight back and sometimes resting is a good strategy."

"How much of what they're doing do they know they're doing?"

What's it like to enter into sacred space uninvited? Do you feel your trespassing, knowing you're done something wrong, and a thought flashes that you know you shouldn't be there? Like stumbling into somebody else's home and everybody looks up at the same time in innocent confusion, and you say, "Oops," and go to your own home. But what if you didn't? What if you stayed despite the baby crying and the food on the stove burning while you insist that you belong there, and chaos and confusion ensue while everyone tries to sort it out, and the family seeks to throw you out of the house? Do you realize the upheaval you caused? Do you know you are trespassing? Ultimately, do you care?

Rapists stalk or stumble upon their victims. Sometimes the victim is not a stranger; the victim is an acquaintance, a loved one or a spouse. No rapist has said they thought they were entering into "sacred" space and while many know they are doing something wrong, most don't explore the reasons why they rape until, maybe, after the assault. That is why they rape.

Rapists don't care about victims, so when interacting with them, a "no holds barred" mentality should be used at all costs, because the rapist is going to rape until his life is in danger, and only then will he seek to withdraw his trespassing. Fighting back is encouraged if you think it will help you. Screaming is more than allowed. Sometimes, the die is cast— there is no escape, law enforcement will not be busting down any locked doors and there's no way the rapist is going to be overtaken by the victim. In that case, one must find the part of the mind that survives everything and follow its dictates. They key concept, thought, and action is that one survives the rape be it by fighting back physically and getting away, or consciously deciding not to fight in order to save one's life because that is what your mind says is the thing to do in order for you to live. Any choice and manner to survive is valid.

* * * * * * * * *

"There are no wrong ways to survive a rape."

"How do I know if the lover I trust will rape me?"

The rapist rapes because:

> he feels like it
> he has opportunity
> he wants to
> he can

There is no rhyme or reason, and none should be pursued for a lifetime. Most times, people do what they do because they want to and can.

We who have survived these imposters who pose as husbands, lovers, significant others, relatives or "safe" acquaintances, have no reason to continue a perpetration by blaming ourselves. In fact, our next step in healing is to make sure the rapist is seen for what he is, despite his many chameleon-like attributes we wish to grant him. Indeed, in the future it would be taking care of ourselves to trust in our doubts and intuition and act accordingly, rather than be a possible victim of raped.

* * * * * * * * *

"Sometimes we don't know a truth until we accidentally stumble upon it.
It is not our fault that we are neither soul or mind readers."

"What shall I do with the pieces?"

Who am I now? What do I do now? I can walk again, but the things I wanted to walk again for no longer matter to me. I am adrift, and each day I wake searching for meaning or interest towards the world outside or my own inner world. I mean, why get out of bed if I must find reasons to make it worthwhile all the time?

Because the world we live in is all we consciously know, we think Earth is the be all and the end all, as if we had some other life culture from another planet to compare it with. Everybody dies, but I want to do so on my terms. When I die, I want it to be a good day, not a day full of emptiness and sorrow and sand dunes that stretch in the deserts forever. I want it to be a day when I am happy and pleased by my achievements and the beloved people in my life. I want to move on to the next world when I can say, "Hey, it was all worth it." I want to be able to live my life in longevity, spend time lovingly with the people who make up my family, and go to sleep knowing I loved and was loved as well.

It is hard to rebuild again, even when all the problems are gone. I grew arms to mother my own child, and now I must create new dreams so I can rebuild another vision for my remaining days upon this earth. The foundation is sturdy. The rest is left up to me and my dreams.

* * * * * * * * *

"Starting over again is like writing a new chapter in my own book of life."

"What boat carries me to the River Jordan?"

"Dear God, if there is a God, please save my soul, if I have a soul.."* We have many moments when we believe we are blessed. However, sometimes those experiences seem to be totally wiped out when faced with the great deceivers: fear and doubt.

Some folks believe deeply in a God or deeply in themselves. Others take flight back and forth, never knowing for sure, but hoping nonetheless that they have a soul, that the world we are born into is not one of deliberate chaos and ugliness, but for which at the end of the road, or as our ashes are scattered above the airways over chosen waters, we will learn there has been a larger plan after all. Many of us would like to believe that with the continuing behavior of the sun, the oceans, the night, and the sky, there are laws of nature that have always been there, created by a Divine Being who has a personal interest in our life.

We survivors know that we have escaped, barely, with our lives, seldom relaxing into the truth that we are truly free to do what we wish. It is sometimes hard for us to even trust that the sun will rise each morning, and yet in truth, morning has always come every day of the year since the day we were born.

*Author unknown

* * * * * * * * *

"None go the Way except by the Spirit of Truth."

"Who am I now that I am free?"

Molestation. Incest. Rape. Sexual Assault. Sexual Abuse. Date Rape. Marital Rape. Stranger Rape. Acquaintance Rape. Age 2. Age 85. Woman. Man. Child. Heterosexual. Homosexual. White race. Black race. Brown race. Yellow race. Red race. Bi-racial. Multi-racial. With weapons. Without weapons. One perp. Many perps.

In all manner of sexual violations, regardless of what sex, race, ethnicity, culture, class, ableness or age group, for an unknown amount of time a victim is overcome, overpowered, controlled, dominated and their body is no longer their own. Eventually if one survives the sexual violation and if one frees one's self, the decision is to keep on running, don't stop, just keep running or he or they will catch up with you, will get you, and you will never have a chance to be free again. Never. That is what you know and you remember most— the time you didn't get away until it was all over and then the feelings of despair and shame that consumed your mind overtook your body.

The challenge becomes then, once freedom is attained, not to rest in the fact that one is saved, but rather, one has the freedom to make a new life.

It may seem like a lifetime has come and gone before one is free from the sexual violation, and then another lifetime before we heal, but always after we are free, it is a lifetime of our own to do with what we will. Sometimes freedom is told in short stories, but mostly freedom is a consuming novelistic saga about a long journey.

* * * * * * * * *

"No matter how long it takes, be patient for your time will come."

"These thoughts aren't mine, are they?"

She didn't know when this part of her began to publicly show its face to everybody but herself. She felt like she hated everybody, and the thoughts that finally escaped from wherever they'd been locked up for years, suddenly became a regular part of her everyday thinking. She only wanted them to stop because she was afraid she might actually say them out loud to others. "If they only knew," she said to herself. "They would not think so highly of me." The part of her that built these thoughts added, "And they don't need to know, either. So there." To whom she was speaking, she really didn't know.

But another part of her, the one that kept calling her into balance every time she was a little off center, would not be placated with the usual "life is like this, and all is well with the world." Her need for centeredness was as great as the laws of day and night, as awesome as sun and moon, and as necessary as the land, air, and sea.

Only this part of her, although she would quickly banish it as soon as it raised its monstrous head, would not stop rearing its head. It would keep popping up, especially during those times when she felt most good about herself. Finally, she was where she wanted to be in her life, and didn't know she had brought along this outstanding and apparently necessary baggage.

She had no idea where all the anger was coming from, especially the anger in her dreams. There were times she would wake up cursing in the middle of the night, literally kicking a leg out, and didn't know why. Or else, matters she thought had been settled would be played out in a series of dream after dream on some nights, always with her standing unnecessary ground and angrily stating her position.

In the old days, she would have been able to send this part of herself away. But this was a new day in her life, once lost and now found. She knew her healing lay in the total exploration of these monstrous feelings. This time, though impatient, she was not afraid.

* * * * * * * * *

"No matter my beginning ignorance
I will come to my light of truth."

"Who is this new me?"

She moved purposely now. No matter where she went she was aware of her environment.

When she walked outside, she carried her head high, sometimes nodding or smiling at other people she passed along the way. She was different now and she knew it, felt the new re-possession of her body. She had acquired the necessary humility of human nature as she knew she was no more invulnerable to the craziness of the streets than anybody else. She was more than willing to avoid danger, but no longer afraid to call attention to herself if need be in order to ask for help or assistance. And physically, she wasn't afraid of being hurt nor of defending herself and hurting someone else if that someone were to attempt an attack upon her. In short, she now felt capable of taking care of all aspects of her physical, mental, emotional, and spiritual self.

Often now, she marveled in amazement that her search for a healing from years of incest and CSA, had lead her to a 180° return to an unburied self. When she went to work with the hopeful, yet at times despairing young girls who also had to unfortunately walk the same path, she often told them in tones and words she wished she'd heard back then, "It's okay. You won't be stuck here forever. There really is something out there waiting for you that is wonderful and is going to exceed all your expectations and doubts, if you're willing to trust who you are deep inside. Most of all, when you are in your darkest moments, remember that deep within you, your warrior spirit will show you the way out."

* * * * * * * * *

"Even as writers, the ending of a good story is not quite what we expect."

"Why doesn't my mother love me?"

You have no idea how you broke her heart. We ought to be able to look at the life records of this world at any given time— records that say, "Attention: All Parents. This is what matters and this is what doesn't." And by your name they should write, "Due to serious spiritual and emotional injury, this woman could not mother her children, no matter how much they needed her. Her children, but especially her oldest daughter, were brokenhearted every time she left them all, never once witnessing her daughter's tears; never once telling her, 'Hush, don't cry, everything's gonna be all right.'"

Because of you, tonight I pray your daughter does not decide in her anguish to kill herself as she seeks to find a good reason to value her own life, since the mother that brought her into the world, apparently does not. One day, your daughter will realize she is worth living for, that her life in and of itself has value simply because she has been born. I don't know how long it will take her to get there, especially when you keep leaving, thereby telling her she's not good enough for you to stay around, raise her, and love her.

I hope this is the last time you leave her. I hope you don't come back after you've solved your next drug addiction, your next domestic violent relationship, or your next need to prove that you really do love all your children, raising that faint flicker of hope that this time you'll stay.

It is one of the most cruel ironies in this life— to know there are women all over the world who can not have children and go to bed heartbroken, wishing above all else that they could have a child of their own. At the same time, there are abandoned children yearning for a mother who loves and wants them. There should be a constant, pulsating Universal law embedded in every human being who brings a new life into the world, that says, "In regards to your children, do the right thing or suffer the immediate consequences. No appeals."

* * * * * * * * *

"One day there will be cells in the brain that automatically stop production of sperm and eggs until a person is ready to be a loving parent."

"Now What?"

If we survivors wish our lives to be different then we must make significant changes. Be forewarned. Change definitely *requires* commitment and practice. Many survivors want to change their lives because it is filled with fear, anxieties and mistrust of self and others. And too, there is something about the human spirit that seems to drive a person to express her life as fully as she can in whatever area that may be, such as work, free time or relationships. When this drive is unfulfilled in positive ways, then it will show up in other ways such as drug use, alcohol use, raging at others, denial and often chronic depression.

The profundity of the power of the aftermath of a sexual assault, rape, incest or molestation can not be over-stated in terms of the way it influences every aspect of a survivor's life.

An inactive healing survivor may find ways to divert her unaddressed reactions to a sexual assault by either burying it for years in her unconscious mind and then acts as if it never happened. Or, another survivor may go through the motions of life doing what is expected of her by her family and society such as going to college, getting a job and getting married, but *always* feeling as if some part of her is missing in every relationship she has be it with family members, friends or lovers.

So what is commitment to change? It means being willing to do the emotional and mental *work* needed to make those changes happen. It is a willingness to consistently show up and work on the changes we committed ourselves to do. So if a survivor says, "I always feel shameful after I make love. What can I do to change that?", it may mean she immediately addresses her feelings with her partner as these feelings arise *during* loving making and because she is no longer a victim, but a survivor, work through the shame so she can give the shame back to who it belongs— the perp; and that she understands this not just intellectually, but in the deepest parts of her heart and soul.

* * * * * * * * *

"Healing means commitment to changing my life even during the uncomfortable times."

"Why should I bother getting out of bed?"

10 REASONS TO GET OUT OF BED

1. You have slept so much in the past 24 hours that your dreams are repeating the same endings. Get up and get new material for your unconscious.

2. You can not work with the public in your job capacity from your pillow and blankets.

3. Even if you wish it a zillion times, you will not get your laundry and vacuuming done from the bed.

4. You are not on the Starship Enterprise and do not have a replicator next to your bed to make you coffee, tea, hot cocoa, eggs, bacon, grits, toast, or anything else your mind might conjure up with which you wish to satisfy your hunger and thirst.

5. The goldfish can not live as long as you without food, and you are the designated feeder of all your pets. This, as you know, requires you to leave your bed.

6. You feel the unrelenting pressure of a full bladder, do not have a portable potty or bedpan, and the reason you woke up is that you were dreaming of peeing.

7. You are already late for work, again, and no one can complete the grant deadline for today except you. It's your project. You could choose to stay home, but missing the deadline would mean loss of funding the 10-year project that's floating the payroll of all the employees at your job.

8. It's payday.

9. There's a sale at your favorite store, and you have enough change to buy something other than time.

10. When you throw the covers over your head to blank out the world, the atmosphere inside the cocoon is rough.

* * * * * * * * *

"One can find any reason to stay in bed and any reason to get up."

"What awesome power has the lie to the truth?"

Some say there is nothing more powerful than truth. There are others that would argue more empires and superpowers have been built upon the lies of men throughout the ages of all humanity. We may disdain lies and the liars that tell them, but there is no doubt that they are powerful.

Still, they are never more powerful than the truth. Unfortunately for us, it calls upon a tremendous amount of patience by we seekers and believers of truth to fight this terrible power. And yet, it is a fact that the truth always wills out, even if it takes ages to do so.

We survivors should and can take heart that the truth does not rest until it is heard. Many of us are lucky because the truth of our lives eventually reveals itself during our time of living. Our stories of surviving CSA will be heard. And while we may not always have justice, specifically as we would want it, we can always tell our truths, for there are ears ready to hear them.

Sometimes the people we want to hear, usually family members, don't want to hear the truth, or if they do hear it, can not bear to hear it for very long. That is why lies have such an awesome and terrible power, because they have so many allies such as denial and misplaced loyalties.

But eventually, the truth stares down most disbelievers. It's powerful opponent, the lie, is so awesome that it can convince holders of truth to doubt even themselves. So it is necessary to surround ourselves with other survivors for validation and support.

We are not alone and we do not walk alone. We walk with our friends and we walk with our truths, and no one can take our truths away from us, no matter how many lies are told. We *know* truth. Our truths. It is something we should never forget. Luckily, our truths will not let us do so.

* * * * * * * * *

"Nothing is more powerful than truth…not even power."

"When will we accept all of our beauty?"

Sistagirl twisted the handle of the locked door. After six heartbeats or so, the door opened and conversation ceased a moment, then it began again very quietly. There was no reason for any of the women to turn their heads, as mirrors surrounded the room. Sistagirl searched faces that might be able to answer her question. Movement went on hold.

A young woman, comb in hand and with curious eyes and a neutral voice, offered help. Sistagirl asked, "Do you sell cow shells here?" The young woman nodded left to a woman in the corner. Obviously In Charge spoke, "Yes?"

Sistagirl asked, "Do you sell, you know, the cow shells folks use for jewelry and stuff?"

"I don't know what you mean," said In Charge.

Incredible, although noting an accent of Caribbean or other island cues, Sistagirl asked her question again, her eyes searching those of the women in the room as if to say, "Y'all know what I mean, right?"

The woman whose hair was being done by In Charge said, "Oh you know, *cow shells.*" In Charge turned back with a smile to Sistagirl and said, "Oh no, I'm sorry, we don't." Sistagirl smiled, said her thanks and stepped lightly out the door closing it gently behind her.

In the span of five minutes, the deeply-buried wound of a legacy of slavery rose up between its descendants in a single social interaction. Sistagirl was mentally swept up with the unspoken suspicions that sometimes entered into these brief exchanges of light-skin meets dark skin and kinky hair meets straight hair and how it interwove the atmosphere of her life as an African American woman. She reminded herself that this was not all of reality, and blinked tears that made her feel that life was just too complicated and just as quickly blinked them off. Opening the door to her car, she closed it with a slam against the jealousies, the disdains, the envies, the mistrusts, and the self-mirrored hatred, took a deep breath, and drove on.

* * * * * * * * *

"Love is beauty."

"Why can't we all make it?"

She had no idea she was being stalked. In this awful time where she and her family had taken refuge like thousands of others in the huge stadium because of the hurricane, she couldn't believe that this was happening to them. She told her mother she was going to the restroom and would be back shortly.

His pouncing on her was quick and anything but quiet as he simultaneously covered her mouth with one hand and wielded a knife at her throat with the other. "Bitch say one word and I will kill you," his harsh voice said as he dragged her off behind a grouping of large dumping canisters. He had no way of knowing that he was not foremost in her thoughts. Disbelief was. And her family. She had a feeling she wasn't going to see them again. And so, while what he was doing was terrifying, she was separated from the full impact of his heinous act.

She was aware of how, only minutes ago, she felt as if she could not breathe, from the humid suffocating air that seemed to be everywhere. Then he came along with his hatred and fear, and put them on her. Strangely, she felt no fear. She wondered if she said, "Look, this isn't necessary. I understand so much and you don't have to do this; you can just walk away," that he would hear her above all his heavy breathing and panting. Mentally letting go of struggling with him, she turned inward to her God and said, "If this is Your Will," and let her body go limp, not knowing it would be the last willful act she did. Her eyes closed and the final word she uttered was, "No."

Having raped her, he shook her shoulders and yelled at her to open her eyes, but she didn't. His anger rose again and so he methodically stabbed her stomach in seven different places. Her head rolled over to her right side; and he ran out into the darkness from whence he came. Her body was found later that night, partially covered with clothing, dirt and the sounds of her shattered family.

* * * * * * * * *

*"Not everyone survives, but those of us who do are obligated
to make sure our sisters have not died in vain."*

"Why do we wish for change and than cringe when it takes place?"

I wish I could salve the craving pain in the belly of my life. I am physically, mentally, and emotionally fine. Yet as I go on about my daily business, this nagging unknown craving will not let me feel life is okay. It is as if a small particle of the Dread of Life decided to settle in the center of my stomach and whenever an opportunity of change that promises success and joy presents itself, the Dread makes itself known with nudging and nagging; and as I seek to achieve my new tasks and goals, it becomes more powerful.

I am no longer a victim. And though I am a survivor, I rarely think in those terms anymore: I survived, and all that belongs to another cycle, another life, another time, another dream although I continue to reap the benefits of my healing journey.

And yet as I move through my new being and new here-to-stay freedom, it seems that my inkling Dread of Life insists on reminding me something within me is still inherently wanting. I am free, and I embrace with great vigor the pursuit and attainment of those things my soul has so long desired; or else I turn away as if I know there's something great there, but it no longer means anything to me.

Perhaps it is the beginning of another level of my healing. Growing causes change and sometimes pain. Perhaps the craving that is ever-present must be recognized objectively as a general indicator for change that can bring growth and meaning into my life now on a better and positive level.

* * * * * * * * *

"Change and growth can bring success."

"Why can't it simply go away?"

While no longer surprised that her intimate enemy returned again, she felt frustrated by whatever *it* was that she hadn't found a way to address, so that this feeling appeared at the most unexpected moments.

She was angry, no doubt about it. She was grown and knowledgeable about the ways of the Universe, and rain falling on the just and the unjust and blah, blah, blah. She just wished she could find a way to make it disappear.

This time she took out her pottery tools and clay and set to work in her special place where she would not be disturbed. In her anger and ranting with overall contempt for living in this particularly planetary locale, she began to streamline her rage into an act of pounding beats upon the foot pedal and strong and focused motions upon her swirling clay.

.Muttering and mumbling, her tears began falling. Her eyes tried to squeeze them back and refusing to be denied, they continued to tear anyway. She was at a place where she knew in her heart she needed to move forward, and knew that such a move would require her to leave behind the good as well as the bad, except for her heart's memories. Right now that wasn't okay, it wasn't all right, but it didn't hurt as much as when she first began spinning the sides of her clay. Sometimes it was moving from one activity to another that helped her see things differently. Glad she was learning from this awareness, she followed the urgings of her mind and the working of her hands.

* * * * * * * * *

"If we can be kind to ourselves, we can give permission to do what we know we must do."

"Why is this so common all over the world?"

There is a commercial being advertised in the dawning of our 21st Century media productions. Generally it comes on late at night and the photography is fantastic. It opens up with hundreds upon hundreds of women walking across what looks like the Saharan Dessert, and arriving from all parts of the global world. These women are overwhelmingly women of color and they are dressed in bright, beautiful and brilliantly colorful clothing according to the customs of their country and culture. The emphasis of the commercial is that these women are one of our planet's greatest resources.

This is obviously a not so subtle reminder to businesses that women overseas are cheap laborers and therefore adds to low production costs and increased product profits. And not so subtle is the message "less than".

Objectification and "less than" are key motivations for predators. Sexual assault and CSA is a health epidemic all over the world. How it's handled depends on where the survivor is born and raised. Predators and pedophiles are not limited in their access to women and children in just the home. They lurk and perpetrate in every aspect of society be it politics, religion, education or businesses.

It will be a mighty day when women all over the world wake up and we notice our potential and power and come to actualize it so that the generations of women after us will not have to overcome the daily oppressions we face no matter what country we live in.

We do not have to wait until that day arrives. The best way to help this awakening is to help somebody else. In doing so it proves to ourselves and to others that we care, that we can make a difference and that some day women will not be thought of as "less than", but rather as individuals who have great and untapped contributions to make to this world. As survivors it really is as simple as volunteering in any organization whose goals are to advocate and protect the rights of women and children, especially the right over what happens to our bodies.

* * * * * * * * *

"Until all women live in peace, no woman is safe."

"When will I be really free to do what I want?"

It puzzled her most when she got what she wanted. When she achieved that which she started off happily pursuing, and then finished, she wanted nothing to do with the end product. It didn't matter so much when it was her own internal creation. And it was even too bad when it fell externally into things she wanted to do with others. But it became awful when it entered her relationships— those trusty, dusty interactions of heart meeting heart, and soul touching soul. She'd lost more lovers that way.

How is it that things got turned around? That bad became good and good became bad all in one moment, one day, one week, or one month. She wondered if it would ever change. After a number of years, it got so bad she dared not dwell on inventing herself, for fear in the end she would disappear from herself, turn and walk away from who she became, even if who she became was who she wanted to be. It did, indeed, get tricky.

It is these most complex theories, twists, and turns that hide the simplicity of our freedom. In a moment of great frustration and sorrow, where she thought she was giving up everything she had worked for, her letting go was what saved her. Her imprisonment by the contradictions of her emotions from the aftermath of her past sexual abuse left her as gradually as it came into her life as she purposefully traveled a path of healing.

At first, her taste of freedom happened only in her dreams, and only once or twice at that. In the beginning, her reality was as if she were lost in a forest. It would be many paths, many bushes and briars, many slides down muddy hills and tumbling in streams and rivers, sometimes sinking almost to the bottom. The only thing she knew for sure, that she faithfully believed, was that she couldn't ever give up on finding her way back to herself. And sure enough, she began recognizing different signs along the way. As she let go of her doubts, she began walking with a surety that where she was going was where she wanted to be in her life. She was free again.

* * * * * * * * *

"Walking in freedom is a powerful way to live."

"What to do, what to do?"

It rains
and there is no going to work today.
Today the world will have to make it
on its own without her
she couldn't seem to stop dreaming about the babies
although she couldn't really remember what the dreams
were about. Just that there were babies
crying in her dreams
and though she didn't make the connection
there would be no schedule to meet today.
She did get up and make coffee
and she did have soup
and popcorn
and ice cream throughout the day and night
and there were some shows she watched
even though the TV was on all day and night.
Mostly what she craved and did
was scrunch underneath the heavy, warm covers of her bed
and she would have written it all in her journal
had she been able to leave her warm bed
and she didn't care if her brain gave up important
significant things that swarmed
insightfully throughout her mind
just that she was covered from the rain
for another day
and she didn't regret about her yesterday
nor worry about her tomorrow
as she snuggled further into her cocoon
and the rain fell upon the earth

* * * * * * * * *

"Sometimes 'only' is good enough for one day."

"How can I lose myself so much?"

Her frustration level was once again at its peak. This part of her was always bewildering, but with each level of her healing, it seemed to manifest itself less often, though more intensely.

It was a part of her she tended to slough off in jokes and barbs; but there were days, like today, when there were no clothed remarks, but clear rage and anger at anything and anybody. Nothing was good enough, no one was worthy of whatever they claimed to be; all that was said was merely a cliché, and people seemed to be part of a matrix they had no idea existed. The world was a dangerous place to be during these times, and the next life seemed to beckon her more clearly and demandingly. She could not help but think the human race was no wiser than gazelles around lions, no more civilized than hyenas at a scavenger feast, and no more loving than the animals that eat their own.

She smiled, as the thought of another life other than earth seemed like the answer; and she smiled at the realization that she wasn't the worst person in the world, nor as despicable a human being as she felt just a few moments ago as her cursing and healing vied to occupy the same space in her brain at once. She cursed her healing, though she continued smiling because she knew she was freer than she had ever been before.

"Apparently, my brain is trying to tell me something I don't know about myself," she thought, as she began breathing deeply for a 4-count that would help her ground herself. This new awareness, struggle, and unexpected clarity of herself caused her to smile, yet again, knowing that during her last episode of "to be or not to be," she began cursing again. It wasn't the best place to be, but it was a place she could pass through as her healing and freedom became a regular part of her, and so did the dropping of the unwanted and unnecessary defenses that were useless in her world of recovery.

* * * * * * * * *

"The self is a moment-by-moment discovery."

"What about us?"

No matter how many wounded people she helped heal and mend, the plethora of victims was never-ending. Like hurricanes, tornadoes, earthquakes and snowstorms, victims and survivors were a recurring presence of life that one could expect on a constant basis. Or, so it seemed.

Sometimes we in the helping professions, in the caring professions and in the human services professions, can be overwhelmed by the problems of the world. As far as we know, there will always be problems that call upon us to have a faith that can sustain us through the darkest hours for not only ourselves, but the sisters we seek to help and heal.

We should not forget that our tears and our sadness are a manifestation of our deep feeling, especially for kindred spirits. It is okay to have a day to cry, a day to let our tears fall even though we want to be strong all the time. We can not protect everything and everyone by ourselves. The truth is always so simple. If we do not take time out to care for ourselves, we can not care for others; if we can not hold ourselves, we will surely fail those we seek to hold and help.

* * * * * * * * *

"Taking care of myself is a survival skill."

"Are achievement and success the same?"

It was different today. There was no panic, only excitement at the challenge. No fear that she would freeze up, but just thoughts on how to relax her body and throat as she stood for all to see; as she spoke to be heard for all that were listening and to share what she knew with those who might be able to use it and make their own contributions. She felt good that she could finally speak again, could give voice again, could talk again, and stand without a paralyzing fear that something awful was going to happen to her and that she wouldn't be able to do anything about it, wouldn't be able to stop that storm that was sure to snuff out her life, sure to have her struggling and choking and racked with physical pain she'd never imagined.

She stood whole and she stood proud. And she was at peace. And nothing had compared to that since after her attack where she thought she'd never be able to feel this good about herself again.

She wasn't angry or filled with resentment of bittersweet feelings vying for her acknowledgement. She wasn't rushing off to recoup or regroup or to hear a voice that would remind her that she wasn't insane, or that the feelings wouldn't take over her body and leave her in an uncontrollable state of helplessness and rage. And she didn't need support to remind her of how courageous or how far she had come in her healing.

She truly felt for the first time that being on her own and knowing all she knew about the world, all she knew about the evils of others who wanted to hurt people, her included, was not the only thing the life offered. Justice could and did balance the scales whenever or wherever it was possible. That was a truth, and today it was her truth. It felt good to be back again in her body, having her feelings, balancing and swaying and moving through a life that was full of possibilities of happiness, purpose and contentment. She hadn't felt that way since her days of making mud pies. Today was a glorious day to be alive and to be living *her* own life.

* * * * * * * * *

"Sometimes the feeling of achievement, for just a moment, wipes all the ugly away."

"How much should I worry about what's fair and what isn't?"

Often, our feelings of unfairness are connected with our feelings of needing to be recognized, to be given witness to, to be heard, and to be visible to ourselves and others. Truth is, whether at work or in our families, or in any of our relationships, we need this recognition.

Our sense of injustice may be heightened by our CSA experiences. Our trust in the colloquial, "things working out for the best" leaves much to be desired, or remains an adage we don't believe in at all. Perhaps we have to acknowledge, on a very deep, inner level, that indeed life is unfair, but that it does not mean that goodness can not and will not come our way. It does not mean that truth is always squashed. And it does not mean that our voices can not be heard, that we can not be seen, or for the deepest rankling, that we can not "be."

We have the right to be as much as any living entity upon the earth—the sky, the trees, the rivers, the oceans, the insects, and the wild animals. We have the right to be ourselves and take delight in ourselves without guilt or self-punishment because somewhere along the way, some predator came around and said "You don't have the right to be. You can only be and do what I tell you can be or do. I control you, and there is no escape."

Testament to the fact that we are free today is evidence we have asserted our "right to be." It is not easy to attain or to always maintain that knowledge. Sometimes we may lose our grasp. But once we have reclaimed the knowledge that we have the "right to be", no one can take that away from us again but ourselves.

* * * * * * * * *

"My life is testament that I have the right 'to be'."

"How long shall we wait?"

I want to know
when they're going to cross the plate,
make the shot before the last bell
drop-kick the field goal to break the tie
cross the finish line with just one nose
I want to know when the others will
break the silence for their brothers,
but mostly for the children
when will they put it on the line
as their mothers and sisters
have done for eons of generations
when will these men tell
their lost and hating brothers
enough is enough
and no more is not soon enough?
when will the men
finally get on board?
incest and rape and sexual assault
of children hurts
everybody

* * * * * * * * *

"Enough is enough and too much is too much."

"How can one smell bring it all back?"

I can still smell those sweet,
sweet summer nights
coming at the end
of winter
on a warm, dark moon
and newly-born honeysuckles
and lilacs breathe freely
on the crest
reminding me
of those terrible, terrible times,
wishing I could go home
with my friends,
wishing I could go home
in safety
instead of a stalker
living in my home
perpetrating
silly, silly, me
who knew?
I can still breathe
after all these years,
and those long, long
ugly sweet-smelling
summer nights.

* * * * * * * * *

"It is a great thing that some memories are viewed from a long distance."

September 1

DISILLUSIONED
Disillusioned students
seek
teachers of truth
of which
are both
and neither
with the passing
of time and truth

"What punishment is just?"

On matters of punishment and discipline, perhaps survivors are not the best judges to make such assessments. We understand the terror one human being can exact to another. We know what it is to be terrorized, many of us day and night. Some of us know long lengths of time where time was forgotten, and to wish for an end to our suffering was to entertain a cruel hope of action. We knew our tormentors had to sleep sometime, had to leave sometime— might even forget us for a few hours. Sometimes we just gave up hope that anything would change. But it did. Some of us even got justice.

So in the light of a new day and a version of an old enemy, we find our country holds "detainees." Are they being treated inhumanely? We are not the best judges. Anybody party to terrorizing is not a good judge of just and fair treatment. Survivors want the act never to happen again, want the perpetrator to be used as a warning that no one should think of perpetrating a sexual crime on any human being, moreover, a child.

It is right, no matter how much we lust for vengeance, that justice prevails even with a despicable and horrific perpetrator. Because if it does not, then the perpetrator was right in the first place, that anyone weaker can be prey. And if we act on the laws of the predator, then we become predators ourselves, and we internalize the hate and the ugliness that runs rampant on victims and the survivors.

Everybody deserves justice, especially the one offended. Such justice must come from calmer and saner minds, because all of society deserves the best it can receive, even in times of sorrow and war. The truth *always* wills out, especially for survivors. Let justice prevail for perpetrators of all guises, forms, and times. True justice means truth prevails, and as survivors, it means we have prevailed in our healing.

* * * * * * * * *

"True justice serves both the victim and the criminal."

"Is there a 'normal'?"

Nothing about her life had ever seemed normal to her. From the youngest years of her life, she felt as though she was always looking through windows to view all outside of her, and always felt as if there were some energetic barrier that separated her from the rest of her tribe.

As she grew in years and thought, she still traveled on that energetic road alone. Most times, she soothed her soul with the poetic thought in her head about walking to the "beat of a different drummer." She sought help for her differences. Therapy was soothing, as it was the only place where she felt safe, no matter that she paid money for the service. However, therapy was not her end-all cure. In fact, in her darkest moments, it seemed as if therapy was a thorough waste of time and effort. In her clearest moments, she knew therapy was instrumental in overcoming many of her lifelong fears, even if it meant some things were scarier than before; at least she finally knew why she was scared.

But no matter what, she couldn't seem to stop wondering how her life might have been if only the "if" had not happened: If only there was not the incest; if only she had not been incarcerated; if only she had not lost her family; and if only she could break loose from the invisible chains wrapped fully around her body.

She *was* grateful for the times in between, times life gave her love, gave her children; times when one or two of the goals she had set for herself she was able to accomplish. Yet, as she marveled at people who were at ease to make life plans and see them come to fruition, she still wondered what it would be like to be "normal." She *was* healing, and in due time, from another of life's significant lessons for *her*, she learned that though she was different from many others, it was not necessary to be "normal," but rather, authentically "natural" in response to what life brought her.

* * * * * * * * *

"There is no normal; just soul waiting to be embraced by self."

"Is there anything to be gained by confronting parents with our truth?"

The highest percentage groups targeted for sexual abuse and incest are children and adolescents. In the matter of incest, some parents are aware of the incest or have an inkling that something "is wrong" with their child that bodes ill for the whole family.

As adults many of us may think that talking with our parents about what happened has to be done as part of our healing journey. The unacknowledged and unspoken incest and CSA in a family becomes an invisible block that halts true communication and feelings, because when not talked about, it takes on an energetic form of its own as the "thing" not talked about.

The most positive thing about discussing these matters is that it no longer becomes the "thing" not talked about it. Whether parents go into denial or whether they accept the disclosure totally or with excuses, it is out in the open for all to know, discuss, pick at, fight out, or even sweep back under the rug. But, it is no longer the hidden secret; every one knows, and the truth will out.

The negative of such disclosure is that we survivors run the risk of losing what we do have with our families, or sometimes losing our families totally. There will be no more family celebrations, no more birthday hoop-di-doos, and no more seasonal holidays of toting the kids over, laughing, joking, arguing, and debating. For some, there may be no more connection to the most primal connections of all in our lives— family of origin.

Sometimes, the point in having the confrontation is about acknowledgement that says, "Yes this awful, awful betrayal did happen." If after disclosure, that recognition is not given, the pain resulting can be as great as the violation itself, but another link in the chain to the past is broken. However, if recognition is given, it can mean a new level of healing with family members and relationships can move forward and grow. Confrontation can be one of great risk with the possibility of great reward involved in our healing, and should be done only when we are ready.

* * * * * * * * *

*"Confronting my family is a big step.
and I do so when I'm ready."*

"Why does society tacitly condone the abuse of a person based on gender?"

Children are often preyed upon because they are helpless and powerless to fight the predator. A whole world can know a society is oppressed, can know the women and children are being raped and tortured, and do nothing until they deem the time is ripe. So the question is begged: when will the time be ripe for world to stopping turning its eyes away from Afghanistan women and female children? Some things are inherent in societies that wish to be considered civilized, or in societies that wish to have relations with other civilized societies.

Yet, maybe there is only so much that others can do before the women of Afghanistan are treated as first-class citizens. Not all societies that strive for equal rights between the sexes are a democratic society. However, one does not have to have a democratic society in order to be treated with fairness, respect and dignity: the majority may rule but the minority has rights as well.

People in general and women in particular, who wait for others to grant them civil rights will wait in vain. Like everyone who seeks freedom from an oppressive environment, individuals must take the initiative to empower their own freedom. The beginning act of healing and freedom must come from the individual herself.

Disenfranchised people must fight their oppressors on every level at some point in their struggle for freedom. Even survivors who may not have been able to get away from their perpetrator, eventually still had to fight for their right to simply "be." There are times we even get our freedom by helping others to be free. Women's rights in America took off during the struggle as African Americans marched for their civil rights.

If we are survivors not of Afghanistan, we can still help our sisters, for instance, by searching the Internet or going to the library to research how they wish to be helped. If we are Afghanistan women, then we can meet those who wish to support our cause. Either way, freedom comes to those who risk the very essence of their lives to have that freedom, including survivors.

* * * * * * * * *

"One woman's freedom is every woman's freedom."

"How can I stop remembering when everything's such a reminder?"

She hadn't planned to watch this particular movie. In fact, she started making fun of it. It was on the "Women's'" station, which meant there was bound to be some woman mistreated by some man or her family. Some kind of rape, some kind of domestic violence, some kind of murder, or some kind of child caught in the throes of incest and all kinds of abuse— name your flavor, it's there.

In her smugness, she'd forgotten how real it all was. She'd forgotten the dread of those times, when just the sight of the perp would take her breath away, and she would feel the air sucked out of her chest, feeling for a moment as though she had no lungs and nowhere to run as that low-sinking feeling came over her with the recognition that there was no escape.

She wished she'd had some righteously indignant uncles who'd seen her scars and went after her perp, like in the book, *Bastard Out of Carolina*, or the town's people in *How Green Was My Valley*. She wished she'd had an avenging angel in any form that would have kicked the perp out of her life and memories forever and ever. She wished. Most of all, what she wished was that the incest had never happened and that she could find a way to reclaim her feelings that had mysteriously disappeared from her body, from that time not so long ago still in her mind.

We who are survivors must, at some point in our journey, give up the ghost, as it were, of being rescued. If it means we need to explore fully the pain that festers most, we must take the risks inherent in touching the wound. There are some things only we can do, especially to heal the most vulnerable parts of our souls. Wishing and dreaming are for children and dreamers, and for those of us healing, it is truth we seek and all the possibilities such a knowing will bring us. Mindful remembering can help us through those memories and to the truths we are living today.

* * * * * * * * *

"Few things are as powerful as the unlived truths of our lives."

"When will we stop killing with rules?"

War is two or more societies engaging in a no holds barred conflict; and the goal is to kill the people on the other side, becoming lawless to all that is civilized until the most powerful dominates the least powerful.

Survivors have difficulty with coming to terms with the concept of war. The September 11, 2001 attack upon the United States stunned Americans into a speechlessness we had never witnessed in our country. An assault came out from the sky, and after the explosion of four airplanes, the result was that almost 3,000 people were killed and numerous people wounded.

Is war ever justified? Is taking the law into one's own hands ever justified? When a person or a nation takes the law into its own hands, then that person or nation must be willing to accept the consequences of such an action.

Taking justice into one's own hands is illegal in most of the world's societies. This vigilante behavior is the one that most survivors do not take. It is tempting to go the way of the predator and strike back in deadly fashion. And ironically, because of our experiences, many of us have a built-in compassion scale and a creed. We don't wish to hurt others. We just want to be left unfettered by another human being to pursue our dreams and our lives. For most survivors, the assault they survived was as unexpected and unimagined as the September 11 attack. It was unthinkable that the world we lived in could be destroyed in a matter of moments, and in a blink of an eye, all that we trusted gave way to the ugliest sight we'd never even imagined. And we were left to pick up the pieces and make it all make sense. At the end of the day, whether we receive justice or not, we go on with our lives, and heal; one day at a time and one step before the other for war and abuse play no favorites.

* * * * * * * * *

"There may be victory in war, but in truth, there are no winners."

"How long do we agree to this charade?"

People look at us and, of course, immediately make a story about us. They have to. It's the way we all survive in life. This new person I'm meeting seems nice. Or, seems mean. Bet things were easy for them. Hmm, must have had a rough life.

Survivors have spent years either fitting into the status quo, or in pretense, finding a way to go along with the program. Sisters of color have honed it into one of the finer, if not more painful, arts of living with untapped and unfinished inner business.

Until we undertake responsibility for the way we live as adults, we survivors use illusions to make our lives more palatable. An illusion is not real. We just think it's real because its props help us believe in ourselves when reality is just too much. Survivors who use illusions as a defense have a hearty world in which to live. Their illusions are greater than their realities.

Illusions work until the knowingness begins to creep in the mind of a survivor that something is amiss. The survivor is no longer satisfied with her realities on the one hand, and her illusions on the other. A hunger for truth begins growing right along with the illusion. And eventually, hunger catches up because hunger continues growing until it is fed. It will be ignored only so long and then it cries to be fed. And if its cry is continually ignored, it will reek a costly vengeance and lay waste to its host— the survivor.

All weaknesses have their strengths. Illusions suggest that survivors want more, that a part of us longs to be fulfilled. Often, we live in the fantasy world because we don't think we have what it takes to live in the outside world, by outside rules. But we do. Survivors that have gone before us and made inroads in society have given up most of the world of illusions. We dare to walk through the veneer of our illusions in order to reach the reality we want. And we begin such changes one day at a time.

* * * * * * * * *

"There is beauty in reality that I can claim as my own."

"How can I be sure of any decision I make?"

The ageless woman sat still before the ocean waves, listening to thoughts she'd cultured over a lifetime, reviewing obstacles she had hurdled and reluctantly recognizing those that were stumbling blocks of her own making. Phrases such as, "I'm afraid," "I can't," and therefore, "I don't." Endless questions such as, "What if I get to the end and it's not what I thought? What if everything I do to get there is rendered useless because the goal was wrong in the first place? What will I do then?"

"What if all my fears are true? What will I do then? Which way shall I go? How many times can I start over? How many chances do we get to 'get it right'?"

"What if this *is* all there *is*? Can I live with that? Can I wake up in the morning and start all over again? How will I know what's right and what's wrong?"

"Having given 'truth' the priority, how long do I stay on the path before I can see what's false and what's true?"

Being on a roll, she could not stop herself from further thinking, "I have depended on my own voice to get me where I am today. I am a survivor. No matter how bad things get, I'm supposed to come out on top, I'm supposed to win the war, if not all the battles. So, why can't I pick up the pieces now and move forward, when I know it is so necessary for me to move forward? Why can't I see the path I'm traveling? Why am I filled only with questions and no solid answers?"

Letting her questions go, she sat on a ragged, wet log and looked at the tides rolling into the shore of the ocean. Her frustration suddenly abated as she came to her own realization. She knew the answer. If her life was to change, the only person capable of doing the changing was she. Noting the vulnerability that swept through her soul being replaced by a strength she had somehow known was always hers, she accepted this truth, picked herself up and started her walk off the beach, one foot before the other as always.

* * * * * * * * *

*"Difficult as it may seem at first, we are the ones
who hold sway to the tides of our oceans."*

"Have we folded our hands too long?"

It isn't that women don't fight— we do. Nonetheless, it seems women, particularly mothers, spend much of their time negotiating, mediating, assuaging, placating, and doing the righteous thing when there is a conflict, whether between children, between relatives, or between their friends. Even an 86-year-old mother, at 4 feet, 3 inches, can break up a raucous fight between two 6 foot 6 inch male siblings, and make them apologize to each other before they leave the room. Maybe it's time we entered the fracas of world conflicts and insisted on peace on our terms.

Women have been cooperating from time immemorial— from watching children in the days of husbandry and agriculture, all the way through the technological revolution. Women run internet companies from their living rooms while their children play in the sunroom with a neighbor's child who needs daycare. In fact, women share in everything except running the world.

Survivors underestimate all too often the tasks and goals we are capable of accomplishing. We think once we were rendered helpless by an act of rape or child molestation, it can happen again in some other form, and so can the fallout that comes with it. As a result, many times we survivors avoid positions where we might have to call on our own power to take care of a situation. In fact, we can spend a lot of time proving to ourselves why we can not do what we can.

When we begin addressing the defenses we have, disarming the useless and keeping the necessary ones we are able to be more of who we are. Our imaginations are the most fertile ground for beginning any foundation to any of our achievements, and that includes using our personal power in the world we live in today.

* * * * * * * * *

"I remember a time when I was brave and my Spirit was strong;
and I can feel that way again."

"What value does money have for us?"

"If I touch your ass you shouldn't be upset. Asses like yours come a dime a dozen," he said to her. His viciousness was without loud rancor, and it was as violent as if it had slapped her— as he'd done many times before. One of his demeaning ways was to measure his actions in terms of money. "Give me a kiss and I'll give you a dollar." By now, she'd become numb to his violence, to his words, and his hands. All things considered, she saw the money offers as an evil blessing.

Was it any wonder that later in life, she often threw her money away, no matter how much or how little she had? When she had it, it seemed to burn a hole in her consciousness, saying, "Buy something," "Spend me," and "I want." She did not think consciously that money was bad, or that it hurt or helped her. And it was almost like an axiom. The more money she had to meet her budget, the more she threw it away on frivolous purchases.

After a number of setbacks, she grew tired of not having money. She grew tired of the power it had over her. Like many other defenses that no longer worked, she hit a wall that was no longer a protection, but destruction. And in that insight, she found it was necessary to disengage her subconscious view of "money is dirty," and learn to view it for the objective value that it was— a means to a financial end. It took the shock of having to borrow from friends to keep her from being "outdoors" to understand she needed control of owning her financial life.

It did call for re-adjustments in her belief system about money and this new way of looking at money was something she had to work at for a while. There was no magic here, no glittering wand to wipe it away. And to her surprise, there were times she cried because she realized she thought so little of herself, hurting herself when the answers were literally in her pocket. She cried because in changing, she felt the feelings of shame attached to a coin, had to feel her center crack inside and trust that the Spirit of Truth that began to overtake this lie was beckoning to her this gift of insight, and the gift to claim another part of her self-worth.

* * * * * * * * *

"Money habits are learned and not inherited."

Weep   September 12

"How many tears can a world shed?"

The women of Sudan weep. No matter how many governments come into power, the women of Sudan weep the tears of women all the world over.

It is horrible to live at the extreme of anything— poverty, abuse, disability, even riches. Each has its own trappings. But, what makes it worse is when everyone's watching and no one does anything at all to stop this obscenity of life itself— the preposterous, arrogant, erroneous and criminal belief of thinking that one can, and therefore one does, own another human being.

There's no support group for those who know they are not about to survive life unconnected with a disease. Just as there are no groups for the children of families who know that no matter how much the outside says it wants to help, for some situations, there is no help.

Our child protection services can visit a home that may be under suspicion of abuse, but if they go in and there's no evidence, for the child what changes is that the stakes may become higher now that the parents know they are in danger of being exposed. Their fear of such exposure almost inevitably leads them to punish the child even more than before, so that the reporting of such abuse will not be made again.

We survivors, who are no longer under the thumb of anyone, know what one kind word, one kind act by another human being can do to give hope to another human being in distress. We survivors also know that the first step must come from and be for ourselves. And once we are free and healing, we must also help our sisters whose voices may be silenced, muffled and distant, whose feet and hands may be bound, but whose dreams have not left the gray matter; and whose souls still flicker with hope, if ever so faintly for the freedom from the bondage of modern day slavery and human trafficking.

* * * * * * * * *

"When one person escapes bondage,
there is the possibility that all may be free."

-255-

"How many layers are there to a world full of illusions?"

She rides in the car listening to the chatter of the voices of her now-growing children and their friends. Despite the passage of time, she still finds herself amazed at how beautiful they remain in her eyes. A song plays from a homemade CD, and it cuts across her gratitude and immediately brings an onslaught of "who knew?"

It wasn't supposed to be like this, she thought to herself. The sun's not supposed to be shining so bright and the air filled with such happiness, while I am suddenly hit with "what hasn't worked."

Could I have done this differently? She looked out to the passing hills. When did it get to the point of not being able to mend the rift at all?

He'd take my hand now. At another time, he'd reach for me and I'd receive him, clasp my fingers and intertwine them with his. I'd be happy with him at this moment, if only the "if onlys" hadn't happened.

Shaking off the loss before being wrapped in its clutches, she became clichéd about their life together. *When it was good it was very, very good; and when it was bad, it was very, very bad, "Don't explain and don't complain,"* and of course the latest twist, *"You backed the wrong horse."*

With a slight twinge of bitterness, she laughed to herself about the irony. Having been disillusioned so early in life, she never thought she'd come to a place in her adulthood where anything or anyone, including herself, could surprise her. She finally had her truth. The illusions were no longer necessary. It really was okay to be who she was without the baggage of the past weighing her down. She only wished this truth had come sooner. The human condition is, if not adjustable, certainly adaptable.

* * * * * * * * *

"The only reality we have is truth;
everything else is an illusion."

"How can I get out of bed this morning?"

A DOZEN WAYS TO GET OUT OF BED IN THE MORNING

1. Especially for coffee drinkers. Make sure your timer is set so that when you wake up, the coffee's ready for you to drink

2. Put on your favorite song and blast it as loud as is comfortable for you to hear. If you do not have a favorite song, find one as soon as possible!

3. Sing your favorite song if you do not have a radio or audio player.

4. Get up and do the favorite thing you want to do and ignore old mind tapes that say, "Only when your chores are finished."

5. Sit up and imagine that for today, you are going to be the person that you always wanted to be. If you run into obstacles, improvise.

6. Go to the mirror. Smile five times at yourself. Then, frown five times at yourself. Then, smile five more times at yourself. Wasn't it easier the second time to smile?

7. Tell yourself a joke. If necessary, find one before going to sleep.

8. Sit up in bed and talk to your favorite cuddly. Explain to your cuddly this is going to be a good day for you.

9. If you are a person who never makes a list of "Things To Do" make a list of "Things To Do" and do at least one of those things.

10. Call a friend, wish them "good morning," and tell them it's just because "You are such a good friend and I am counting my blessings."

11. Count your blessings. If you think you don't have any, make up three blessings you want to have.

12. If you are a person who loves to take showers, give yourself an extra five minutes. If you are a person who hates to take showers, do a quick wash. Accept no guilt-thoughts this day.

* * * * * * * * *

"We eventually are responsible for our own reality;
let's do that which bring us joy."

"Who needs a period anyway?"

Many women at some point in their lives are shocked by the fact that they bleed a couple of days a month from the first onset of their period in youth, until some 45, 50 years down the road. To a young pubescent or adolescent girl, such a length of time may seem like a life sentence, even unbelievable. Many survivors often experience difficulties with their period— heavy bleeding, terrible cramps, mood swings from rage to silliness, etc. And for some women, the menstrual experience can simply be horrendous.

Some survivors have been taught by their perpetrators to hate themselves when they bleed. Along with all the rest of the cruelty of a perp, the time when a survivor is menstruating can be an opportunity for the perp to be even more derisive or humiliating. And unfortunately, the survivor may internalize the message and add to the already-building fortress of self-hatred.

Here's a truth: Menstruating, while a time of blood loss, is also a life-affirming process. The body automatically rids itself of what it no longer needs. The body also prepares and maintains itself for the one of the monumental experiences a woman can have, and that is to be a co-creator of life by giving birth to a child. One doesn't even have to draw up the design plans for such a creation. One simply says *yes* to the concept and possibilities— bringing into existence the breath and life of another human being.

Only women have the ability to carry a potential human being within their bodies. What a fantastic and awesome honor.

Traumatized by sexual abuse/assault, a survivor may not see any of it as a gift. However, as she heals, she may yet glimpse the beauty of all the physical aspects of her body, and be able to embrace all of what she can be if she so chooses— a carrier, mother, and co-creator of life with a Divine Deity.

* * * * * * * * *

"The very thing that symbolizes loss,
contains the nucleus of life itself."

"What is this thing about 'touch'?"

There can not be enough said about the importance and beauty of touching. To survive meaningfully in this world, safe touching is a necessity. Perhaps by touching a petal of a flower, we see the delicacy of such action. Or maybe even more so when we touch the face of a newborn child— the vulnerability, trust and power the adult is held responsible for in the eyes of the Universe and the child. Is it any wonder that survivors fear touch so much? Is it any wonder that survivors also crave so much that which we hold so much in fear?

Many survivors express their longing to be held in safe touch. Safe touch means unconditional acceptance, not owing your holder anything, and not being bodily invaded by the holder. It seems like a simple enough act, something simple to ask for, and yet it is such a difficult thing for a survivor to ask from another human being. One always runs the risk of being misinterpreted, of perhaps sending off the wrong signal and being misunderstood or simply of being rejected. Even when a person offers to hold a survivor in trust, it may be a while before the survivor takes them up on it.

The image of the Madonna cradling the child is powerful for one very good reason: it breaks through all cultural barriers and everyone understands the collective need to be held in safety. The mother bear is revered in the United States, both from our Native Americans and societal folklore that continues to be held in high esteem— the mother bear that protects her cubs under any and all circumstances. Such fierce love is still held in high-esteem.

We survivors, we women of many shades and hues, owe it to ourselves to be very gentle with ourselves when we come across the need within. There is nothing wrong, nothing needy about wanting to be held in safe touch. It is a very primordial memory from the days we grew in our mothers' wombs. When that need is fulfilled, no matter how old we are, we will have healed one of the largest injuries to our psyches.

* * * * * * * * *

"Someone touched me today, and the beauty of it suddenly brought tears to my eyes."

"What place does art have for those of us simply trying to survive?"

What is art and what meaning can it have for survivors? Who cares about a painted picture, a stream of words, a sculptured moment or a printed photo? What can any of these things have to do with healing and growing?

Most works of art express the beauty of something— an idea, a concept, or even a memory. It's as if an artist captured a moment of time and froze it in form for all the world to see. We survivors owe it to ourselves to bring something of beauty— art— into our lives. Doesn't have to be expensive or huge or humanly made. Just something of beauty which gives our souls relief and respite from the busy and tiring world, which in its way, symbolizes a constant source of hope.

Many artists are survivors of great grief. Perhaps that is part of the human condition. Who goes through our world untouched by some grief unappeased by the heart? Many survivors find that they stumble upon their art. Some learn from an exercise in a book. Another from a homework assignment from a workshop, or from one's therapist. Others have always known they were artists, but never found a medium in which to express themselves.

Here's a simple exercise. Close your eyes and imagine you are doing the one thing you've always wanted to express creatively— like writing a poem or essay, or painting with watercolors, or making a collage, or taking a picture— anything that expresses how you feel, even making up a song. Then go do it. Nothing fancy. No judgment. Just do your heart's desire, and when finished, place it where your eyes can rest on it always, and remember it contains part of your heart, and for some survivors, part of your heart's dream.

* * * * * * * * *

"All of us have the ability to express the beauty held within our souls."

"Are there people who really, really care about me?"

Often, it is at our darkest moments, and when we need help and need others, that we think no one cares about us. Who hasn't asked themselves more than a few times, "Who really cares?" and even more personal, "Who really cares about me?" It is a tough imprint to erase, when as children, we thought everybody knew what was happening to us, yet nobody cared to do anything about it. There were adults who did know, and because they didn't do anything, we thought they didn't care, as well. Those adults who knew and didn't do anything, even though they may have wanted to, couldn't do anything. And there were, for some of us, some "silver lining" adults who *did* help us and who did care and showed it, even risking their relationships with our families for us.

Helpful as these wonderful people were, most of the adults that inhabited our world did not or could not help us. And that is the imprint we remember most. For some of us, the time of need or help was frequent, and the sound of the empty response was as loud as it was invisible.

Nonetheless, one day many of us did get out of our circumstances. One day we were free. And few are the folks that can say they did it alone. Some help was clear and direct, and some was like hot popcorn on a cold winter night. Some of us could turn to help from family members and neighbors that cared. What we didn't know as children is that people help people all the time, checking in with them to see if they are okay, or participating in celebrating one of life's events that mark our milestones.

One never gets too old for help or to reach out to others to let them know they care. *Everybody* has a need to know that they matter to others, and that others matter to them. It is one of our ways.

* * * * * * * * *

"Dropping our defenses often lets us open doors we have always wanted to enter."

"Am I up to this battle?"

She tiredly walks up the stairs and then into the kitchen and turns on the light. Last night's dishes are still there, but those were the least of her worries. Figuring out tomorrow's schedule would cause her plenty of anguish for the rest of the night.

For now, it is always a matter of making it through until the next day. If she stops the battle, drops out of the fighting, lets up for one minute, she thinks she will lose this war, and she's come too far in her life to lose now. At least that is what echoes in her mind and that is what she tells herself. "I've worked too hard and I deserve better than this; and if I just hang on, something will come my way that I can use to get out of here, and then the war will be over and I will have won."

It is a very consuming battle. The days are long and wide, and the nights even longer. Her stomach rumbles for all the gases imploding in the hidden crevices of her muscles. The medicine she takes can not hope to compete with the long-time embedded brain cells that carry the memories that rumble her stomach. Still, she swallows the meds that will still her anxiety and takes a chaser of antacids every two hours and then some.

Before she hunkers down for the night, she wipes the tears off her eyes and runs in place for 5 minutes to stave off her night leg cramps, eats a package of crackers to soothe the river of acid that continually flows. *This must end sometime*, she wearily thinks to herself as she lays down for the night. Her supplies are dwindling and so are her funds. If she can just hold on a little longer, all of this will change. She just needs to stay in her patience, give her spirit and body some rest, and remember why she came there in the first place. "It is a good life, is a tough war and I am a stealthy warrior," so said the spear of her thoughts as it flew through the cold, tired, night and she reluctantly closes her eyes.

* * * * * * * * *

"Sometimes life is a battlefield, and we are its warriors."

"How could I forget my sisters?"

Some sisters are by blood, and many are sisters by kindred spirit. We meet these sisters, we connect with them, and then when we need them most, we may forget they are there. They are strong, like us. They carry their own weight, and some of the weight of society. We are peers, and we come together in community, working to make our lives and the lives of those we meet a little better. And then when we become the person in need of help, we forget about the sisters we can go to.

We don't always have to be strong for ourselves. Sometimes we can let our sisters carry us. We travel with a group that "has gone before," women who "know whereof I speak," soul women who have walked the "valley of the dead," and who have risen.

The fact that we need help outside ourselves does not mean we have lost our strength. It means a new personal challenge. And those who have gone before us teach every new step taken.

Our paths may diverge, but we live in a holistic world, not a linear one. And this means, amongst other things, that all roads travel back and through the main path of life. If we are deterred from our original path, it may mean a spiritual opportunity is waiting for us to get back on the original path.

Just as we are our "sister's keeper," they, as well, are our keepers, too. They know us almost as well as we do, and when we are mired down by blockage, they can often see the way better than we can. Just as we reach back to help others, there are those who have gone before us who are also willing to reach back to us, no matter how long we've been on the path of healing. All we have to do is risk our pride and our fears. We have risked so much to get where we are now. One more risk is not going to hurt us anymore than *not* taking a risk, wondering if we've done the right thing.

* * * * * * * * *

"It is so easy to reach out and touch a sister's hand and heart."

"What is this awful horror happening in my body?"

They dump us in the garbage. Sometimes they just throw us out the car. And though we don't always think so, we are the lucky ones. Don't ask us, "Wasn't there something else you could've done?" Don't bother castigating us for leaving ourselves vulnerable— we've already done that. Do ask us, "Is there any way I can help?" We will probably tell you "No," but just the fact that you asked such an ordinary question in a very unordinary time for us, makes all the difference in the world.

There is no way to explain the horror of rape: the taking and over-powering of another's body by penetration of an other offending body so that this offender can do what he wants to the body he is violating for sexual gratification through domination and control. For one unthinkable moment, a survivor knows what is going to happen to her, knows the die has been cast and there's not a thing she can do to change it. In the realization of knowing what is about to happen, a survivor does one of two things: decides if she can escape or overtake her perpetrator, or she accepts that the worst of what she fears is going to happen, and doesn't have any fight left in her. At that point, a survivor's mind will do whatever it can to protect her from the reality of the assault upon her.

The survivor's job after an assault is to heal. Whether she begins— immediately or ten or twenty years down the road— she will be brought by life's circumstances to address the healing that needs to be done. The best thing for a survivor to do is talk to another survivor who is on her way to healing. A healing survivor will know the roadblocks, the obstacles, and the challenges needed to be faced in order to begin healing. She will know of the rape itself and what it means for one human being to enter the body of another without permission. She will know the pain, the fear, the shame, the horror, and the yearning and the hope to be whole again. And she will be able to show her sister the way. Anything else from anyone else is a bonus.

* * * * * * * * *

"Fear is an awesome and lonely road when one objects
to well-proven methods of healing with others."

"What must I do to walk in safety?"

She walked the streets in freedom. If she went out at night, it was a calculated risk, for she carefully weighed the dangers against what she needed to do. Still, she feared very little of the dangerous and loathsome creatures that also roamed the night, uniquely hidden in the shadows that dropped behind her.

On this particular night, she turned the corner and walked the half-mile to the store, and if anyone came upon her and could see in the darkness, they would see a smile on her face. For some reason, she felt she could breathe in the sweetness of the night's sounds, and she was overcome with a sense of gratitude. Despite the dangers, she was unafraid and she rested in that alone.

The parts that were once frozen had defrosted a long time ago. Now her body actually listened and worked in cooperation with her mind. It didn't matter if she was afraid; her body no longer failed her mind. And her mind no longer failed her needs. The road to her transformation was not an easy one, yet neither was it impossible or improbable. The only requirement on her part was the exercise of trusting herself and worthy others.

She still marveled at who she had become. She had found a way to get a second chance to repair the damage she once thought was irreparable. With guidance from her teachers and support from her classmates, she was able to relive it again, and this time, she could and did win the fight.

Afterwards, she continued to practice her self-defense training with martial arts. Slowly, over time, just as she had been told that it would be slow, that it would take time, and that all she had to do was commit herself to healing, she indeed regained her sense of viewing the world through clearer lenses. It wasn't that the world had changed or that life was any safer. She had changed and her life was safer. She made better choices. She lived better. And she was better. She said a prayer of thanks for all her teachers, counselors and therapists who helped her help herself walk again in freedom.

* * * * * * * * *

"Trust in self can make dreams realities."

"Will this scab turn into a scar?"

There is a pain that seems as if it will never go away, will never be healed, will serve up reminders week after week and sometimes in it's exquisite lifeline, minute by minute. Most times, it returns unexpectedly— always. Like death, when you think you've cheated it or when you feel you're on guard in case it dares to strike when you're not watching. But death and pain are mighty hunters. And because they are natural and inevitable, they always hit their mark. The survivor's role is to meet it at its most strengthening moment.

There's no sense in putting all our energy into fighting pain or running away. Running away just allows for a moment in our life when the pain will simply catch up. It can not be outrun as long as a survivor has any consciousness in her life. Sooner or later, the mind and heart of a survivor will tire, will need rest, will give in; and if it takes that long, pain is patient and will wait, even if it has to come upon the survivor when she isn't looking.

It doesn't do us any good to compare our reason for pain to others, except to find a way to heal it. It does no good to say I shouldn't feel this way, or I should've healed a long time ago or whatever other reason one can come up with to deny the reality of our pain. We are not bad people for feeling untreated pain for such a long time. We suffer because the pain is there, that in some instances of life, a grief of loss will take years to get over, and for some, to never get over at all.

This is not about wallowing in pain. This is recognition that in matters of health, even in the realm of the psyche and the emotional, some wounds take longer to heal than others. As survivors, we are better off accepting such truth, than picking and tearing at ourselves some more to add to the pain that's already there. If nothing else, we can picture the most beloved scene we know, and know that Wisdom of the Creators holds us with their folds. It may not change anything, but perhaps it will bring a moment of peace; and peace stills all pain.

* * * * * * * * *

"When the last holdout tear is shed, the wound shall be healed."

"I wonder if I can get back at 'em?"

Unfortunately, revenge is never as good as it looks in our mind's eye. Only a feeling person can think revenge. Revenge is but a backwards way of wanting justice, a justice that is never forthcoming. Revenge does not soothe the pained and saddened heart, does not heal the grieving soul.

Fantasies of revenge should run amok. They are just fantasies. Because of the nature of revenge, it is simply a stop-gap for the real feelings of injustice, righteous indignation, and it can never fill the wounded cut of the betrayal.

Wanting revenge reminds us that we are deep-feeling people. Nonetheless, to continually harbor revenge in our hearts, to give revenge refuge in our souls, is to slip and slide on the slime of debris and hatred on the outskirts of our healing path. Revenge, in and of itself, brings good to no one.

On the upside, turning a weakness into a strength, revenge is the cry for justice. And it is the cry for protection against an act of inhumanity. Revenge harbors a peek at the shadow of our being. The fact that it is there, that it exists, is not conclusive, nor a cause and effect axiom. However, in its shadow, it is there for all to see that it in fact does exist. But like all shadows, its essence is neutral, allowing all kinds of projective thought. One is not ordered, compelled, or driven to act on revenge unless we give it our permission. We do not have to do that to survive. We only have to create a space to hold these feelings and see them for what they truly are— reaction to a knockout loss. They are also a reference point to be acknowledged as we continue to seek justice during the journey of our healing.

* * * * * * * * *

"Revenge ought not to be confused with justice."

"How can we go on a journey without a dream?"

She had spent the past week doing everything but that one thing she really wanted to do. She'd found this, that, and then even more to divert her creative energies from that which she loved. When she could no longer pretend to be busy with pitter-patter work, she'd practically sit in stupor, and wonder why she couldn't do what she wanted to do.

There were no locks on her doors, no bars on her windows. Her hands were neither chained nor tied. Her mind was free to roam in comfort and feed off the many fascinating tidbits of life and imagination that phased her brain, but she could not do the thing she wanted to do most. Over the years, she raged, screamed, cried, and had migraine headaches galore over this very stuckedness. Still, she had not found the way to release her from the binding energy to do what she most wanted done.

A few days later on a particular bright, sunny, autumn day, she went outside and after walking only a few yards down the road, ended up having a conversation with a wise elder that lived down the street from her. The elder invited her to sit on the porch and rock with her awhile, and then told her to close her eyes, as she had a story she wanted to share with her. With the aged, melodious voice that carried rhythms of the Ancients of the Continents, she transported her to another place where the very thing our survivor feared swooped in with gifts upon its wings. Before the elder transported her back to the present from the few minutes which seemed like hours, the survivor was reminded that she could do whatever she wanted to do with the gifts she had been given.

As the next few days went by, she'd close her eyes and think, *If I did it before, I can do it again.* Tuning into the energy of the Ancients and with her mind acting as if *it* had a mind of its own, she brought herself to the place the wise elder had led her earlier. Opening her eyes and smiling, she forgave herself for temporarily forgetting who she was and that she had what she had been looking for all along. She began again to finish her work now connected fully to her mind.

* * * * * * * * *

"We need our dreams to begin our journeys."

"How can I take leave of my feelings for this person?"

10 MORE REASONS TO LET GO OF THAT PERSON WHO SAID THEY LOVED YOU BUT DIDN'T:

1. Ever since you met this person, your life began unraveling.
2. The day seems wonderful, but then "bam!" this person shows up.
3. They made promises to you that you didn't ask for, and didn't keep the promises.
4. They made promises to you that you did ask for, and didn't keep the promises.
5. They didn't make you any promises.
6. They broke your heart with your permission.
7. They broke your heart without your permission.
8. You told them you didn't think it was a good idea for the two of you to get together, but against your better judgment and all the red flags, you got together anyway.
9. You're the only one who knows how this person really is and so you don't have to listen to those who say otherwise and,
10. Because you can!

* * * * * * * * *

"We must protect and provide a refuge from that which would harm us."

"How do I protect myself from the hatred?"

10 REASONS NOT TO HATE SOMEONE:

1. Hating is ugly and it nullifies the one who hates more than the one who is hated.

2. Hating displaces a tremendous amount energy that could be used for something positive.

3. Hating takes a soul where it's harder to get out than to get in.

4. Hating fills your stomach with worms and your eyes can't see right.

5. Hating repels, and even those who you don't hate, don't want to be around you.

6. Hating is not anger, and therefore, has no righteous outlet.

7. Hating is not the opposite of love, and therefore, can not grow on its own.

8. Hating stagnates and degenerates the person who is doing the hating more than the person who is hated.

9. Hating is not a reward in and of itself.

10. Better you should learn to love yourself 100-fold than to spend one ounce of energy entertaining a concept that has the ability to consume your very soul.

* * * * * * * * *

"Do not clothe yourself in that which you do not wish to wear."

"How did this happen again?"

She opened her eyes and the reality of her life began unfolding into her awakening consciousness. She tightly closed her eyes again, anguish rushing up from the pit of her stomach into the veins of her brain, and thought, *This is a terribly, terribly bad joke.* How could she have lost so much in what seemed like a single night when in actuality it was over a few years ?

Last time she felt this embattled was as an adolescent, and in one day, she lost her world in the setting of the day's sun. One day she had friends, was a good student, loved her family, and her family loved her. Suddenly, the home and family she was so grateful for had no room for her. Safe kisses turned into sloppy, gooey, wet ones; and sleeping no longer gave over to sweet dreams. Her nights were splintered with sharp awakenings from creaking floor sounds and doors that slid not so silently open. Unwanted touches began to invade the most protected parts of her body, and her soul began experiencing some of the most terrifying feelings known to a human being.

She thought she had left such ugly times behind, thought she could no longer be wounded by any of life's surprises or unexpected visits. And yet, here she was some forty years later, and some of those same life sounds were echoing loudly in a home she called her own, thinking she was safe from loved ones who may turn ugly and show a skin she'd not seen before.

She was stronger now than when she was a teenager. While she might be somewhat world-weary, she'd been fortified by her many travels, knew dangers she had to beware of, and knew much of what she was capable of doing. She would not acquiesce to anybody's tyrannical reign with her as victim. She was a survivor. This time, she would not lose her feelings on the new path of her life journey. She opened her eyes again and began anew, the beginning of another day that waited only upon her.

* * * * * * * * *

"We do not have to laugh when life is not funny to us."

"How can I shift the energy?"

THREE WAYS TO GET OUT FROM UNDER:

First: Harness your energy. Maybe for some folks it's lying in bed, gathering up the morning's light, and breathing it in for a few minutes before getting up. For some, it's puttering around, piddling with different little things in the bedroom or kitchen until the soul, the mind and the body become synced again from the night's dreams and sleep. For others, it could be a routine for awakening oneself such as going to the bathroom and staring sleepily into the mirror, acquainting oneself with one's reflection.

Second: Focus. Once the different parts of the self come together, catch up with one another, the mind must begin the daily journey. Some folks focus through their routine. By the time they finish their morning's ablutions, the mind has the clarity to tackle the wants, desires, and needs of the soul. Others purposely choose a definite way of focusing to meet the day. Some pray, some meditate, and some do physical exercise, as they begin to harness their soul energy in a focused way to achieve their goals and tasks.

Third: Do it. Begin each task as if it were the first task you set for yourself. Do not allow past mindsets to dictate your course. Mind tapes such as, *But, I can't* or *This never works*, are not allowed in this exercise. Remember, this is an experiment. If it doesn't work, you can always try it again or apply it to another task. If it does work, then you have found another way to accomplish a task you have set for yourself. Remember, one step at time, one task at a time.

* * * * * * * * *

"Sometimes trying new things actually works."

"How can I tell I'm healing?"

Healed or healing does not mean we will not have any more crises, or that our lives will be exempt from doubts and anxieties of everyday living. What it may mean is that we develop skills not to collapse in the old ways, and we have new lenses to view our situations so we no longer need defenses to get us through new challenges and problems.

Healing means feeling better about ourselves, our life situations, and other people in our lives. Healing means having more of what we want in our lives. It means feeling again and it means feeling more deeply. Healing means taking new steps on unknown paths, faltering every now and then, and being able to stay the course of our new pathways. Healing means the new replaces the old. Healing means being more connected to others, but mostly to ourselves. Healing means we have lives we can live, and we will do any and everything to do so, despite faltering steps and doubting ourselves.

Healing means recognizing we are women, we are human beings, and it is okay to have weaknesses and imperfections. It means we can depend on others again, we can trust others again, and we can love others again. Like any art of beauty, healing takes time, takes thoughtfulness, takes vision, and needs to breathe like the release of an old, fine and succulent wine. Perhaps most importantly, healing is more than a concept or a possibility. At its essence, healing is itself, and means all the value its word implies. It means to treat a wound, to re-grow new tissue— scarred or invisible, and to know a past life-threatening experience with long-term consequences that happened in our lives can, or for many of us has been healed by our souls.

* * * * * * * * *

"It is the nature of the human being to fulfill its own beatific perfection."

October 1

COMPELLED
We are compelled
to repeat the lessons
and revisit the pain
over and over again
until we set it right
in our souls

"How shall I go about healing my life?"

Bleak. Gray. Endless horizons and infinite vastness. In bleakness, there are no tomorrows, no better days; just the same ol' stuff. There is no hope, and without hope there is no change. To change that the horizons must have an end in sight; and the vastness must have a beginning, middle and end (although, not necessarily in that order).

Many of us learned at an early age, and through a number of years, that things were hopeless. We had to endure abuse because nobody knew or else those who knew turned their heads, closed their eyes and sealed their lips. Their denial about the abuse made the feelings of hopelessness in us very real. And so perhaps some of us fell into the emptiness and vastness to counteract the sinking feelings of hopelessness; if one is empty one can not feel.

We are the architects of our lives. We lay the foundations and add the structures as we go along. We clean out the debris and bring in new materials to fill the spaces of our minds and our lives. If we look at the whole picture before we begin building, it may seem too much to do. But if we begin to enclose the vastness one step at a time, and maybe get some people to help us, then we begin the enclosure and can see the containment.

Our healing is like that; no straight and narrow path, but one that is flexible and gives way for adjustment. And our healing may call for us to remind ourselves that hope for us must be nurtured. Nurturing ourselves may call for a walk in the park, the viewing of a beautiful sunset, the kindness of the smile from a stranger or a relaxing meal with a good friend. Then the world doesn't seem so vast or infinite and neither do our lives.

Every time we nurture that hope and close that vastness we unfailingly gain a piece of ourselves back. Reclamation comes in all forms and in so many ways, and sometimes the simplest ways are the way back home to ourselves.

* * * * * * * * *

"There is wisdom in the old adage
'with hope, all things are possible.'"

"Can mantras really help me?"

10 MANTRAS OF USE FOR THE TOUGH, BORING, AND INERT TIMES:

1. "Suffice the problems the day thereof."
2. "One day at a time."
3. Listen to your spirit and hear it say, "Trust me."
4. Talk to your mind and say, "Fear not."
5. It's a done deal.
6. I am my own Creator
7. I've been here before and know the way home.
8. I have more lives than a cat.
9. I'm the one I've been searching for.
10. Today is always a perfect day to fight the good fight.

* * * * * * * * *

"One mantra might just get me through a very trying day."

"When will I be able to see my own truth?"

With head bent down and gray hairs spread throughout her thick hair, she looked to be about 60 years old. Her limp, seated body, while not telling her true height, told of her unspoken ordeal. Her dress was spotted with crusted liquid; her bedroom slippers looked as if they'd never seen a day of washing; and her slight snore clearly said she did not want to be disturbed. And her smooth, brown skin played shades of old broken autumn leaves.

Truth be told, she was yet to be 40 years of age. Her already-damaged body bore long, scarred tissues on her upper arm. She had been kidnapped, assaulted and almost raped, but had managed to overcome her two attackers and escape their clutches. She wandered the streets for the next three hours, begging for help, pleading as she stumbled and mumbled. And she kept the scream that she was blind, to herself, until finally someone called the police.

It was no surprise to anyone in ER that she nodded off periodically, and she frequently winced when her arm was moved. She asked for medication for the pain in her arm and fell asleep in the midst of her request. Despite her ordeal and her obvious distress, she did not want to make a fuss or accept our offers of refreshments. She apologized for taking up our space and time, having no idea that the strength of her spirit seemed to emanate inches of energy off her skin.

As her numbness seemed to leave, her head began to clear up, and her face became somewhat animated. She began to speak in tones of resignation about the way her life unfolded. Fighting off her attackers was small pickings considering the murder of her three children some 20 years ago. Her boyfriend killed them, and then put her in a coma. A month or so later, she woke up to the knowledge that her children had been buried, and that it was not dark outside, but in her eyes. Her face, despite its markings and ravaging, was beautiful and enhanced by some unknown grace. While she thanked us for our help, we remained quite speechless at being blessed by the presence of such beauty befallen by a criminal. He did not know her will to live was unassailable.

* * * * * * * * *

"Truth is beholden in my eyes and in my heart."

"Must I always have my guard up?"

It can be no surprise that many of us survivors are a bit wary, leery, and doubting of words spoken to us, regardless of the who the speaker is. Seldom do we take words at their face value. Almost always, we connect them to the one giving voice to the words.

Many of us have been under personal attack since early childhood, and therein, our saving defenses were finely honed and sculled. In resting in our healing and giving up the defenses we no longer need, we may find ourselves a bit more vulnerable to the impact of the sound of words and the actions of bodies.

It may be that many people are almost inculcated with the desire to receive respect from others. It isn't something we survivors grew up with; actually, it is just the opposite. Disrespect was frequently thrown our way, particularly when we knew we should've been treated better, treated with respect by those who violated our boundaries and assaulted or molested us in the ways they chose. Perhaps in realizing that it was wrong for us to be mistreated and abused, the question for many of us seems to be, "Why?" We may have had thoughts such as, *If you loved me, if you cared about me, if you cared about my family, and if you didn't want to hurt me, you wouldn't be doing this.* So we are sometimes haunted with a longevity we wish we never had in the realms of our memories, which keeps asking the question, "Why?"

Our healing gives us back our respect for ourselves. A personal injury thrust upon us may catch us off guard momentarily. If we find ourselves dwelling on a particular person's action or words that cause us offense, if we can name what it is we are feeling, we can recover from our highly sensitized reactions and see the situation for what it is and separate it from our past. When others are not respectful of us, it is their problem to work out and own, and we can take heart that an old pattern is being diminished as we move forward along our path of healing.

* * * * * * * * *

"Respect for myself, while given or earned, can only be sanctioned by me."

"What's different with my eyes wide open?"

I don't know how
I'm broke again
I close my eyes
and it's way back then
I open my eyes
and I'm broke again
Wish I could close
my eyes
and find that star
that everyone dreams
wish I could find that star
and open my eyes again
seeing my dream

* * * * * * * * *

"I am the dreamer."

"Why do we have such deep feelings of hate and self-hatred?"

I hate myself today. I am trusting my indwelling Spirit to get me through this self-hatred. I hate the way I look. I'm a failure and I know it and I hate it. I hate the dreams I have lost that keep coming up in my memories. I wish there were something that I could strike, hit, anything that would make a difference, or at least make me feel better.

I hate it that I am not a success, not only by my measurements, but by other's successes. I hate it that I've lost my vision to move to the next dream. I hate that I lost my dream. I hate it that I start projects and really get into them, and just as they're almost finished, I stop working on the projects. I hate it that I'm so far behind in paying my bills. I hate that I've lost the intimacy and sharing in my marriage. I hate it that I can't and won't complete a damn thing. I hate the way I manipulate the world to get what I want

I hate the world today— all the confronters, conflictors, warmongers, and the lying media trying to make us accept a war. I hate it that it is more important to get rid of a dictator at the expense of hundreds of thousands of lives of children and other living things, just so some politician can say, "I won." I hate it that my protests or actions are not enough to stop the momentum of the erroneous warrior's scream. I hate it that there is so much work to be done to change society, and that society must change or all we shall know is war.

I hate it that so much hatred is boiling inside of me, and the Creator I seek apparently hears me not. I hate it that I don't know why we are born and live the particular lives we live. I hate it that the simple emotions of want, love, and need are so hard to come by with friends and family; and I hate that those same needs are met by the kindness of strangers.

I am very unhappy with the world and myself today; yet, I still believe in Divine Creation and Purpose. But tonight, I go to sleep hating all of it; therefore, I am giving it all to my Creator to help me make it through another day and night and hopefully minister a healing to help me with tomorrow.

* * * * * * * * *

"Sometimes the inexplicable can remain so, and changes I want can be so."

"How can I bring peace to my nation?"

The drums of violence are currently pounding the beat of war in so many parts of the world. Many of us who are survivors side on the part of our nation's heart, and advocate for laws that call for non-violence in solving problems.

We survivors are almost automatically skeptical of anything said from a politician or government official on any level— local, state, or national. Perhaps one of our leftover defenses now acts as a strength for us. We can *feel* the truth, or the lack thereof. We seem to have a sixth sense when a person's feelings genuinely match, or don't match their expression. We learned early on to read the coldness and deadness of the eyes that lie; yet, on matters of forgiveness, if we sense sincerity we are willing to give a person who's made a mistake a second chance.

In healing from the abuse we suffered, we learn not to blame ourselves and, instead, to hold accountable those that abused or hurt us as children, and we have transferred over that same insightful thinking to those in political power. Many of us have also learned that when circumstances present themselves, we can join others, and prove the simple adage that "there is power in numbers." When elected representatives, from the national office of the president to a city council person, ignores the directives of their constituents or abuses their power, then like all perpetrators, they should be held accountable; and they should be replaced if necessary by those who are willing to listen to the voices that elect them.

As survivors, we can work on any level in our society to see that peace and sanity prevail over the machinations of lustful and devastating warmongers. We know the necessity of setting boundaries for ourselves, and we can now, as part of our healing, participate in setting boundaries for our country. No matter the situation, we can join other kindred visionaries as we exercise our right to vote and elect people who are willing to work for a peaceful and non-assaultive world.

* * * * * * * * *

"As survivors we can take action to make our world safer for everybody."

"How much of my personal history should I share with them?"

If we are survivors with sons and daughters, we can expect a bumpy ride in family life, just like everybody else. The teen years can be an especially difficult time for survivors and their children. Many of us skipped the normal growth of adolescence, of independence vs. dependence, and/or boundaries vs. freedom, with our families of origin. Having a personal history of incest, molestation, or continual and ritualistic control of our lives by our primary caretakers, left little room for us to follow the average course of teenage emotional development.

Admittedly, we may be a bit "weird" to our teens. This particular time of high parental embarrassment and finding their youthful identity in their social groups is difficult enough without having a survivor parent. Nonetheless, we exist; and those of us healing bring a richness of love and connection to our children, even if a bit quirky.

Sometimes we bring real disconnection and pain to them. Some of us are clinically depressed; some of us have multiple personalities; some of us are obsessive and compulsive about how a family should do things around the house. They may find it frightening, and may directly attack us venomously, spewing out their misunderstandings of why we are in the place of our healing during their teen times.

Nonetheless, in healing we must find a way to protect those parts of ourselves that need such protection from our children; and at the same time, we must provide our children a safe and loving environment. Sometimes it is heartbreaking to be unable to explain why we do some of the things we do or act the way we do. And like all truth, "in the fullness of time," we, as well as our children, will understand why things are the way they are now. We must be kind enough to be patient with ourselves and our teens on this particular path and in this particular age.

* * * * * * * * *

"We were creative enough to survive, and we can be
creative enough to solve many of the problems of our families."

"How many times must I feel like I'm starting all over again?"

How could she explain the feeling of having chronic and constant emotional pain, sadness, and loss, while trying to gather the energy to live and rebuild some semblance of a sane life? How can she tell anyone, but especially herself, that she is not the person she wanted to be, and not the woman she could fully be? How can she explain her deepest disappointment in herself? She looked around at the women in her room; some she knew and a couple she didn't. She wondered why they bothered at all.

Forgiveness, you say?

This time she suffered a relapse deep into despair and anguish; of beating herself up and letting herself feel the pain. She had been at the point in her healing where she believed she should be able to handle this herself without seeing a therapist or counselor, and here she was doing a stint in a psych ward. And too, despite the presence of other patients traveling a similar road, she felt she had no one to talk to, and she felt painfully isolated and alone.

Her thoughts drifted throughout the day and she found herself speaking with Quan Yin, and for the first time in a long time, she felt the same peace of presence that she felt when with Christ. For a little while, the pain was let go. The feeling was brief and she took advantage of the respite and went to bed early rather then continuing to hazarding the experience the pain that suddenly had lifted from her heart.

Lying down, she wished she knew the way home.

Drifting off to sleep, she heard murmuring of voices of women bouncing softly off the dull, green walls in her hospital room. Ancestral murmurings brought comfort she couldn't name, and unspoken prayers fervently coursed through their blood that one of their daughters might indeed heal from the night. All of them knew the journey would be a long one, and so each and every one of them whispered soothing words of hope and truth as one of their own took refuge in sleep.

* * * * * * * * *

"Just because I can not see a life line, does not mean it is not there."

"And how will I know I am healing?"

10 TOP SIGNS TO KNOW YOU'RE HEALING:

1. The pain of it all is excruciating and seems never to end, and everything in your life— job, family, education, beliefs, and creeds, seem out of control.

2. Old defenses do not work, and you haven't figured out new ones, ergo making you feel awkward and confused in many social situations.

3. You can make a list of things to do

4. You can make a list of things to do and not do them

5. You no longer feel compelled to make a list of things to do.

6. You have plenty of free time on your hands and feel bored, not anxious.

7. The pain that is excruciating and seems never to have an end in sight now has an end in sight.

8. You do what you have to do for as long as you have to do it, recognizing the law of the jungle in civilization.

9. There is very little difference in perception of awake time and dreamtime, and you are aware of when you are awake and when you are dreaming.

10. The part of you that stopped you from going forward has ingested experientially the sayings, "One monkey don't stop no show," and "You're all that and a bag of chips!"

* * * * * * * *

"There are healing markers along the trail of our journey."

"Can I find the one I love?"

You can't make someone love you if they don't. You can't make yourself love someone you don't.

You can love someone madly, even if they don't love you back in return. Someone can love you madly, even you don't love them back in return.

You can long for, desire for, want for, crave for, even die for, but it won't change the fact that the other person doesn't have the same feelings for you. You can want someone and not have them in your life, and acknowledge that truth in itself, and still move forward in your healing.

You can't have every toy in the toy store, and you can't have everyone who comes into your life come home with you. But, it is helpful to know that at some point in your life, you will satisfy this need and wanting in a reciprocal way. You will find someone who loves you as much as you love them. It has been proven over time and in the Chronicles of Love that for every Ethel there's a Harry and/or for every Doris there's a Barbara. And, sometimes when you stop looking that person will find you even if it's 40 years down the road.

* * * * * * * * *

"Be patient and love will come to you.."

"Who's to say who's fragile?"

Walking the path of mainstream society was not a trail she would walk in the days following the rape. In fact, those days back then were often filled with crying, nail biting, smoking cigarettes non-stop and drinking alcohol as if prohibition were about to return again.

Her beauty was held in a lithe shapely body encased in dark, reddish brown skin as smooth as an ancient rock, and her head of black hair was a ringlet of curls that stopped short at her neck. In this embodiment she walked the earth and returned another's eye contact with a penetrating look from deep within her. Deceptive really because a quick look at her and one would think a gust of wind could sweep her a few inches above the earth and sway her gently if it had a mind to.

His objective was similar to the wind, but unlike the wind, he would not gently put her feet back on the ground. And he didn't. He snatched her off the street unseen as dusk settled upon the day, and dragged her to a bramble of tall bushes. She screamed, "No, get off me!" and fruitlessly struggled against his overpowering weight. He punched her in the stomach and then muffled her sounds with his heavy arm under her neck suppressing all noise as it choked her breath. When he finished raping her, he punched her in the face and head until she was totally still. This was how the police found her, brutalized and almost dead.

Her strength that kept her alive also helped her to testify against him in court, and he was convicted and sent to jail. It didn't cure her of the fears she had collected from his attack, but she began healing, journeying on a path many had walked before her and with others who now walked beside her.

* * * * * * * * *

"Every survivor walks the healing path at her own pace."

"Were clichés originally born of truth and change?

10 CLICHÉS WITH NEW ENDINGS FOR THE MILLENNIUM:

1. 'Tis better to have loved and lost, than to never have lived at all.
2. What comes first? The victim or the crime?
3. A bird in one hand will probably make somebody call the ASPC.
4. Be not a lender or borrower— but credit cards are okay.
5. When you walk through a storm, hold your head up high and hurry.
6. Look for the silver lining, and see the Sunnyside products in select grocery stores.
7. She who laughs lasts was probably disassociating and came back just as the punch line was being told.
8. The grass is always greener on the other side, unless of course you live in the desert.
9. Seek ye to know the truth, and it'll help if you're willing to walk that walk and talk that talk.
10. Patience is a virtue seldom practiced by people in fast food lines and survivors on the healing path.

* * * * * * * * *

"Clichés, like survivors, can change."

"How long will it take me to be free of my internalized tyranny?"

It is said that Americans are spoiled and unaware of "true" poverty or of "tyranny" by a dictator. It is said that Americans don't understand how any immigrant could believe the streets of America "are paved with gold." But most of all, it would appear that many Americans can not understand how immigrants are so willing to accept paltry wages and work under horrible conditions. Americans, they say, fail to understand why immigrants who seek refuge in America seem to either be incredibly satisfied with a life that appears materially marginal, or why the haven-seekers work 25/8 to be the best, to do their best, to prove to the family "back home" that they are successful and hard workers. Americans are in awe that so many immigrants seem to settle for so little, and do not understand immigrants working two jobs just to live paycheck to paycheck and call that success.

Survivors seem to have an understanding of both sides of the coin: (1) Anything is worth freedom and safety and, (2) Climb as far as you can go, even if it means sacrificing all of yourself and your family "in the pursuit of happiness."

Here's what some folks may not understand about survivors who appear self-satisfied with their lot, or who seem to want to succeed "no matter the cost." Perhaps for the one, it is enough to be free from the tyranny of another who takes away your power, security, or ability to protect yourself or your loved ones. Just to be free is enough. On the other hand, they miss the fact of the survivor's knowing how lucky she is to be able to pursue healing, to be away from her captor perps, and to finally have the chance to excel at what she chooses to do. And maybe, overall, to make up for what she feels she missed along the way during her years of captivity.

No matter how it appears to on-lookers who have never lived a day of imprisonment and unspeakable abuse in their lives, survivors are willing to travel the healing path even if their sweat turns to blood on their journey.

* * * * * * * * *

"Sometimes 'extreme' is the temporary salve of healing."

"Is there a timetable and only one way to heal?"

She didn't ask for this, at least that is what she told herself a hundred times a day. Wherever she went, there they were— rapists, con artists, thieves, gangs, and drunks— all of them waiting for her to make one move, one mistake so they could enter her world and take what they wanted— all her things and worldly goods, her car, books, statutes, and of course, the most coveted of all, her body. They wouldn't leave her alone until they finally killed her. They tapped her phones, had someone follow her wherever she went, and tried to break into her house whenever they had a chance to get in the door.

The cops were useless, calling her a nutcase. They tried to put her in the county hospital, but you couldn't trust those folks, either. They tried to poison her with her own medicine, and if she took it, she got worse problems and had to see other doctors. Her therapist was the worst of all, prescribing medicine that could kill her with all kinds of side effects, even brain damage.

They just didn't know how she had to stand guard all the time, and the minute she didn't, something bad happened. For example, while she was waiting at the bus stop and talking to one of the others waiting for the bus, somebody stole her pocketbook and took all of her money.

Even the hotline people couldn't be trusted. But they had to listen because they had told her to call. Most times, they didn't understand; but sometimes some of them would. Tonight, they did not understand. She could call back again, and probably would if her mind got to spinning again. If just for one moment she could let her guard down, she might get back some of the other parts of herself that were stolen from her that day.

Getting into bed, she set the TV timer to shutoff within the hour. She might be able to doze off into a bit of sleep, maybe even sleep until the morning, right before sunrise. She burrowed herself under her covers and tried to figure out how she would make it through the next day, reminding herself that if nothing else, she made it to this night.

* * * * * * * * *

"I sometimes heal moment-by-moment, and sometimes that is enough."

"Does it really matter to keep trying to anticipate the surprises of a new day?"

Her morning started off a bit askew, rushing around getting ready for her big day at the office. She had to get to work early to look over a report before her meeting, where she would be making her first presentation as assistant administrator to the law staff. She took her time with her makeup, and the choice of what shoes she would wear with her outfit and those were her only concerns for the day— the report and how she was dressed for her meeting.

Her meeting couldn't have gone any better. She had gone through the half-minute jitters and butterflies, and conducted herself to the standards expected of her and more. So happy was she with her success that she had let her guard down when walking back to her car to drive home. Consequently, in a movement that seemed to happen all at once, a car slowed down, a door opened, and a man stepped out and grabbed her towards the inside of the car.

Not this time. The voices came back and she reacted instinctively. With her mouth, she bit his hand, turned around up and struck his face with a palm strike as hard as she could. She could hear voices somewhere in her head, shouting her name and telling her to scream. And so she shouted, "No! Call 911!" She took a step back, twisted her hips, and threw a side kick into his knee, as the other man drove off, leaving his buddy on the ground to fend for himself. A couple of people came up to her and asked if she was okay and told her the police were on their way.

Later that night when she thought about the day's events, she still couldn't believe it. She was walking on air; bruised maybe, but walking on air and feeling as she hadn't felt since she was five years old— invincible. "Hell," she thought, "sometimes shit does work out."

* * * * * * * * *

"'Always be prepared' is not just for Girl Scouts."

"Will I be able to hold my head up high again?"

Every now and then, one of life's nightmares became reality in front of her eyes. This time it took the form of a crumpled woman upon the hospital bed. She was everyone's image of the homeless woman who seemed to have given up everything except breathing and angry muttering.

"He made me beg for my life. I had to beg for my life!" And then she began a wailing of her humiliation.

The advocate remembered what it was like to beg for her own life. The confusion, the disbelief, and the gruesome acts of the perp that waited for her if she didn't escape; bits of her soul, embedded in the terrible plans he had for her while he touched parts of her body he had explored before. And so she resorted to the only thing left for her to bargain with— a plea for her own life and a swearing that she would tell nobody if he just let her go this time. Her fear contained the thought that even if he let her go, he'd change his mind before she escaped out the door.

The advocate returned her focused to her client and viewed the damage of what was done to the woman. There were old burn scars spread out upon her body like undeciphered tattoos, and the new scratches on her face competed with scabs from days before the fresh-blooded ones. Her wig lay beside her knee like a prosthetic, and a soiled baseball cap covered most of her short, cotton-tight hair. It was as if chickens had pecked at her head and then scattered bites upon her neck.

What to do to help? Such a soul needed containment; such energy needed to be reigned in and shifted through the strands of healing atoms from one who had already walked the path. Luckily, such human beings existed, more than one might expect in a world where every six minutes a woman is assaulted and raped, and in a world where every three minutes, another is battered. There was no other way than to plow into the earth with her client and retrieve what was needed to coax the soul to try again for another day.

* * * * * * * * *

"There is no end of souls in need of healing."

Telling   **October 19**

"Why couldn't she just tell them what happened?"

They seem so perplexed, some of the health care folks and law enforcement. Can't the victim see that if she gives them the info, if she gives them the evidence, they can get the perp, the criminal, the monster who hurt her so badly? They can stop such a person from hurting anyone else. Why are victims so reluctant to help themselves the "helpers" ask themselves?

We all want to forget bad situations. We want to fix the problem immediately, and get on with our lives and our projects and our families and so forth. However, recovering from a sexual assault— a rape, a rape with a gun at your head, a rape with a gun at your head and the picture of a dead woman who told— well, what comes first? The victim or the law?

Secondary witnesses must exercise as much patience as is asked of survivors, for as witnesses, they become one with the survivors. Temporarily.

It is enough that victims tell someone. It is more than enough that we seek help. And the final "enough is enough" is when the survivor says so and then acts accordingly.

* * * * * * * * *

*"Survivors and secondary witnesses are in the same boat,
and each paddle is needed."*

-292-

"What happened to my memory?"

When the clamoring in her mind settled down, when her ears stopped ringing so that her eyes could focus in front of her, she laid in the hospital gurney alternately looking at the people grouped around her, or staring at a spot in front of her that blurred with her peripheral vision. In fact, she actually saw nothing, but heard clearly what was being said about her.

She didn't want to cry. She knew she wouldn't stop if she did. It took a while for her to get to this place of acceptance. She had at first fought off the hospital personnel that had tried to help her when she was admitted to the emergency room; hence, the leather straps on her wrists. She had told them she didn't belong in the hospital, that there was a mistake, that the things the doctor was telling her were all lies. But her clarity of mind was returning, and she was beginning to accept that what was going on was real. She'd been raped.

Most everything was vague to her, but some of what they said rang a bell though most were nonsensical words to her ears. All she knew is that prior to being in the hospital she had gone to a bar with some friends, left to go to the bathroom and the next thing she knew she was running and limping through an alley. And then she was in a police car and now she was in a hospital and they were saying she should do a rape kit and were asking for her consent.

That was as much as she could remember although she felt a burning between her legs and a soreness in her neck and shoulders and there were red and purple bruises on her arms. And yes, she felt she had been drugged, even though she took regular medications. And yes, it was possible that everything they were telling her was the truth, and if so, she had survived, and that would have to be enough. She didn't want to hear anymore, and didn't want to talk anymore about it. For now, she was just glad to be alive even if she kept wondering how such a thing could happen to her on what had started as a bright sunny day.

* * * * * * * * *

"Some memories are non-recoverable; it doesn't mean I can not heal."

"How come I feel so bad today?"

Here's a bad day:

The sun is shining and you have reason to celebrate but have no one who cares enough to celebrate it with you. Or, those who care about you are really, really pissed at you, and you are raging at them so you can't celebrate with them either.

A bad day also feels like you no longer have first place in anybody else's heart, and it's too late and there's nothing you can do about it.

When you wake up on a bad day your thoughts are already in the framework of "I don't want to be with anybody" and "I don't care about nothing", but inside your heart you wish you could be with someone you really wanted to be with and you wish there was something you cared about.

A bad day is realizing all of this before you put your feet on the floor for the first time that day. You just know nothing's going to get better, and you just can't figure out how you're going to get through the day.

A bad day is to see and know the world as it really is in the most sobering place of your mind. You know the only thing you can do is to go through it and you know that in a day or two, you're going to feel a lot better. Hell, for that matter, you could be a lot better in two hours. But for right now, just after you've woken up and weighed your options for the day, it's just a fucking bad day.

A bad day feels like the deep void in your belly and the unending ache in your heart continues to override any good feeling that may come up to counter those bad day feelings.

But.

A good day for us survivors is knowing that a bad day can happen, and it has nothing to do with our sexual abuse histories; just that it's a bad fucking day.

* * * * * * * * *

"A bad day is just a bad day when it can
be summed up as just the "blues.""

"Am I a good mother?"

She wished she could tell her son so that he might comprehend some things that affected them all as a family. However, she was bound by the unwritten parental rules, true and tried, of certain matters not appropriate to share with your children. She wished her husband, his father, could be more supportive of her, and too, not dismiss her arguments or her discipline of their son as "crazy" or that she had "issues" and therefore was not to be taken seriously.

She was tired of being seen as the "bad" parent, or the "enforcer." Any parent could say yes to whatever their children wanted, if it was within their means to do so, and of course, everything a child wants is neither good nor healthy.

"You're crazy," said her almost 14-year-old son, this time raising his voice to an unacceptable yell. She was tempted to go to the library, get the DSM (Diagnostic and Statistical Manual for Mental Disorder), and copy the pages that talked of PTSD and clinical depression. Instead, she sat down with her son and began a dialogue of acceptable and unacceptable behavior within the family.

Despite her son's getting older, he was still not ready to hear a truth that was not his own, and that was not his burden. She was also saddened that perhaps she hadn't done a good enough job, despite her healing. Yes, she knew her son was a being unto his own. Still she was tired of explaining her decisions about why she made the kind of decisions she did, especially to a child she brought into the world. This time, she rested in the fact that a personal history of sexual abuse does not make one exempt from wondering whether or not one is a good parent. The truth is like many of her kindred sisters, she was more than a good enough, loving mother.

* * * * * * * * *

"As mothers we often hold back certain knowledge
until our children are ready to hear and understand our truths."

"Must my fight always be to the death?"

She woke up from a deadened sleep and suddenly a thought popped into her head, "I will not be defeated." Nonetheless, she moved slowly as reality invaded her presence. Again. She had yet to find a way to block the grief, sadness, loss, confusion and emptiness that couldn't seem to be countered or blocked by anything she had at hand. No booze. No drugs. No sex. No food. No proverbs. No secret and sacred words of wisdom. These feelings simply invaded her body and rarely lasted for a minute or two; just long enough to embed a weariness of living her own life.

She brushes her teeth and it occurs to her that she knows there's a healing somewhere. She knows that the place where she came from with all the people who cared about her and loved her and made her their own, had gone to other parts of the world or else were literally dead. She knows, now, she must linger here where there are different people, but they, too, care and love her and make her a part of their own. She just doesn't know how to live with a freedom she's fought for and won. She thinks she can win this battle, once and for all, but she has her doubts and there is no getting around this particular fight. After all, she's fighting for her life, her right to live as she so designs and desires for herself.

If she wishes to be undefeated than she must identify this invisible enemy she seems to be fighting on a daily basis and the closest she can come to being undefeated is a draw. But she doesn't want a draw, she wants a win.

She realizes in one moment that while she was a warrior who no longer needed to fight an inner self ongoing war, her skills as a warrior have to be translated into her new world and her only enemy now is herself.

There is no fanfare to her victory from the outside world. But inside, her soul celebrates the triumph of her spirit over death to her in any form.

* * * * * * * * *

"All wars shall end, and the spirit of my ancestors
continue to show me the Way."

"Why do I bother at all to make any plans when anything can happen?"

10 CHALLENGES YOU HAVE SURVIVED IF YOU HAVE EVER:

1. been in a long-term domestically violent relationship and escaped with only the clothes on your back;

2. been threatened with a weapon to do as another person says or die;

3. been incarcerated and/or imprisoned by a government system unjustly and without legal representation;

4. been certain that your absolute saving grace as a soul was to unselfishly give birth to another soul;

5. awakened and had the reality of your life come to you in streaming clarity, and it makes you feel that this should be your last day on earth, and you're the one to do it, but didn't;

6. been addicted to drugs of any kind and kicked the habit;

7. lived through CSA on a regular and ritualistic basis and can't fathom that you will be healed wholly;

8. been physically, sexually, mentally and/or emotionally abused throughout your entire life, except for now, and you know "one day at a time" means for you "one minute at a time";

9. ever had to start all over again more than once in your life;

10. learned that you are the one truly in charge of your life and that forevermore, whatever happens is because you accepted and/or made the choice for such a situation, and you're going to hang on until your "time has come," then:

you are truly a woman of great courage. You know the heart can mend itself unexpectedly and more than you could have dreamed of simply because the Universe truly loves all Her creations, of which you are one.

* * * * * * * * *

"Hope has been known to produce more than a few miracles in a person's life."

"What's different about things now?"

In our 21st Century, some things have changed for children who are sexually assaulted, abused or incested. Many of them have lawyers, social workers, or therapists. And society actually says it will listen to them. There was a time when society did not listen and, in fact, moved on the assumption that any child and/or adolescent that stood before a judge in family court was simply a bad child, an incorrigible runaway or a future criminal dressed in teenaged insolence. As a result, many a youth, male or female, was hustled off to a state reformatory school, if not the state hospital, to be or not be diagnosed, but definitely to be locked up for some indefinite agreed upon time in the future.

Many adults now still remember the shock and loneliness of wanting to go home and not being able to because of a legal authority higher than one's parent. Many of us remember that it was the perpetrator that was free to go and we were the ones to be locked behind steel doors with diamond criss cross peek holes and shaded glass windows so one could not look out and see the outside world and hear the voices of people freely walking outside the window.

One would think these things would go better. While it's true now that many a perpetrator is moved out of the home or arrested upon the complaint of a child, it is also true that many a child and/or adolescent is thrown out of their home at the same time, while clearly hearing the message, "Don't bother coming back home anymore." We still have much work to do, but some things have changed for the better even if it doesn't seem like it at times.

* * * * * * * * *

"In our healing we have the opportunity to help society heal as well."

Rapists

"How can we tell the difference between one rapist or another?"

I do not have to tell her that her life, as she once knew it, is forever changed. Since she is here, with her body and emotions assaulted, having been raped, and she is offering up the remains for evidence to catch the criminal, she knows this. My job is to help her, at this moment, get from point A to point B with as much of her sanity intact as possible.

I must remind her where she is so any triggering effects will be properly referenced to the hospital room and not a replay of the violation she has so recently experienced, only now presented as metal clinical invasiveness, intrusion and medical attack, and in the presence of us all.

She tells me, "He dressed nicely and smelled good and his shoes were shiny." Actually, she continues, "His uniform made him look impeccably good," a fact he used to beam his intended message, "I will protect you." He was addressed, "Yes, sir" and "No, sir" and "On the double, sir." His intellect was as huge as his presence, and it was no surprise he worked on matters labeled "Top Secret" and "Classified."

Some of the nicest men we know are rapists. When they are public figures and are identified for what they have done, i.e., rape (something that is becoming more frequent), not only do we have to provide resources for the healing of the victim, but that of society. Most rapes are committed by close family members, spouses, partners or acquaintances and society needs to start focusing on that truth and not the myth of its opposite: that most rapists are derelicts, homeless, uneducated or strangers.

* * * * * * * * *

"Trusting our intuition and being safe is better than worrying about what others will think and say."

"When is 'letting go' not running away?"

There are different ways of letting go— sometimes in organized order, or sometimes in random pack-it-ups. One may have to let go of something because it was stolen and will never be gained back, or if found again, will have been damaged and just doesn't feel the same.

Another way of letting go is to recognize that which you have in your possession is not what you thought it was. The gold jewelry necklace is really just gold-plated, and the anklet is not platinum, but simply shiny silver. Perhaps the relationship we are in is because of comfort and safety and not love.

And then there is the letting go because we know that do to so is in our best interests, either because of health, welfare, or for other necessary matters of survival.

We survivors frequently have to sort through such gradations, often wondering what our motives are. Are we letting go because we should let go? Are we letting go because we just don't care anymore? Are we letting go because it is the way for us to take the next step in our lives, be it a relationship, a job, a house, a car, etc.?

"Letting go" decisions often start on our subconscious level, and when important enough for the change to take place, begin agitation in our consciousness until we make the adjustments needed to be in balance.

Letting go can be one of the most life-affirming decisions we can make. It speaks of trust, faith, and more importantly an unshakable hope in ourselves that in letting go, we are moving forward, and in our journey that is our healing.

* * * * * * * * *

"Letting go' is often the first step in my healing"

"Why can't I get what I want?"

Poverty is not just about not having the means to attain material products. For survivors, it often means thinking we are unworthy and/or undeserving of receiving those things our hearts desire, that are not consumer goods.

In order to survive, we may have told ourselves not to expect anything from anybody, and not to want anything from anybody, including our own selves. If we didn't have expectations then we wouldn't be disappointed. If we didn't hope for a rescue from the awful situation we were in, then maybe we would find the means to escape ourselves; and if we couldn't escape we would learn to endure. But of course, we weren't able to escape until after the damage was done. Therefore, we set about fixing it as best we could, and now that we are healing, we may find that we are still impoverished in our thinking of what we deserve or don't deserve such as:

Poverty of mindfulness in:

Thinking

Trust

Love

Faith

Hope

Great Expectations

Reaching beyond one's grasp

Support from others

We are so deserving of all these things and more. Our healing can and does lead us to a richness of thinking, when we break through our defenses, risking whatever fear of entitlement that stands in our way.

* * * * * * * * *

"On this journey I am learning to receive what I want."

"Was it possible to have a day that didn't question her right to exist?"

She was tired of being different. She was tired of her illness. She was tired of feeling almost every day, with the exception of a few years betwixt thirty and forty, that each day Hamlet's question, "To be or not to be," was proposed to her by some part of her mind.

She would've thought that one day she would be free, sometimes even felt as if it were true. The old fears mostly were non-existent, and the ones that remained were manageable or easily dismissed as untruthful.

The absence of her fears allowed her to feel what her life was like, and she did not like it that it made no sense, that there were some important human connections she was missing. And she was pained that an intimate love life, which had been filled with work and a labor of love, now bore bitter fruits that withered to the ground.

She believed that the "Kingdom of the Spirit" dwelt somewhere in her soul and sometimes she felt and received its availability offered to her. But those visits were few and far between, and so she had also turned to nature as if the intimate social behavior of lions and wolves could help her explain the complexity of her emotions and love for a man she could no longer abide in her heart or share in her life.

At night, she reminded herself that the remains of incest was a war she had survived well, and while she still carried some scars of the many battles it presented, it seemed at times she felt she hadn't really survived anything at all. She also reminded herself that she was part of a grand plan of which she was blessed to have glimpsed occasionally throughout her life— even now, sometimes through the eyes of her children. There were many she knew that were happier and much better off than she, and there were many who were unhappier and worse off. Closing her eyes, returning to a corner that always held a vision of hope, she drifted off into her dreams for the restful sleep she needed to continue her journey seeking answers to her newest riddle of life: could she finally stop questioning her right to be?

* * * * * * * * *

"'To be or not to be' can be answered daily with a resounding 'yes'."

"What have I learned?"

Sometimes when I wonder about the value of my life, I think of my sisters who have walked before me. Or I think of my sisters living in the depths of despair, finding within themselves the strength to keep hoping and having faith that the world will present more goodness more times than it does evilness. And hoping that heinous acts committed against the less strong, downtrodden, discouraged and those that feel they can not be consoled, will see the light of justice and mercy in our time.

I know I am wiser now. I know that I can be hurt, and that short of death, I will live to mend and re-enter, again and again, the dance of life. The fact that I survived as I am is a triumph in itself. My life is no longer filled with nightmares from the past, and everyday no longer holds a flashback of something— a quick swish of movement to remind me of a slap nor does my body go into full anxiety mode at the sound of a cracking twig being stepped upon, reminding me that someone is chasing me and means me harm.

In the latter stages of my healing, it is not the remembered past acts of rape, assault and battery that is the hardest to survive. It is the living afterwards. Having faced the demons of my past, conquering them in fact, now means I live a life with no illusions; that I can now make a life for myself free of my fears, doubts and past history. It is this living of the new and healing way that occasionally makes me wonder, still, if my life is of any more value than that of a falling dried leaf in autumn as it drifts to the ground and completes its circle of life.

While full of wisdom from lessons finally learned, there are still those moments when my faith in "more" than just what I see, and my despair of humanity of ever reaching peace for just one day, is seemingly tested beyond my endurance. Nonetheless, I have learned that the present is indeed the only place one can be when choosing to journey this path of healing.

* * * * * * * * *

"One can stand on the ground of adversity
and still be in the midst of beauty."

"What is this thing called empowerment?"

Breaking the legacy of powerlessness may be our greatest challenge. Maneuvering through the world from a position of strength and power is to embody the "I am" in all its facets. It is to embrace who we are holistically. The secret of our empowerment is to accept ourselves totally. We may have weaknesses, but that doesn't make us "weak." We may have strengths, many of them, but that doesn't necessarily make us "strong." But, being able to recognize our weaknesses and being able to utilize our strengths to get what we want and need is to embrace our power within.

There is no shame in recognizing what we can not do. In fact, it is that process that allows us to do the so-called undoable. If we want an intimate relationship, free of the fears and defenses we have accumulated throughout the years, it is the recognition of our weaknesses that enables us to build our strengths. If we can not trust because we are fearful our partners will hurt us, it is in traveling such a fear that we overcome it so we can take the necessary steps to trust again.

A number of us are great sprint runners. We see danger and say, "Uh oh. I'm outa here." Works when there's real danger. But in truth, we go on about our daily lives; and most of the time the day ends without external danger, so our signals are no longer useful. But it is the learned fear response that once worked and is no longer needed which becomes our "weakness." It is the recognition of such bogus fear that is our strength. It impels us to move forward. And many of us are courageous enough to take the step to move into an area that may be excruciatingly uncomfortable for a short while, knowing from ours sisters around us, that such steps lead us to a path of empowerment. And life is like that, is it not? Circle round circle we travel, repeatedly touching the core of our souls with each peeling away of the impeding layers. Such is our power.

* * * * * * * * *

"I am so much more than I think I am."

November 1

GRATEFUL

Sometimes I think
I have so little
and then I think
of you
I am so grateful
to be alive

"What can I do when I feel overwhelmed by my inner children?"

There are times when we are so mentally anguished that we slip on the unexplored inner landscape of our mental discord. It is unknown terrain we wish to stay away from, and yet are compellingly drawn to; a terrain best visited with guides, lest we are unable to find our way out of this unexplored terrain. Too, many times it is the place where our inner children, or for some, alters, reside. Their needs during our healing will not be denied.

Though such inners of intense feeling may come into our lives with tremendous force, we can find ways to adapt, adjust and accept these parts of ourselves. We know during such moments, sometimes the best way to deal with it is to go with it. At other times, we just can not do that. We have lives to live and need to function in our everyday activities like our jobs, families and other external commitments. Functioning on multi-levels can be difficult to do even if one is not wrestling with mental leftovers from our personal histories of sexual assault, rape, molestation, or incest.

If we gently talk to our inner selves and to the clamoring voices of our inner children, we can leave the difficult corners of our minds and move on to the business at hand, which may include simply getting out of the bed and getting dressed. If we pay attention to our inner children and let them know that as soon as we take care of business in our outer world, we will come back and take care of the business within that they are trying to tell us about, then the angry, young inhabitants of our minds will not claim us with so much power, and can have the capability to help us through our day. And if we keep our promise to deal with the issues they wish to speak of, they can, in fact, make space so that we can address our issues and still work a life that has dependable and manageable routines for our many daily tasks.

* * * * * * * * *

"We can overcome obstacles when we are honest in our work of healing."

"How long will my rage be with me?

Inner Raging. A life form living in a space of our inner world that assaults many of us like any other assailant— unexpectedly, sneakily, and with no warning like the proverbial thief in the night...our night. And we are always so unprepared no matter how many times in the past we have warned ourselves against its possible invasion. Suddenly, we are caught up in our ranting, raging, and banging our heads against invisible walls (or not so invisible). We rage at the force of our own powerlessness, not understanding the making of our ingrained prison. Being our own cell guards, we do not unlock the bars surrounding our escape, and can not hear our unvoiced screams, only the voices of others. Two or three days spent with our inner rage is enough to know that something must be done. But what? Surrender to a Higher Power, a Merciful Spirit, or a Divine Creator that lives along with the inner rage. And what does that mean? Just that we don't know everything, that we don't know what's coming around the bend, that indeed life can, if we allow it, produce an ordinary miracle to occur in our everyday lives if we take a moment to breathe and remind ourselves during the raging.

We women who have histories of incest, child molestation, child rape, or any other sexual violation may find ourselves faltering in the face of this nameless rage that attacks us, this intimate enemy of ours, on every level of our lives— personally, spiritually, mentally, emotionally, and physically.

Our greatest hope and, indeed, our greatest triumph is that despite our lack of understanding of our inner rage, we continue to have faith that one day this leftover rage will recede, be removed and its taming is part of our journey. If we allow ourselves to be guided by the Spirit of Faith we may well replace our rage with other feelings of truth, beauty, and goodness which indwells our hearts and have carried us through times worse than the raging. Such faith in ourselves will lead us to a healing of empowerment over our rage that no longer serves a purpose in our lives now.

* * * * * * * * *

"I am more than just my rage."

"Who are the selves I do not know?"

Sometimes our thinking goes like this: "I don't know who I am. All the roadblocks are gone, all the defenses I erected came down, and now I am face-to-face with who I am, and I don't know myself at all. I thought if I got rid of all my monstrous fears, or even one or two of the most powerful ones, I could finally get going where I needed to go. Yet, when the defenses finally disappeared and some of them finally bowed out on their own, the person left behind in me is a stranger. Suddenly what had meaning was gone, and what was of value is no longer. People I thought I knew and loved are not, and those I thought knew and loved me are gone. This new path, tentatively welcome, makes me feel as if I were still a young child, with the day getting darker, and the way home, though familiar, feeling somewhat scary."

During our CSA, time may have seemed liked an eternal measurement of all that was going on within us. Then, we became adults and at some point began our recovery. So much of our healing was wrapped up in reliving the pain of the feelings and truth we hid deep inside. But we healed, and now we are older and time is no longer infinite, but rather a daily reminder of our mortality.

Complex as it is at the moment, this is our time to paint that "new" picture of life we always wanted. It is our chance to start over, and even better, we now have a drawing of where we've been and where we can go. True, we may not be as young as we would want to be; and we may know we have some weaknesses that will always be at our side, but at least we know what they are. More importantly, we know who we are.

* * * * * * * * *

"My paintbrush is calling me to my untouched canvas."

"How can I champion my own self?"

Morale termites tend to turn up at the worst times. Sometimes we don't even know they're there until a friend notices something out of whack and says, "Are you sure things are okay?" But most of the time we're on our own, and these little infested destructors are busy gnawing away at our ego form, busily chewing at our foundation until some part of ourselves we've always trusted to carry us through isn't there. Suddenly, we take a step, and we trip because we didn't see the damage that was being done to weaken the foundation as we went about our daily schedules, unmindful of anything calling from the inside for our attention.

When we are on a jagged mind-bender, it is then that we are made aware that these morale destructors are at work. When in our eyes nothing we do is right, and when in our minds nothing we hear is positive, we know that these bugs that snack inside the thresholds of our thinking must be removed. Unlike other situations, we can not bring in others to remove this annoyance. We must do it ourselves; we are the ones who have to patrol the borders of our consciousness to see that innocuous and untrue thoughts do not permeate and bed down in the crevices of our brain veins.

There's no magic to it, and it's a simple formula to defeat an old, but persistent, enemy from negative thinking. We must replace the old that doesn't work, with the new, which most of us have not tried. We must remind ourselves that we have goodness in our hearts, that we are lovable, that the things and goals we want to achieve are doable, and that since we are here, in this world, our lives were meant to be not only in pain and sorrow, but with goodness and love. There is no reason that ugliness and negativity should reign in our inner worlds with our consent— especially when we know the truth.

* * * * * * * * *

"'Seek you to know the truth, and the truth shall set you free.'"

"And who can love me and not hurt me?"

Will sometimes not forgiving keep us from moving forward in our lives? What is it to forgive what we consider a most heinous and unforgivable act? For many of us, "betrayal" and "abandonment" are the boundaries we draw on unforgiving; maybe anything else we consider forgivable.

Is there a standard, a list somewhere that says, "These things you should forgive, and these things you should not"? Or is it a place where, once again, only we can make those decisions for ourselves? Do we forgive the uncle that betrayed us? The father that abandoned us? The lover that left us? The friend that didn't want to be a friend anymore? The boss that didn't promote us? The children that turned their backs on us?

We survivors have difficulty laying down boundary lines. As women, we are culturally inculcated with the ability to forgive unstintingly. We sometimes see *only* the big picture, so we make for allowances and have hearts big enough to forgive the slights and the hurts and the misunderstandings, for a trade that allows us to be in relationships and have loved ones in our lives. We are not forgiving so much as making a trade.

There are no rules to forgiveness other than the old-time wisdom that one forgives when one tries, wants to and can. Like love, forgiveness is not something that can be forced. Our hearts must be big enough to accept others for what and who they are. Our minds must be wise enough to know which persons to let in and how deep the path they share with us will be. And forgiveness, like love, must be something we want to do. A big and gracious heart can do many things, but first and foremost, it must be true to itself.

* * * * * * * * *

"I will forgive when I am spiritually ready to do so—
no sooner, no later."

"Where was the Creator when this happened to me?"

"God lives within you," they say. "Oh yeah? Where?"

Some of us, and with good reason, don't believe in a God or a Goddess or to take it out of the spectrum of gender, Deity. How could we? What Holiness would allow such terrible things that go on in this world to happen to us...especially to children? What Righteous Being would allow such awful, ugly, and evil things to happen?

Perhaps a Deity whom has built into the body human— the ever-perfect, breathing physical machine— defense systems to withstand almost any horror; a defense system that shuts down the mind when it can no longer accept the reality of the violation offending against it; a defense system that assists in the disassociation of a mind from its soul, unable to bear witness to the iniquity being assaulted upon its physical inhabitant, and surely most egregious of all, a child's body. What is this inner bastion that allows no assailant beyond a certain point?

And where is this Deity, then, after the assault? After the war?

Is it the voice of the Deity that allows the wounded soul to move forward? What is this innate urge we have to push ourselves beyond our limits? The urge that won't accept annihilation without a fight? This urge to survive despite everything we know of ourselves and others? Despite everything we have gone through? This urge— does it come from us? Or, from the Spirit of the One within?

We who do not have the wherewithal to create the sky, the ground, the sun, the wind, the oceans, the stars and the moon...not even the lives we may carry within our stomachs without such a bestowal by a Deity are, nonetheless, the descendant beings of such a Divine Creator. Something is greater than ourselves or we would not have lived to tell it.

* * * * * * * * *

"In my heart, dare I find the Spirit of a Divine Creator?"

"Will I ever freely enter the world of loving sexual intimacy?"

Having survived sexual abuse and/or incest causes more than a little difficulty dealing with our sexual feelings. It may cause us trouble with owning feelings for an act that seemed to have brought on tremendous pain, and in some instances, pleasure, and left the pain imprint more than the pleasure imprint. In many instances, the imprint of both were left mixed in together. In an effort to deal with our psychic, tumultuous world, we may have chosen to disown these feelings, denying we have any sexual feelings at all.

We can, and we do, deny certain aspects of ourselves to adjust to daily living. Everyday living calls for constant juggling; sometimes even for suppression of many feelings towards many people. We don't go out and tell our bosses exactly how we feel about them if we don't like them. It just wouldn't help us as employees. Therefore, we make certain adjustments so that we can keep our jobs. We do not always have the same latitude and flexibility with our innermost feelings, of which our sexuality is one.

In our world of sexuality, this particular dance with life is wrought with potholes, is filled with trick mirrors, and is an area that, in the beginning of our healing, can cause us to be blindsided by the very feelings that ought to offer us pleasure of ultimate physical and emotional intimacy. We may, at the very same time, experience two opposing feelings with equal intensity— one of deep ecstasy surpassed by no pleasure we have ever felt on any level but a coupling. And the other? A self-loathing we experience on no other emotional level fills the cells of our bodies with memories of betrayal and repulsion.

In a perfect world, we would not be needing 20-something-plus stop signs all over our internal hemispheres, seeking to desperately protect ourselves from an act that has so many different and diverse meanings for all of us. Hence, we walk the path of healing, a road of challenges, contradictions, obstacles, confrontations, and if traveled with a deep trust in the ultimate goodness of ourselves, on a path of emotional, mental, and spiritual healing.

* * * * * * * * *

"Every experience presents a chance for the soul to grow."

"Is there an end in sight to this path I'm traveling on?"

Wouldn't it be great if during our healing we could shelve our feelings for a few days, or a few weeks and get back to them when we feel stronger, better, or more up to dealing with them? The thing about healing is that many times it is so inconvenient. Many of us have projects from our jobs and careers that need our full attention. Some of us have projects we have committed ourselves to in our communities or our churches. Others of us have one or more children that need every free moment of attention we can muster, and healing at these times just seems so impractical for everybody involved.

Dealing with our issues on our own schedules is wishful thinking on our parts, because we know that's not how it works. Once we begin to look at our lives— at the abuse and its effects upon ourselves and our loved ones— there is no turning back, and our healing is not based on an external timetable. In fact, it may be the external world that has kicked off our healing. Something happens on the job that triggers our memories; a child of ours may come to the age when we were first molested; or we get married. Some of us may have already been in therapy and we "stumble" across a forgotten incident as we pursue other issues.

Whether we are in the beginning of our healing journey or in the thick of it, we may feel that it is never going to end, and that we are stuck with feelings that are painful and disturbing. But the truth is nothing lasts forever, and when we heal, we let go of so many things that are no longer necessary or useful to us in our lives, especially our fears, anxieties, and phobias. To be free of these defenses is worth the pain of being born by the fire within. When we are in doubt about whether or not our healing is working, we need only check with our friends, loved ones, support resources, and most importantly, ourselves.

* * * * * * * * *

"When I lose my way, my Indwelling Spirit leads me ever forward."

"How do I get out of this frozen moment of time?"

If a poll were taken of survivors and our remembrances of the moment when the "die was cast" and we were trapped with our abuser, and if there was one defining moment that was outstanding of that experience, it would probably be the realization that clearly neither the cavalry or superman was coming to save the day. Our minds were filled with indescribable terror. In that moment, with our hearts banging wildly against our chest, and our ears sounding a roar like the crashing waves of the ocean, and because of the tremendous fear we embodied at the time, we retain a long-standing *memory of clarity of that singular moment of terror* for all time as we were checkmated from escape from the perpetrator.

Perhaps such an experience is forever branded and imprinted in our psyches, and perhaps it is this experience, this knowing of the reality of being over powered and at the mercy of another person, that becomes a constant and unwanted life guest in our minds, and played out in some way in our everyday lives. Sometimes it is disguised as procrastination, sometimes as sabotage, and sometimes as non-interest in our very own lives. But whatever its mask, it is sooner or later revealed as the inability to act either positively or negatively on behalf of our self; cogently put as being frozen in time.

How to unfreeze that part to move forward in our healing then becomes the question and the solution. We may not know the solution, but we do know that somewhere in our being lies the key to releasing this frozen part of our self. For as surely as we were once frozen in fear, we became unfrozen to do some things or we would not be here today. But, it is the unfreezing *to do what we want* that is at stake. It is an honorable and necessary battle, what with the flashbacks, body memories, and acceptance of what we survived. It is our spiritual birthright to make and live our life choices, and be free of fear, helplessness, powerlessness and terror on any level.

* * * * * * * * *

"I am the me fighting for my freedom."

"And now who's the saboteur?"

Why do we survivors sabotage ourselves? What happens when things are going in a good direction for us, when we are feeling pretty good about ourselves, that we become disconcerted and start feeling the tentacles of disenchantment in our lives? With our lives? What is it about us that allows the saboteur entry into that which we have spent so much time cultivating and nurturing? What is it that almost allows us to cave in to that which in reality has no strength except by our permission? *What is this disbelief that our healing is real?*

It is hard to break a lifelong habit. When we have for so long lived in a world that said we were undeserving of contentment, or unworthy of happiness for ourselves, it is difficult to remove the depths of such thinking and imprints, especially when we have been told by those who were to nurture us that we were, in fact, unworthy of nurturing. We took in their message and embraced the value judgment of no value as our own value.

In terms of mountain ranges that peak high and low, this is one of our difficult ones. Coming down the mountain can be just as difficult as climbing up. We just have to learn how to enjoy the achievement of having climbed the mountain and take in the success of our descent along the trails leading back to solid ground.

* * * * * * * * *

*"We can replace our need to sabotage
with a committed belief that our healing is real."*

"What does it mean that now, of all times, I feel a need to retreat?"

There are days we wish to speak with no one. Why should we? To what avail? Some days it seems that everyone wants a piece of us, and then there is nothing left for ourselves, and so we retreat, making ourselves unavailable.

Some days we are reminded of the pain that we left behind, that we have not quite exorcised from our minds. Sometimes we can not remove all traces of where we have been. And so we retreat. We need not falter so much during such a retreat. We need not give in totally and begin a descent totally into the netherworlds of our minds— one of those free-for-all falls.

During such times, we can remember that everything is temporary, even our feelings. If, for some reason, we see a need to retreat, it doesn't have to mean total withdrawal from the human race. It may seem like it at the time, but we need only remind ourselves that this is *now* and that was *then*. We can be kind to ourselves during this small hiatus. If somewhere in our psyche we are telling ourselves that we need a break from the outside world, during this time of our healing, we can be gentle and understanding with our souls. It really is okay to retreat every now and then regardless of the reasons.

* * * * * * * * *

"Today I will be as understanding with myself as I am with others."

"How come I'm not healing as fast as I want to?"

Experienced gardeners are well aware of the necessary processes for growth by nature. There is a basic premise that says, "Everything in its own time"; there is an old biblical proverb that says, "To everything there is a season." So it doesn't matter, and it doesn't pay to become impatient with time or to rail at the Gods and Goddesses that the seeds are not growing as fast the gardener would like, nor the petals blooming in a manner deemed by the gardener. An experienced gardener knows that a plant grows in season and according to the dictates of nature— no amount of rushing, pushing, hurrying up, or artificial means will produce the sustenance for the way a healthy plant needs to grow.

We, too, are like plants that must abide by the natural laws of nature. When we begin our healing and/or are in the thick of our healing journey, we can not force anything— memories, change of behavior, feelings— before its time. We can not make ourselves feel a certain way if we do not have that feeling; however, by honestly and mindfully exploring the issues that lead to certain feelings, we can certainly make progress from whatever is holding us back from progressing in our healing. We can not force a memory stored in our brain just because we think we are ready to deal with it. Certain parts of our repressed memories are hidden and stored for good reason, and they will become available to our conscious psyches when the body whole knows we are ready.

Changing our behavior to what we want it to be will happen in its own time. We have certain behaviors because they are what helped us survive, and while we are growing new, inner directions and expressions in changing, the way we move through our internal and external worlds must also be paced with our new selves that are being revealed as we shed old defenses.

* * * * * * * * *

"Old and surely true: Everything happens in its own time."

"Who will hear me now?"

Why is it that it seems whenever a Black woman addresses the sexual pain in her experience and community, there is an attempt to silence her? It happened when Ntozake Shange came out with *For Colored Girls Who Have Considered Suicide When the Rainbow is Enuf*; when Latoya Jackson came out with her autobiography; when Anita Hill testified before the judicial hearings on Clarence Thomas; and when Alice Walker wrote *The Color Purple*.

Communities of color, and in this instance, the African American community, are vociferous and uncompassionate in their reception, digestion, and rejection in response to women who speak out our truths of sexual abuse, incest, rape and assault. We women are vilified and/or denounced as men-haters, insane, jealous, and just plain wrong, as if none of the things we speak about ever happened to anyone. Conversely, when was the last time anybody ever heard of anyone accused of rape or incest say in public, "I'm sorry. I did it."

If 1 out of 3 girls experiences some type of sexual abuse, and 1 out of 6 boys experience some type of sexual abuse prior to the age of 18, then it's safe to say that they are representative of families in our country. Imagine the magnitude of such a crime upon the collective community of society and its families to experience a victim and a perpetrator in their personal histories in such large numbers.

As a society, we have a long way to go because of our collective denial. However, we are fortified, strengthened, and hopeful by the sheer numbers of women and men coming forward to tell their stories, to break the silence and begin a major shift in societal behavior. To break the silence is to shake off the shackles of shame, is to free ourselves, and in so doing, to free the next generation from the same experience and pain. We have survived a grave violation of personal experience, and we have truths to tell to ears willing to hear.

* * * * * * * * *

"'...and let it begin with me.'"

"When does the pain stop?"

Sometimes we can't fill up. Sometimes the depth of our pain is so deep it feels like trying to fill a hole as big as the ocean with a never-ending pouring of a glass of water. Sometimes our pain is so deep we think we shall drown in it in the next breath we take. In some ways we do. Some of us physically start choking for air because we can not breathe from all the thoughts rumbling around in our heads, rushing down into our chests, and drowning us with what we know and feel of our personal histories and how it plays out in our present lives.

Sometimes the pain is so deep and excruciating we stuff ourselves with food and drink and lovers, thinking if we can take in enough external things it will fill the empty, painful void that won't stop hurting.

Nothing goes on forever. We must remind ourselves during our healing, and especially at times like these, that the abuse is over, it is in the past and we have survived it. We are no longer the helpless and powerless children we were; and what we are experiencing now is healing, even if it causes us new kinds of pain— pain that seems that it will never end. But it does end. As long as we are open to honest healing, slowly and surely, the pain that stayed stuck deep inside us is released with each new risk we take to bring ourselves to balance. Each time we learn a new skill to fight the fears and anxieties and the panic attacks, we lessen the depth of our pain. Each time we risk trusting and loving a friend or a partner, we loosen the grip of the pain. And each time we take the risk to become more of who we are, we feel the pain lessen, until the pain becomes that which is natural to everyday living. We are survivors. We are victims no more, and we need not fear the change that will lead us into light of our healing.

* * * * * * * * *

"Nothing is forever including my pain."

"Why is my heart full of sorrow?"

Grief. Sorrow and sadness at the loss of someone important to us. Being a part of, and watching the process of having to separate from a loved one causes us grief. Sometimes it is because of our CSA that we are separated from those we love very much. A family member or close friend of the family molested many of us. We were shocked by what they did to us. Some of us were even disbelieving of what we went through at the time it was happening. And after it was all over we couldn't believe that such an act could have been perpetrated against us. All that really mattered was that we were betrayed by a loved and trusted person who held a very important relationship to us in our lives.

And of course, sometimes death is like that, too. Some of us are given the experience to witness one who is dying over time. It is not unlike the loss of our innocence in childhood. We were powerless in childhood to change events and we had no control over our lives. It is the same in death, only it's a bigger picture and yet, who we love is being taken away from us, is going away from us and we are helpless and powerless to stop it.

But unlike molestation, sexual assault and incest, death is a natural expectation for everyone and society supports our need to grieve the loss of our loved ones. Child sexual abuse, while quite common, is not a natural expectation, and so there is little support for the need of the survivor to grieve her losses— all of them. Some of us may not grieve these losses until we are in our 30s, 40s, 50s or 60s. Whenever we begin the process of healing, we also begin the process of grieving. This includes the recognition of many of our losses— our childhoods, our families of origin, our jobs, our career steps, our children, our spouses and partners. We may have suffered the loss of one or all of these because we are survivors. Fortunately, there is no statute of limitations on when we can begin to grieve for ourselves..

* * * * * * * * *

"And when she had shed the tears, her soul grew lighter within."

"Why are beginnings the hardest?"

Everything in our lives starts with one step at a time. Every endeavor, every enterprise, every new vision begins with a first step— and beginnings are the hardest. Sometimes even in taking that first step, we want to give up. Taking that first step can reveal to us everything that may be involved in attaining our goal, and such knowledge may be overwhelming...at first. We may immediately want to give up. Our minds are assailed with our inner doubts and those old memory tapes of our perpetrators. "You can't do that." "You'll never be able to do that." "Who do you think you are? Bitch. Prima Dona. Worthless excuse for a girl."

Sometimes the inner voices are not so strident and are voices we internalized. "You don't want to do that." "That's not what you really want." "Let's do something else." We can sometimes lose the stride of our visions simply by imagining their outcome, with ourselves, of course, at the helm and instead of success, we see failure.

Healing first steps can be quite awkward and reclaiming who we are takes time. It is not like the coal can not shine into a diamond. It is that it takes, sometimes, an enormous amount of time to see the first sparkle. And of course, one has to dig first to find the coal; one has to dig deep and labor before its discovery. And then one has to polish it to see the beginning glints of a shine. And one has to respect the underground mine one is working in. All of it encompassing time, gentleness, patience, sweat, energy and faith.

* * * * * * * * *

"Every successful beginning starts from its simplest point."

"How do I change into the woman I want to be?"

It is not hard to wish, to be like another person we see excelling in something we'd like to do, and to start castigating ourselves because we are not excelling like them. Some of us even begin a litany, telling ourselves, "I could do that if I weren't so scared...so dumb...so stupid...so untalented...so weak...or so ugly." All of it, the string of doubt-litanies, can go on ad nauseam. We forget, during these mind-doubt-boggling times, of where we've been and who we are. And we assail ourselves with outrageous expectations. We expect to speak with poise and grace in front of a large group of people, when many of us lost our voices at a young age. We expect to make love with our partners uninterrupted when, of course, our path to intimacy was violated by our perpetrators. We expect to take the risk of trusting our closest friends, when it was someone closest to us who first betrayed our trust.

It is not that we can not attain these goals, but rather, we need to use a different measuring stick. The person we wish we could be like is not the person who has been where we have been. It really does no good to compare ourselves to another. We may have all walked the same road, but in different shoes; some with no shoes at all.

When we honor where we have been, it is then, if we wish, that we can reclaim our voice. It is then that our most intimate times with our partners can become more intimate, and we can even take the risky step of disclosing some part of ourselves to our close friends.

These defenses we have designed to pilot ourselves through life are there with good reason. We can not just dismantle them magically. They may come down slowly, but they will come down because of the healing work we do. There is a part of ourselves that always remembers where we've been. We have trusted it thus far, and we can continue to trust it as we seek a healing for our lives.

* * * * * * * * *

"It is my Higher Self that I can completely trust."

"When will I get over this?"

Do some wounds ever heal? What happens when we think a wound has healed and then something outside of ourselves happens, something beyond our control, and suddenly we are once again facing an open wound instead of lumpy scar tissue?

The layers to our abandonment are many-folded, like tissues out of a box; how many are there before the box is empty? There is a first and lasting impression, imprint if you will, to all our experiences, hence our coined word "primal." Perhaps at the core of all our pain, abandonment has status of primacy. Admittedly, some may think it's a toss-up between "betrayal" and "abandonment," but perhaps they are sides of the same coin.

There is a difference between letting go of and abandoning a child. Even our perpetrators abandoned who we were, substituting instead their fantasies for our realities. Abandonment at its cruelest says we are not worthy of another's love and so we are left behind, and at its kindest, keeps us around and at the same time neglects us.

Those of us who have reclaimed our feelings know at the seat of all our feelings is an unrequited call of rage that is never answered by the chorus. For many of us, it is the last barrier to our wholeness, to our reclamation. To acknowledge it is to touch the acrid wound, to take its sting while its healing takes place. It is to acknowledge the wound of love lost.

There are no easy words, no short-cut paths, no soothing balms to stay the wild pain. There is, however, the knowledge that our sisters have gone before us and have healed. We know that others have gone through the fire and returned to the fold unscathed by the flames surrounding the heart. The heart will not rest until its powers extinguish the fires that burn within because of the wound. And it is only the heart that, in its innate wisdom, has the ability that in doing so heals us.

* * * * * * * * * *

"It is our hearts which reclaim our lost souls."

"What shall I do with this energy draining off my Spirit?"

And what shall I do with my rage? This unquenchable, raw, chaotic and fiendish feeling that cruises through my body without rhyme or reason to me? How to appease this monster of betrayal to my self-control? When this rage arises, I want to strike out, I want to destroy everything and everyone in my path and because I can't, it is difficult to focus on any task at hand, difficult not to stuff it back down and implode so that instead of my body expressing the rage I feel, I end up having headaches, or irritable bowel syndrome or sink into some dark, deep depression. Stuffing my rage or turning it against my body are not choices that help me heal.

Rage doesn't just pop up out of the blue, even if it seems to us to come from nowhere. We are simply not in touch with the real parts of ourselves that bring it screaming out of our mouths. Or, sometimes we're in a conversation with another person, and something that person says suddenly sets it off. We find ourselves holding back certain responses because we think it just wouldn't be appropriate to say what we're truly thinking and feeling and that our feelings of rage are so powerful, if expressed, it will destroy everything and everyone in its way. And so, we shove it back through the recesses in our mind.

If we are raging and at first think we can not connect it to anything, we have to think again. As survivors, we wholeheartedly believe in not giving up. Such a belief has kept us alive, our hearts pulsating and longing for that which is righteously ours— a fulfilling and joyful life. And we haven't gotten this far from running away from the truth.

What shall we do with our rage? Own it, embrace it, love it, and tame it. Once it carried us through the most perilous waters of our lives. Once it helped us to set things right. Once it helped us to move mountains out of our way. Now we must possess it, transforming it from an intense mix of angry feelings to expression of these feelings without harm to others or ourselves.

* * * * * * * * *

"And if I am patient, I can bring even my uncontrollable rage into balance."

"When will these intrusive thoughts and ghosts leave me alone?"

Can we ever have intimate moments with our lovers without intrusive thoughts? Can we have quiet, shared moments without the ghosts returning? Can we go to our spouses and partners in loving embrace, wrap our arms around them, and rest into their love without the old ugliness interfering? We can.

Nowhere are we more vulnerable then when we make love with a beloved. This would be so even if we did not have a personal history of sexual abuse. We just don't know it from our own experiences, but other men and women who have lived without the trauma of CSA are, too, at their most vulnerable when making love with their lovers. It is the nature and essence of true coupling. One must strip away, must put away, and must go through defenses we ordinarily hold up in other areas of our lives, to make love with another individual.

Intrusive thoughts have a way of making this difficult for some of us. They often come of their own accord. Just when we think we've laid it all to rest, when we think we have dispelled every mirror of our past experiences, we see and feel yet another reflection of what we do not want: a perpetrator's face image; a particular touch to our body reminding us of what a perp did and causing us to push away from our lovers; or a smell that brings back an unwanted scene, and the end result is our being left in pain, shame, and feelings of self-loathing in which we have no timetable as to when it will end.

It would help to remember that we need not brandish a clubbing iron or a loaded gun to rid ourselves of unwanted and intrusive thoughts and ghosts. Sometimes gently stepping back is what works. Sometimes waiting patiently for the intrusiveness to pass over and closing our inner doors temporarily to these unwanted marauders is the best way to address the panic that may arise from their presence. If we take the risk of trying new ways with our lovers in handling these intruders, we may find ourselves in unknown, but loving territory.

* * * * * * * * *

"Intruders have no real power— that is why they are called 'intruders.'"

"Is this an area I can heal?"

Sometimes it seems as if we can not allow ourselves to love unreservedly and without trepidation, our intimate partners who share our life. We often find ourselves holding back our deep emotions for this person even though at the same time, we ache to share all our life and our love with them. Not only is it puzzling to us, but even moreso to our partner. As a result, our love lives and relationships are often fraught with daily confusion, mistrust, misunderstandings and miscommunications. We may find that our perceptions about love are so skewered that it hugely interferes with our having a healthy and intimate loving relationship.

For instance, what others may *know* as loving and caring, we may see as possessing and controlling. If we are fortunate and truly have a loving partner who will be patient and ever-steady in their communications with us, we can bring our skewered visions back into a healthy focus. What we may see as the ultimate trap of being chained to another person, may in reality be the ultimate commitment— someone willing to travel with us wherever our healing leads us; someone who is unequivocally unafraid to say, "I love you, I'm here for you, and I support you."

When we were children, our trust was betrayed, many, by a presumably loving family member. But betrayal of love does not change our need for love. Love is love. Someone may attempt and actually pervert it; but then that wouldn't be love; that would be perversion. It is different now that we are adults, and so it is up to us to filter out that which bleeds through, that which leeches to our thoughts of the past, and that which blocks our thoughts of the present. If we have a significant other who loves us and is willing to commit to us, especially through our healing process, then it is worth the risk to love wholeheartedly that person and heal those feelings of mistrust, fear and doubt that would deprive us of a deserving loving relationship.

* * * * * * * * *

"I am not only capable of loving, I am deserving of it!"

"How can I tell the difference between an argument and abuse?"

Domestic violence never goes away by itself. We can not, if we are in a volatile relationship, sit back, cross our fingers and hope that our spouses or partners will somehow magically get better by our wishing or praying. More women have died by wishing and praying that their lovers would change their abusive behavior.

The abuse can be verbal, emotional, or physical. We seem to attract, quiet as it's kept, predators of the spirit. In psychological terms, we might say the ones we attract are obsessive-compulsive in their attachment to us. And any time their attachment to us is threatened, they act out. Or else, they are controllers wanting to control all that we do and say to their standards of what we should be for them. In the best possible light, these partners are fearful that we will reject them and abandon them, and so they seek to control everything, including us. In the worst situation, they are predators feeding off the energy we bring into the world, more specifically, their world.

There are signals they send out: possessiveness and jealousy of our time with others, cutting off relationships with our friends and families, a quick temper, stuck on female and male roles, testing with "light" hitting and shoving, use of drugs and alcohol. Some of these signals may be red flags that a couple is in trouble and need couples counseling. But, if all the signals are there then they are pointing to volatile living situations.

If any of us are in a violent relationship, we need to get out and need to get help for ourselves and our partners and especially if there are children involved, or we need to get help to get out of the relationship if we can not do it ourselves. Every major city has a domestic hotline. We can begin our healing by picking up a phone and calling someone there who knows the way out.

* * * * * * * * *

"I deserve to be treated with respect, dignity, and love."

"Why can't I be like others?"

We sometimes go down the road of, "If only," when we see others move at a pace that we would like to be moving; when we see others in intimate relationships with another; and when see others in families we wish we had. Going down this road is really only another way we rake ourselves over the coals. Of course, "if only" is a cruel, self-inflicted teaser.

And what is "jealousy" anyway? Those of us who have survived CSA missed some necessary developmental stages of human growth. We made a big, gigantic leap to maturity...because we had to. And now that we are dealing with our unfinished business, we have entered this new realm. What does it mean to suddenly start wishing we had what others have? What is it to wish that we could be like somebody else? Never mind the "grass is always greener on the other side."

All the shouldas, couldas, and wouldas won't make us the woman we are not. We can only be who we are, and for each and every one of us, that is a special, unique somebody. We can not use the measurements of others to gauge the distance we have separately traversed. No one else has traveled in our proverbial moccasins; no one else has carried that which we know intimately.

If we are to drop our jealous longings, we must fully embrace who we have become, regardless of whether who we are measures projective standards others put upon us. We are the only ones who can say, and who know, what we are capable of doing or not doing. All things are not equal, and it is unfair to judge ourselves by others who have not gone before us cloaked in our garments. Only we have worn these particular cloths of life. We do what we can, and like everybody else, we can and do strive for our best. But our best is not anybody else's. It is ours. We triumph when we recognize that we are who we are because of where we have been, and we have lived to tell it. We have done that with a little help from others, but mostly from ourselves.

* * * * * * * * *

"If I were meant to be someone else, that's the way it woulda been from jump-street!"

"Why can't there be the same sexual healing for everybody?"

We may ask ourselves, "Is there no end to the kaleidoscope of sexual healing?" Once we begin our healing journey, we can never return to who we were previously. We can not use those old defense systems, and can no longer find refuge in what we trade for reality and truth. In acknowledging where we have been on this journey, we no longer pretend the things that used to bother us, bother us no more.

Sometimes it seems as if we take two steps backwards for every one step forward. Having banished one flashback sometimes means a new one takes its place. Having rid ourselves of all the flashbacks sometimes means we must now create a new reality for the erased pain.

Sometimes we may share an intimate, sexual experience with our lovers, and it may seem as if all our demons have been vanished. We feel centered and complete in our relationship to ourselves and our lovers. Then, the next time, it's as if the previous experience did not happen at all; and though our inner landscape has changed, it's as if we don't know how to navigate the new marks. Our previous triumph seems pithy.

Living in the present means reassessing all new, incoming information with a different measuring stick. Every intimate encounter we have does not have to be met with silent (or for that matter, noisy) inner trumpets. Sometimes our sexual experiences are like all other parts of our lives: routine, humdrum, and par for the course. And sometimes they are exciting, renewing and rejuvenating experiences. And no matter how far we go or how many times we slip back, we are still the captains of our personal sailing ships. We can allow it to stray unguided by any input from ourselves, or we can set the course for bringing it back to our original path.

* * * * * * * * *

"Individuality and uniqueness are as prevalent in sexual healing as in any other healing."

"When will my sentence be over?"

Some of us think we can not do the things we really want to do, or pursue the dreams that burn in our hearts for fulfillment. It is as if these dreams and wants are locked behind prison bars and we, like visitors who love them dearly, can only peer through the bars, hands curled around a cold steeliness, and stare longingly at that which we love, wishing fervently it were free and we were with it.

We are judges without mercy, juries without compassion, and prison guards supremely doing our duty. We have sentenced that which we love away from the rest of our inner achievements and away from that which we can accomplish. We have decided that, for some reason, we must be punished, that somewhere along the line we have committed grievous sins and terrible acts. For what? Being alive? And so, we have arranged for our dreams and wants to be banished, to be locked and imprisoned.

Day in and day out we visit, hoping that someone else will free them. Unlike real prison, we are the gatekeepers to these dreams locked on the other side of the prison. Unlike real prison, we can free that which is a part of us and on the other side. And unlike real prisoners, we are, in truth, free to pursue that which we want and love.

* * * * * * * * *

"We are always free within our hearts."

"Why do I have to take medication to heal?"

Healing and recovering from trauma means that some substantial emotional pain will be encountered along the way. Some of us may need to take medications as a temporary tool in the healing of our emotional and mental health just as we may need medications for physical illnesses such diabetes or high blood pressure.

Proper use of medications prescribed by a physician to help us with depression or anxiety, or to aid in the chemical balance of our brains so we are not dictated by uncontrollable mood swings, can either be a temporary healing tool or a lifelong medical necessity.

However, there is the danger that some of us abuse our meds in the name of self-medication, doubling or tripling up on pills that tranquilize us and make us feel immune to all our anxieties and fears and rationalizing this behavior by saying we're taking the drugs so we can cope and make it through another day. Or, we stop using them prematurely because we feel better although we haven't fully addressed the underlying problems for which the medications were originally prescribed.

Abuse and misuse of these drugs may actually ward off the feelings that would lead us to healing. They would silence the indicators that tell us we must actually do something different to effect change in our lives and change that heals. Misuse of our medications may give us the false impression that we are healing when in fact we are only masking our true pain and fears with the drugs.

If we need drugs to help with an emotional or mental imbalance, then we are better off taking them under a physician's care rather than deciding when and how we will medicate our selves determining when and how they should be taken. To self-medicate or abuse our medications is to purposefully interfere with our healing.

* * * * * * * * *

"To heal purposefully sometimes means doing what we do not want to do."

"I wonder what it's like to be them?"

One does not have to travel in this life with an intimate partner. We can all be self-sufficient individuals if need be. We know of many women who spend the majority of their lifetime alone. Some out of conscious choice, and some because even though they want to, they can not find the one person they wish to share their lives with.

We who have partners, spouses, significant others, and key intimates and are healing from sexual abuse know that not only is the road rocky for ourselves— so it is for our beloveds. We know that when things get crazy for us, they also get crazy for our beloveds. Our loved ones are sometimes the only stabilizing force in an otherwise frequent stormy passage in our lives. They take our steps forward with us, and they step backwards with us. Even when we think we have healed certain issues, but leftover wounds reveal that they are not completely mended, our loved ones are there to experience those times with us. It is not easy for us. It is not easy for them.

Our problems are not always crisis-oriented. We are participants of everyday life, and so even with everyday life problems, we may experience things coming from our sexual abuse histories: distrust, paranoia, and isolation.

Healing is a package deal when we are in relationships. Both people are affected and there are no easy answers when a problem having to do with our healing arise between ourselves and our partners. Only when we are authentic in our communications with our beloveds can both of us move forward. We can dispel a doubt about the relationship our lover may have, take risks in our lovemaking to reach higher ground, and trust the actions of both our selves and our lovers so our love does not become static. This may mean daily renewing our commitment to our relationship, and to one another.

* * * * * * * * *

"Our relationship deserves commitment on both our parts."

"How is it that some of us did not die by the wayside?"

We who are healing have been given a second chance at life. Thousands of our sisters and brothers walk this earth and never get the chance to heal their lives. Some don't have the money, their human spirit has been thoroughly damaged, or they have simply given up on life. They may have chosen to go through life drugged in a daze, in an alcoholic fog, or just as human beings who believe life has nothing to offer them, and they have nothing to offer life and so they have numbed out. They are presented opportunity after opportunity to turn their lives around, and yet each and every time, they sabotage it. In turn, they never move beyond the "What if?" or "I could've been," or worse, "It's everybody else's fault my life is so messed up, and that's just the way it is."

But we who are healing have been given another gift of life. We have been given the gift to move our lives in the direction our hearts want us to move in. We are presented with one opportunity after another to move through our all-encompassing pain born of trauma, to heal and to find new dreams and new visions.

It is not necessary that our lives reflect this renewal in massive doses. It is not necessary that we heal drastically and lay our new foundation all at one time. Our healing, individual to each of us, takes time, takes small steps. We may have to continually remind ourselves of this, as taking the small steps may be something we become impatient with.

Our sexual trauma history may have placed us in a space where time was non-existent and we could not see anything but what we had become. We did not differentiate between what happened then and what is happening now. We could not bear to think of what the next day would bring. But we are healing. We are beginning to shed the cloak of the past. We are beginning to keep our feet firmly rooted in the present, no matter what quandaries beset our paths. And best of all, we are able to see and live in the present— our present.

* * * * * * *

"I have been given a another chance to live my life and I am blessed."

"Must I change it all by myself?

We can not change the whole world alone. If so, someone would have done it a very long time ago. But, we can change *our* world, and in fact, it is the only world we can change. No matter how bleak the outer world may look to us, the only changes we can make are those that happen and affect our world. This is not to say that when we feel moved to give of our time to a cause, an organization, or a person to make the world a better place, our efforts are hopeless or ineffectual. This is not to say that some leader (even one of us) can not effect change on a societal level. Look at Rosa Parks! But everyone who participates to make a great societal change does so on an individual level, and sometimes the results have a collective resonance.

Most change for survivors and to the world happens in the individual arena. Those of us with CSA histories know where some of the most profound changes must take place. We know that homes need to really be safe places for children. We know that schools and daycares need to be safe places for children. We know relatives and friends *we* trust need to be safe people for our children. We know that communities must be safe places for children to play and grow. We know that some of the most devastating abuses and some of the most unspeakable acts take place in those living arrangements that are supposed to be the safest.

If we try to fix all the problems of the world at one time, we will fix nothing, we will be unable to offer solutions; and we will be ineffective in helping to rid the problems of the world. But if we begin healthy change in our own individual lives, and in the lives of those we love and in our work and social lives, we can help tip the first domino for the rest of the dominoes to fall in place.

* * * * * * * * *

"The only person I can wholly change is me."

December 1

BLESSED

I have been blessed
many times with
"peace that surpasses all understanding"
and too,
I have been tossed
into the abyss
of the oceans
by tornadoes and storms
not knowing
if I would surface
again for air
peace be still
I am breathing

"Why is it we never seem to be on the same hill?"

It may seem at times that survivors end up with partners that seem to be "needy." Sometimes, much more needful of the survivor's energy and support than the survivor is that of her partner. But maybe not. Maybe survivors are so tuned-out to their feelings that it takes a relationship to see how distanced we are from our feelings as reflected by our partners.

Many partners say all they want to do is love us, and have a normal sexual, intimate relationship. Since sex was anything but "normal" and "intimate" for us, we may find ourselves questioning the love of our partners. To those of us to whom love never comes without strings, we want to know what they want in exchange for our love. No doubt, many of us think it is sex and sex only is the reason they want to be with us and the reason they love us. After all, why would anyone love us for any other reason?

Love and relationships are difficult for even those who are not survivors, the difference being that their perception is not clouded or violated by a history of sexual abuse. And we survivors are a suspicious lot, all the while questioning, and at the same time wanting to believe that when our lover says, "I really do love *you*," it really is true.

No one ever received loved by keeping only to herself. Love is reciprocal. Love is many layered and includes, by its very essence, trusting another being with yourself as much, if not more, as you trust yourself. And love in an intimate relationship without sex is a wound still waiting to be healed. To never have loved another at all is probably the worst legacy that CSA leaves behind. Knowing this and knowing how much we survivors long for a loving and intimate relationship with another person, it is worth the risk to trust in the Spirits of Truth and Love to help us on our healing journey.

* * * * * * * * *

"I am deserving of having an intimate and loving relationship."

"Where do all these inner critics come from?"

Self-hate is different than self-loathing. Actually, self-loathing tends to be spawned by self-hate. Self-hate is active, seeking, ever ready to pounce on the mind host. While self-loathing tends to have shame attached to it, self-hate is a party all its own, getting its energy from some hidden reservoir in the mind where the self does not know its location, only that it is there and appears frequently.

Self-hate is that part of ourselves internalizing all the doubts and fears we have for success in any area of our lives. We can't be good lovers, good spouses, good partners, good friends, good employees, good entrepreneurs, good parents, or good anything because of self-hate. And it is powerful, made more powerful than we know because many times it is quiet. A thought here, *Oh, you jerk*; and a thought there, *What an asshole. Who do you think you are?* is said ever so quietly in our minds as we go about trying to perform our daily tasks. We are never, never good enough in a self-hate mode.

We heal ourselves from self-hate the way we do everything else— with time, patience, and the *truth* of who we are. We confront it whenever it shows itself, and we say, "I am not stupid," or "I *can* do this." We confront it the way we do all our enemies— with the truth, our truth. We can even do like the kids, and throw out a hand to our side, close our eyes (or roll em' if you like), and with the hand stop signal say, "Poof— be gone."

* * * * * * * * *

"A daily act of self-love feeds my strength in healing."

"And how shall I survive the holidays?"

It seems that the holidays swoop into our lives in one big rush. Maybe it starts with the weather and the way the air smells that brings us memories of holidays gone by. It is the hustling of people hurrying off to parties, to homes, to gatherings to celebrate whatever holiday is here— Thanksgiving, Hanukkah, Christmas, Kwanzaa, New Year's Day. Looking at other faces, every emotion can be found— the delightful surprise, the momentary anguish of missing a loved one, the off-guard glance of saddened eyes, or the deep-felt joy of a child's twinkling eyes.

Sometimes we survivors seem besieged by the onset of these wintry days and its celebrations. While others seem to storm the stores and arm themselves with gifts and party knickknacks, we seek activities and caldecotts we can hideout in until the days pass, and we are once again transported back into regular time, of everyday routines and expectations. Sometimes we forget to dodge the celebrations, and suddenly find ourselves stuck right in the middle of the emotions we so desperately seek to escape.

We need not pretend to have feelings we do not have during this time. We do not have to be fake or hypocritical during a time that may not have very many happy memories for us. But neither do we have to be stuck with old habits and behaviors. The holidays are best survived by honoring whatever feelings and thoughts we may have, regardless if they are contrary to holiday cards and party themes. We need only participate at whatever level we can, if we can. We do not have to pretend anymore for any one that it is a day we wish to celebrate, including ourselves.

* * * * * * * * *

"Taking care of myself during the holidays is a sure sign of my healing."

"When will I believe in myself?"

The "Midas Touch" is a story that has evolved so that in modern day history it means that someone realized that no matter what was going on with everybody else, they got their heart's desire. They saw something they wanted, planned, organized and worked for it, and in a space of time, idea became reality. And it was a pattern that repeated itself again and again and ergo whatever they touched, turned to "gold",

We survivors are good at, well, surviving. Give us a crisis or a deadline and we are, indeed, Joanna on the spot. We get the job done and we multi-task and have everything completed on time and not a second late. Or else, we do the impossible for an organization, a group and agency, or another person. We meet the expectations of others, all the while ignoring the voice inside of ourselves saying, *"Hey, what about me? What about what I want?"*

It is no secret that our personal histories have lent us to this way of being. But it doesn't always have to be like this. We do not always have to make ourselves last, to make ourselves less than others. We don't have to wait until somebody else says it's okay to be who we are. We only have to give the go-ahead to ourselves. We are the ones who give permission to ourselves, to our wants and dreams. We are the ones to make the plans for ourselves, organize for ourselves, and work towards what we want for ourselves, as hard and energetically as we do for others. It's called believing in one's self. We start to believe in ourselves at any moment we choose, at any time we wish, to move forward in our journey of healing.

* * * * * * * * *

"Believing in myself allows others to believe in me as well."

"Why do these unrelenting thoughts beat about my head?"

It's always the same. No matter how we may try to orchestrate it, the plot has been written, the die is cast, and the hero stands alone in the end.

As many as there are of us in this collective war, there are some battles that only we can fight for ourselves. The ones that count so much— the ones that call for courage...for bravery...for consent to continue on another day...for resurrection of untapped life forces buried deep within to fight one more battle for one more day— those are the fights that we battle single-handedly. It is here that each of us faces our she-monsters derived from our very own perpetrators.

We gather strength from one another, for it is our sister travelers that give us strength. It is the ones who have gone before us that forge the path that we must all individually journey. It is our sisters who remind us that there is a reservoir of strength within the soul worthy to take on any and all residue when we think we can not take another step. It is their wisdom that gives us the strength to say to our own demons, "I can do this," and that indeed we do whatever it is we think we can not do and the victory is ours. Our triumphs seldom come with accolades and brass trumpeters. They are often quietly won in the deep, deep recesses of our minds and souls. And though none other are the wiser, we know where we have been, all that was at stake, and that the battle fought and won was from an unassailable place from our souls.

* * * * * * * * *

"I will never give up on me again."

"And how many steps forward and how many steps backward?"

We have traveled this road a long time, some of us. And some of us are just starting on our path of healing. Nonetheless, in one sense, it is all the same. We wonder when it will, if it will, be behind us, and when we will be able to "get to living our lives."

A balanced life seems like a worthy goal, where all parts of us are in harmony: spiritually, mentally, physically, and emotionally. Regardless of where we are on the healing path, we seem to always be balancing these parts of ourselves, some with much success, and others nothing, as if each day we were writing from a clean slate.

There is no magic to healing. One does not wake up one day and say, "Oh. Now I am healed. Now I can get on with it." Actually, one wakes up and deals with the emotions that are occupying our bodies at the time. For some of us, it is the constant companion of fear and/or anxiety. For others, it is indignant anger and righteous rage. And for some of us it is the simple feelings of joy, a knowing that all things change and that we are up to the task that life presents to us.

Too, there are no shortcuts to healing no matter how much we wish we could heal faster then the time needed to do what we must do. We eventually all come to the conclusion that it is up to us, that indeed, the answers are within us, and we do have access to them if only we will seek them out and follow the path that leads us to our healing. There are no time limits, and it matters not what is going on in our lives at the time. It all comes back to us and to our own realizations that we are the ones to allow the healing of our wounds. Others that have gone on before us have done so, and so are others clearly doing it in the present. We need only commit to ourselves that we, too, can join the ranks of those that walked the path before us, healing as they do.

* * * * * * * * *

"I am entitled to the healing of my soul."

"Could this be the day I rid myself of my old nemesis?"

Survivor issues sometimes just seem never-ending. Waking up some mornings can be like waking up to a friend you know is in deep trouble. Lillian Smith once wrote, "The human heart does not stay away too long from that which hurts it most. There is a return journey to anguish that few of us are released from making."

When do we, as survivors, make peace with ourselves and our histories? When do we finally accept the past as it was? As it is now? Because surely making peace means we move forward in our lives, we live our lives, and for some of us, it even means "getting a life."

We make peace with ourselves when the wounds are healing. When we have looked boldly at what was done to us and how it continues to affect the lives we live in the present, we take action to change our lives the way we want them to be. It's hard work at times and it's okay to take time out, but we don't ever give up no matter how bad it gets.

We do not have to do this alone. Daily, groups are springing up to address this health epidemic, this hideous phenomena of the sexual abuse of children. Daily, women who are living the after effects of such a life are saying, "No more." If we can not afford counseling, there are community groups that offer sliding scales, some no fees at all. There are numerous self-help books written by others who have healed and who offer hope to those just beginning to heal, and those needing to know they are not alone. There are 12-step programs specifically for sexual abuse survivors.

We are adults now. We make our own choices for healing or not. Like the day of the emancipation of slaves in American society, we became free and a new day dawned, and now we have new lives to forge; now we have reasons for hope that no one and nothing can ever take from us again.

* * * * * * * * *

"This day is my 'Great getn' up in the Mornin' day."

"When will my changes come?"

Part of the survival defenses of sexual abuse survivors is to discount the things that have happened to us, minimizing what happened to us, saying, "Oh, it was only once," or "It didn't really hurt," or "I'm a really strong person. Nothing bothers me." Later, when we seek to make changes in our lives, we may find that this discounting is something we do so habitually that it is one of our most difficult defensive enemies to overcome.

Often our progress comes in small steps, in small actions, in minute changes of thinking, and our discounting and/or minimizing may block our recognizing when we are making progress. If yesterday, we were petrified to look in another person's eyes (something we have always been afraid to do), but today, we take the chance to look into another's eyes, then even if in the next hour we feel we can't look in the same person's eyes again, that first movement was progress. That one shift in our behavior may have released us to risk taking that step again at another time and so we shift not only our external actions, but our internal thoughts and feelings as well.

When we think one thing, but say another thing instead and then wonder to ourselves, "Where'd that come from?" it may just be one of the times some of our inner kids are struggling to be heard, and the grown-up us is not in charge.

When we make the commitment to change and heal our lives, the grown-up gets to be the adult for real— that grown-up gets to take care of "business," to take care of the wounded child/ren within and get our lives on the tracks we choose to ride. So when we change a given behavior, like not looking at people in the eyes to looking into their eyes every now and then, even if we think it doesn't make a difference, the truth is that every *little* step that we take, no matter how seemingly insignificant in our eyes, is progress.

* * * * * * * * *

"Every movement, no matter how small, counts!"

"Why do I have to keep this secret?"

Probably no one stays longer in therapy than survivors of CSA. For those who want substantial change in their lives, at some point it may be necessary to seek help from a professional. There are some folks that do it alone— explore their issues, make progress; but almost everyone has to connect to another person, intensely, to bring about the changes that will eradicate some of the legacy of sexual abuse such as distrust, inability to make commitments, sharing one's thoughts and self, and connecting deeply with others. Often, when we seek to break the cycle of this legacy, we find ourselves in the therapeutic milieu: individual therapy, group counseling, 12-step programs, hotlines, etc.

When a survivor connects with a therapist, there is probably no other voice more influential in that survivor's life than the therapist. Therefore, the process becomes intense, and it seems to so many participants to be the guiding post in our lives and the therapist holds a special place in survivors' lives.

It is in therapy that survivors may finally come out of hiding. It is in therapy that survivors may, for the first time, trust somebody else with their thoughts and feelings, and with their inner kids or their other identity parts. It may only be in therapy where a survivor will say for the first time, in fact, may be the only place where she says, "This is *who* I really am; this is what *I* really think; please don't hurt me." It is in therapy that the survivor may, for the first time, believe someone actually *wants* to listen and hear what she has to say. In the world of the silence of a survivor, self-imposed and otherwise, it is a gift to have someone who can both listen and help us on our journey. Therapy can be one of the greatest gifts we give to ourselves for our healing.

* * * * * * * * *

"Therapy is not for weaklings."

Locked Up

"Who will come for me now?"

Some of us know what it's like to be a child who is locked up, to be closeted up, to be tied up, tied down, to have our movements restricted, to have nowhere to go while our minds scream for freedom. With our little minds, we thought we could escape, we could break loose, we could run away and no one could see us, no one could hurt us, no one could come with a switch to bring us back. Sometimes we would just hide ourselves in a ball, roll ourselves up and just wait until we were free, however long it took.

We were so happy to be free from the pain of being tied up with ropes, or clotheslines that it didn't matter what we did next. In fact, we may have done nothing. We may have just gone off and sat in a corner staring off into outer space, waiting for our lives to begin again by the command of some adult voice.

Unfortunately, even when we grow up many of us internally carry the voices that said we couldn't do anything or go anywhere, for these imprints and conditioning are not easy to break: these invisible ropes, these invisible chains, and these invisible jails that we carry into our present.

Some days we feel it strongly and deeply in our core being, and it feels as if we are locked up all over again, as if the progressive steps we have made in our lives have never happened, that the personal goals we thought we achieved have never been reached, and that tasks we have set for ourselves have not been completed. This is not true. So here's a contradiction we may need to live with every now and then during our healing: "Some days it is enough to say, "I have survived." At different points in our journey with its many intense memories, flashbacks and other emotions we experience in our healing, a difficult day in acknowledging to ourselves we have survived and are free *is* good enough for the day. It does not mean we are back to square one and locked up again. We are here and we are free.

* * * * * * * * *

"I can learn to bend like the great, awesome Willow trees."

"How honestly am I willing to look at the truth of my life?"

How many of us are willing to be truly open and honest when confronting one of the biggest boogiemen of our psyches? For instance, how many can accept the truth that our mothers and/or fathers did not love us? How many can look that in the face and consider that healing? Forget the buzzwords and psychobabble talk of "abandonment" and "trust" issues. If a parent knows their child is being sexually abused but pretends or denies it is happening and consequently leaves the child unprotected, then clearly that is not love. Parental love inexorably includes the duty and responsibility of making sure your children's safety in life is a priority.

Many survivors have parents that knew their children were being sexually abused but chose to deny it, ignore it or minimize it. Perhaps what is worst is that many of the parents themselves were the perpetrators to their children

Nonetheless, what some of us are willing to say is this: "In their own way, they loved me." or, "They loved me as best they could given their life circumstances." And in some, cases this *is* really true. Many survivors have a deep capacity to love and how can one give love when one has not received love? Perhaps this is one of the biggest contradictions in healing from CSA. While some parents are incapable of loving their children enough to save them from being abused, they show their children love in other ways.

This is where we survivors break the cycle. When we are committed to healing, we release the tenuous hold we have on life and replace it with an energy that returns that which we seek— self-acceptance and self-love— so that it becomes the legacy we take joy in passing on to our children, and simultaneously breaks the cyclic chains of child abuse in our families.

* * * * * * * * *

"I am my own liberator."

"How Do I Do this?"

Then there is Pavlov's theory: if you chain a dog to a tree long enough, once you remove the chains, the dog will still not stray far away from the boundaries of where the chains used to stop. Or, the other older story that says if you cage up a bird long enough, when you leave the cage door open, it will not fly out. There are times, as we heal, that we too act like those who have been chained and caged up. We have no concept of what it means to be free, and during the healing of our wounds, we may find this particular obstacle in our path. We may find that we, too, like the unchained dog and the cageless bird, do not know where to move with our newfound freedom.

Moving in freedom is a difficult thing to learn how to do. Part of the truth of this is that during different stages of our healing, we are often in psyche pain. Emotionally, mentally, and spiritually, we are at a loss and plenty of times confused. Often, our lives may come to a standstill, a place where we do not want to be and yet, do not know how to get out of the situation.

Learning to respond to what "we want" and being emotionally free of our sexual abuse histories is a new experience. Making choices for what "we want" is a new experience. Doing for ourselves because "we want" is so different from our personal history reference points, that when we have attained the freedom to do so, it may be more difficult than other obstacles we have had to overcome. No matter how long it takes to get through to our core selves, there is one thing we can eventually know and own: We have the inalienable right to choose what "we want," to do, to follow our dreams, and to express our creativity that has so long been denied to us by others and ourselves, especially now that we are in charge of our own lives.

* * * * * * * * *

"Everything I do starts with one step at a time."

"Why should I cry?"

We know that crying is an expression of our sadness or our pain. Sometimes, it can be tears of happiness, but mostly, it expresses our hurt. So many of us do not cry. It may even be that our decision to not cry was a noble one. Who else could protect that little girl of ours who was always getting hurt? What better way to protect her than to not let her feel the pain? Not to express the hurt by cutting off the tears? No tears, no pain.

It's too high a price. We begin a journey where that little girl, still stuck in the past, yearns to release the pain, yearns to let her eyes cry, yearns to be whole again, to grieve that which was recklessly taken, so thoughtlessly stolen.

If we haven't done something in a long time, we may forget how to do it. All this means is that we have to learn to do it again. We learn how to cry again. We find the part of ourselves that *knows* that it is safe to cry now; it is now okay to express the pain; it is now okay for that part of our life to be open to our feelings, to open ourselves to our deeply buried and hidden feelings of sadness, sorrow and grief. We know, if by nothing else but time, we can take care of ourselves. And now we have the time to give ourselves that long-deprived permission to "let go and be."

* * * * * * * * *

"A good cry starts with one tear drop, and can touch the ocean of our souls."

"Who said, 'It is better to know the truth?'"

When nothing is working in our lives, why are we the last to know we need help?

Dysfunction means that something that is supposed to function in a certain way is not working according to design and plans; the application works, but the system is not programmed to work for newer versions. Knowing this, we still try to apply old ways to new problems. We try to use old defenses that no longer work in a healing life. At best, we are surprised that something does not work; at worst, we can not progress in our lives, can not attain the goals we set for ourselves, because we have not found a way to adjust our defenses to protect us in our new reality.

It is all too easy to give in, and all so seductive to give up, to raise up our arms, to shrug our shoulders and say, "There's nothing I can do. Nothing's ever going to change, and that's just the way I am; this is the way my life is."

The truth is that each new day, we are offered a new opportunity to make a desire, a wish, a dream, a longing or a yearning, a reality. But it is only when we step into reality and acknowledge what we need to do, that we can then lay a foundation to begin our work to do it. Otherwise, we can fool as many people as we want. It is one of the ways we survived: People ask, "How are you?" and we say, "Oh, fine." However, it is our inner selves we can not fool. We can not fool that part of our heart that says, "I want to know the truth of where I've been so I can live my truth now."

* * * * * * * * *

"It takes more energy to lie than to tell the truth."

"Why is it taking so long to heal?"

Healing seems to take forever. Some of us have been working on the same issue for years, and we are tired of it. We are tired of the roller coaster ride; we are tired of getting our hopes up when we think we see the light at the end of the tunnel, and of plummeting into the depths of despair because reaching that light begins to seem like an impossible task.

For some of us, these feelings of up and down rage on for days. For others, it may be either hope or despair that rages on for days, leaving us spent and foggy, as we pick ourselves up to continue to face our lives and the battles to be won...or not.

We can take solace and refuge in knowing that other survivors have walked before us, have lived before us, and have tapped into the desires of their hearts. They have tapped the longings of their souls, the fears of their hearts and piloted their thoughts to have their dreams come true— freedom from the tyranny and fear that we all experience as survivors. What we forget is how much courage, patience and faith it takes them, and consequently us, to put one foot forward in front of the other on a daily basis as we seek to recover from our past CSA histories. We need to remember that one of the most important factors in our healing is an unmovable, unshakable, unquestionable commitment to ourselves and to our healing, no matter how long it takes.

* * * * * * * * *

"I will have a healing for myself."

"How can I make my today different?"

Today I will make me a new day.

When I get out of bed and my muscles are heavy with the burden of last night's demons, I will say, "Nope. Not today. You must go away and move along without me today."

As I brush my teeth and look in the mirror, and critical thoughts come which tell me "I'm ugly, I can't do anything right, and that I have no right to exist, to take up space upon the planet," I will say, "Nope. Not today."

If, as I move around, a dark shadow is cast and I catch it from the corner of my eyes, and memory threatens its presence, rearing its ugly and painful head, I will say, "Nope. Not today."

As I mingle with other people, and one of them says something, and a flashback threatens to become cinematic in my mind, I will say, "Nope. Not today."

Today I will give me a break. When it seems as if all my efforts will be blown out the window along with the dust particles that permeate the rooms of my mind, I shall take a warm, saltwater bath, submerge my body and thoughtfully say, "Nope. Not today."

I will act as if I'm not afraid of everything; I will act as if I have healed, as if the worst is over, and everything else that comes up is an afterthought. Today I will dismiss my fears, disengage my anger, placate my anxieties, stow away my panic attacks, and will move smoothly throughout the world as if I trust myself so wholeheartedly that I know where I am going.

I will act as if I were deserving of just one of my heart's most secret wishes— that I am glad that I am alive and have everything to live for— if just for today.

* * * * * * * * *

"Today I am glad to be me."

"Can I be a twosome?"

We are, some of us, disturbed by our seeming incapacity to have intimate relationships. Even those of us in long-term relationships frequently question whether we can continue to be with our partners after some argument or long-standing disagreement comes up for discussion. So much emotional turmoil comes up that it seems easier to throw it all aside and, instead, move into old securities with our need to be alone, away from intimacy and closeness. Such intimacy and closeness would be threatening to our sense of self-protection, would threaten to trigger all those reasons we shut down for not being close and intimate. We enter relationships over and over again, hoping this time things will be different, hoping this time our sexual abuse past will not be an impeding presence, or interfere in our personal happiness and in our ability to find love with another person.

We are pained by our inability to move forward, and we want to give up. If heartfelt yearnings came true just by wishing, then all we'd have to do is close our eyes tight, click our heels, make a wish, and immediately we could have relationships without all our abuse baggage being opened up during close intimate times with our lovers.

It is has been proven over and again that those of us who are brave enough to look at our sexual abuse histories, those of us who will take the risk and summon the courage to walk through our valleys of memories, and those of us who will commit totally to our healing, can have intimate relationships. We are not hostages to our abusive pasts. We are really truth-seekers to our deepest emotional wells of healing, of which love is definitely included.

* * * * * * * * *

"Courage always has fear as a companion."

"Who is this child that keeps following me?"

Based on our timing of healing, she comes of her own accord...laughing at us, holding us in contempt, and fervently hoping we will look at the "real" truth of our lives, as if she knows a secret we do not. She is right. She keeps all our secrets. She knows where we have been and who we have been with. Now, she will not let us run. Now, she will not be quiet. Now, she wishes us to know of our rage and pain, and wants us to own it all so she no longer has to stand at the doors of our hearts by herself. She wants only our fullest embracement.

There are times during our abuse that in order to survive, we have had to cut off part of ourselves to continue to maintain or to move forward in daily activities. We could not afford to keep what *she* knew in our conscious thoughts, and so we buried her along with those thoughts and memories. Buried her for good, we thought, until we began our healing.

Much as we may think so, she is not our enemy. Though she appears to bring us bad news, what she actually brings us is wholesomeness and balance to our everyday living. If and when we embrace her, we reclaim that part we thought had died when a part of us had been pierced and we couldn't stand the pain. It was unthinkable, some of the things that were done to us, and so we followed suit and didn't think of it at all afterwards. Some of us even created new "us-es" so we could go on.

We can go on further if we are willing to risk listening to her, to her voice, to her memories, and listening to that part of us she carries like a two-edged sword with laser beam precision to appear whenever she feels we are threatened which, during our healing, is almost always. We are adults. Unlike her, we can reason, comprehend, and understand now; and that is what we can give her. She can give us back the depth of our feelings implanted so that we might feel deeply the joy, love, and goodness of our lives, as was intended the day we were born.

* * * * * * * * *

"I can and will embrace my little girl."

"What and who do I want?"

Sexuality is purportedly one of the areas where we are most vulnerable with ourselves and with others. Some of us want to be with women or we want to be with men. Then there are those of us who want to be with both men and women. And then, there are those of us who aren't sure, who question who we are in the sex arena.

If we choose to be with men, and yet have so many sexual problems with them, does this then mean we shouldn't be with them? Does this mean that we should have women as partners? Others of us who are with women and are experiencing intimacy and sexual difficulties, may begin to question whether we shouldn't be with men. For many people, and all things being equal, these choices are made or known in adolescence and sometimes even at the early age of 5-years old or earlier. A person may feel a strong preference for one sex or the other; they may not even consider it a choice, but an attraction they are naturally and biologically drawn to. For those of us with CSA histories, we may suppress all our sexual feelings until later in our adult lives, and then find we are stuck in adolescent identity choices and don't know what we feel towards either sex. We didn't have time, opportunity, or energy to enter the realm of making choices in relationships and develop sexual identities of our choice.

Society stresses that we make heterosexual choices and simultaneously sends out the signal that same sex choice partners are not the desirable ones. While slow, this message is changing for societal acceptance of choice with same sex couples having the same rights and recognition as heterosexuals, including marriage. This can be a supportive boost for those of us wishing to or who have made same sex choices for intimate relationships.

Truth be told, there is no wrong or right decision in these choices, but only that the choice we make is the one we want and not the one we feel pressured to make, whether it be from society or from our own inner fears. We will learn nothing nor heal in this area, unless we are willing to look honestly at our inner landscapes, trust ourselves and make our own choices.

* * * * * * * * *

"What is of value and has meaning is that I am true to me and the person I am in relationship with."

"Am I crazy or what?"

How do we decide if we are crazy or not? When we survivors are growing up and a perp decides to target us and forever change our lives, we think we are very different from everybody else, especially not knowing that many children experience what we do, unbeknownst to us. We carry this belief that "Something's very wrong with me." We feel there must be, or else, why would we have been chosen for the abuse?

When we begin our healing from this abuse, we find it necessary to revisit the memories in our minds that causes us the present pain in our lives. We begin traveling in that time again; and our emotions and expressions from the abuse are finally allowed to come out in a healthy manner. Such an experience could lead us to think that we are going "crazy." After all, how sane can it be, we say to ourselves, for a grown person in their 20s, 30s, 40s, etc., to be acting in their emotional lives as if they are 3, 4, 6, 12 or 15 years old? Insanity is thinking that we can not change, that the past has forever stymied us into emotional and mental deficient being. Insanity's thinking that the perpetrator was right all along, that something is wrong with us, and deserve what we got and we'll never be free.

It is a sane act to find a defense that will protect us from our reality when we are powerless and helpless; our feelings must go someplace. If we have been attacked on almost a daily basis, weekly basis, yearly basis, whatever the time schedule, it is only sane that we find an escape in the inner-mazes of our minds. And it is a sane thing to do, when we are enabled to empower ourselves and reclaim ourselves to step into our pasts and confront the very things that make us feel so crazy in our adult world, even if it means reliving an experience, going through flashbacks, or doing things that make us question our sanity, while all along, we are healthily bringing ourselves back into balance.

* * * * * * * * *

"Sanity means I can change if I want to."

"What's real and what isn't in my memories of the abuse?

"False memory" is a phrase coined by an organization made up of parents who are in deep denial that they perpetrated sexual abuse against their children. It is an organization that continues to protect the perpetrator, while denying the truths of the survivor.

Unlike these deluded parents, survivors are willing to travel a road that requires them to honestly, sometimes brutally, examine their thoughts and feelings towards what has happened to them. And while false memory people are willing to deny, survivors are willing to accept the truth, since that actually is the path we are walking— learning and living the truths of our lives.

We do not always know what is real or what is not real when memories come up that we've forgotten. We can be in the midst of experiencing all sorts of emotions and call into question if the emotion, itself, is real. We are the first ones to doubt what we have experienced. Who wants to believe that a trusted caregiver would harm us in a sexual manner? Who wants to believe that a parent will sneak into your bedroom in the middle of the night to fondle or rape you when you are a child? Who wants to believe that all manner of abuse can go on in our own households with the outside world never the wiser? And who wants to believe that there is an area in our lives where we can be terrified into silence? Where our only salvation is that we will be able to endure it all until we are independent and away from any contact with the abuser?

Here's what we survivors can do while seeking to heal from sexual abuse: Trust all memories that come up. In time, we will learn what is real and what is not real, for that is the nature of life and the seeking of truth. Here's another truth to know: While statistically, we know hundreds of thousands of children are sexually abused, the confessions of the perpetrators are few, if any.

* * * * * * * * *

"I will not allow any organization or person to deny my truth."

"Must I live this life?"

Suicide, though often talked about, is still taboo. It is a subject not to be taken seriously unless in the event of a real suicide. Otherwise, those that consider suicide as a solution to their problems are considered merely to be "just talking"; and sometimes they are categorized as "just wanting attention."

Discussing suicide amongst survivors is a two-edged sword. It is necessary that we speak of our feelings and thoughts. The danger is that we often confuse thoughts with feelings. We feel extremely depressed about something, a matter that leads us to feeling despair, and what we say is, "I feel suicidal." It would be more helpful and truthful for us to say, "I feel so badly that I am having suicidal *thoughts*."

Some of us may become fearful of the power of our own thoughts. "I don't want to explore that or look at that 'cause I might kill myself," we say, when something incredibly painful arises and we can not alleviate that pain immediately, or we think we will never stop the pain.

Suicidal thoughts are a wake-up call. Something very deep and tender needs addressing in our souls. When that wound is healed, thoughts of suicide disappear. This is hope for all survivors to know that suicidal thoughts are indicative of psychic pain levels, and when the pain is attended to, suicidal thoughts tend to dissipate. We survivors come into contact with this particular process somewhat frequently prior to and during our healing. While it gives us the false security that we can end the pain anytime we wish, the real truth it imparts is that some part of ourselves needs healing, a laying on of the hands. Day after day, survivors of all manner of CSA carry on in their lives, healing and seeking fulfillment of their dreams and desires. They are inspirations to us all and they too have had suicidal thoughts. We do not have to end our lives in order to end our painful feelings from our personal histories of sexual abuse.

* * * * * * * * *

"My memories will not be cause to end my life."

"How shall I celebrate the upcoming holidays?"

Holidays bring up thoughts of loving families for many people, in the media and in our surrounding environments. If we go into stores, we are reminded by holiday decorations. If we go into schools we are reminded by the recognition from the children with their posters and drawings and essays. Sometimes we look at our neighbors and friends with their families and think *They must be the ones everyone's talking about— families that care about each other and help each other.*

It is no secret that survivors dread the holidays. For many of us, such times are painful reminders of what we did not have then and may not have now, and are often intermixed with memories of abuse and the hypocrisy presented to the outside world from our family of origin. We think, *If they only knew the truth.*

Some of us may now have families of our own, with children and grandchildren clamoring for us to celebrate these holidays. Those of us who are healing can now create holidays that have meaning for us. We can choose to celebrate the holidays in our own manner and establish new family traditions. Some of us may turn to our family of choice— people we have chosen to be family because of our loving connection with them. Some of us may choose not to celebrate the holidays at all, and instead, may choose to attend to things that will make us feel better on that day.

* * * * * * * * *

*"I may or may not choose to celebrate a holiday;
either way, the choice I make means healing for me."*

Christmas   **December 25**

"What shall I do this day?"

Here's a day that brings dread and grumblings from survivors. Those who can, have made plans to be away from their families of origin. Those who can not, for whatever their reasons, have made some kind of peace or compromise such as, "I'll go early and leave right after dinner," or "I'll make sure I am not alone with any one of them at any time. I'll make sure my partner is glued to me all day long."

For many survivors, the idea of a Santa Claus coming down the chimney and delivering gifts and sneaking away is too reminiscent of the perpetrator who came into our lives, took our milk and cookies, and then snuck away. For some of us who are women of color, the idea that a strange white man should come into our homes and give our children gifts that we worked so hard to buy, seems too preposterous an idea to celebrate. But still, none of it changes our personal histories of abuse or our present relationships, or not, with our families of origin. Even the celebration of a Savior who came to save the world is painfully ironic to those who prayed for God to save us in our most needed hours, and in our eyes, we were not saved.

None of us need defend our views on this day, whether we choose to celebrate it or not, and/or be with our families or not. What really matters on this day is that we take care of our inner children, making sure none of them are subject to abuse again. If we celebrate anything, then let us celebrate that the fact that the greatest gift we can give is to take back and receive the power that was so wickedly taken away from us.

* * * * * * * * * *

"The greatest gift I can have is that of my soul."

"What beginnings shall I undertake today?"

Today is the first day of Kwanzaa, a celebration of seven principles, which speak to respect and self-determination. We who are women of African American descent, and with our friends and families, may choose to celebrate this holiday, a holiday started in this country from our ancestral roots in Africa. In fact, much of the seven principles speak to our survival: unity, self-determination, collective work and responsibility, cooperative economics, purpose, creativity, and faith. Each and every one of these principles is a concept and belief that has allowed many of us to survive whether we consciously invoked them or not. And they are tools that move us from surviving to thriving.

Many supporters of survivors have helped us and done so, frequently at their own cost. Supporters and other survivors have founded organizations to address our needs and concerns. Some have found purpose and pooled their resources so that another survivor might receive services from a health clinic, or be able to take a self-defense class to empower themselves. And some have utilized their firm beliefs in creativity and faith to make it to the next level in their healing, while helping others who must also travel these same roads.

If any of us is newly traveling this path, we might wonder what we did to deserve such goodness that allows us to have people in our lives that will gladly meet our needs. In gratitude, we might pass such kindness along to someone who may come behind us, someone newly starting out on our oftentimes long, but promising healing journey.

* * * * * * * * *

"Great things can be done when there is a meeting of kindred souls."

"I wonder what I've accomplished this year?"

Some of us are quite happy to see the year coming to an end. We think we can get out of the year like others get out of a bad job situation. Actually, getting out of a bad year is not unlike getting out of a bad relationship. There is a residue that follows us until we have resolved it all.

We often make silent contracts with ourselves while waiting for a suitable time to leave a bad relationship. Just as when a year is ending, we start making silent agreements of things we will change in our lives or about ourselves as the New Year approaches. We are hoping for a clean slate, hoping for a brand new chance.

We are a fortunate group of creatures. Not only are we conscious of having a new day, we are conscious of the gift of having a new year in which, since we know progress takes time, great things can happen to and with us.

We survivors are often a mass of contradictions both in our inward and outward behaviors. Sometimes the contradictions collide and we find we are stuck in our inability to make a decision about something in our life that needs attending to. But as far as new days and new years, we need not struggle with that. They come of their own accord.

The truth is that each day of each New Year we are given the blessing to start anew; we are given the blessing to begin a new project, a new lifestyle, a new way of looking at the world based on what we have learned from the days before. We are given gifts to mend the old ways and to have faith in the new ones. As long as we are alive, we are given the gift of hope, for it is hope that allows us to continue to have faith in our ability to eventually thrive with joy in our lives.

* * * * * * * * *

"To survive with hope is a wonderful gift."

"What changes must I bring into my world?"

Our emotions, at times, can reflect our abuse history. Like our childhood, things seemed to be going smoothly until, out of nowhere, we were sexually assaulted. Later, as adults, we may find that happening to us emotionally; or we may find that life itself is like that— things are going smoothly and then, out of nowhere, we feel we have been sucker-punched by some event or some person.

For us, as children, our lives were like a roller coaster ride. Something out of our control was happening in our lives. It was a ride that there was no stopping until the guy with the lever stopped it. But that perception is through the eyes of a child.

We are adults now, and the truth is that life does bring us ups and downs, not unlike amusement park rides, regardless of goals we are pursuing for ourselves. We have the ups and downs in our relationships, even when our relationships are good and healthy. It is the nature of life to constantly be in flux, to continually be in the process of change.

Change doesn't have to mean that something bad is going to happen, but rather, that something is shifting. Sometimes change does bring crisis, but we have the skills and strengths to handle them; in fact, some of us do our best work in crisis. We need not fear change of events or change of our emotions. If at first we are feeling good, and then suddenly we are feeling bad, then that is a barometer to our inner world; it is a signal of something going on within our inner lives. And that is not a bad thing.

* * * * * * * * *

"Change is always an opportunity for my growth."

"Dare I dream that I be healed?"

What is it to be healed? Is there such a thing that we can be totally healed from sexual abuse, that we can reach a glass ceiling where all the ramifications of the abuse in our daily lives can reach no more? Are we ever finished with healing specifically from the abuse?

Maybe it's just sort of hitting the milestones. Maybe we don't have to hit all the spots and times we were abused, but just the ones that are representative of the abuse. We need not dredge up every moment and time, unless they come up on their own accord.

Because the abuse can seem so all-encompassing and touching every facet of our life, we may think we will never be healed, will never reach balance. While it is good, and actually necessary, to have contact with those who are healing and feel their lives are working for them, we must keep in mind not to make comparisons. But, the fact that others have healed and have found a happiness they thought they would always be deprived of, can serve as inspirations to what can be achieved when healing from our abuse histories.

To be healed means to be able to handle the problems that arise in our lives in a way that is healthy and in balance for us. Life is ever changing, and there will always be new problems, and new crisis to attend to in our lives. And when we are in balance, there will also be new joys to share in our hearts, new days in which to celebrate new achievements, and new loves with whom we can share our lives.

* * * * * * * * *

"Others have traveled a path to healing that I can walk."

"Well? Just how many times did he do it?"

Some say
"It was just once."
One night
he crept
into her room
seizing everything

her dancing legs
her songs she made up
all by herself
and
    even
her unspoken words
he stole
from her silent lips
while disregarding
the strength in her heart
she blew away her soul
with leftovers
from her baby's breath

fleeing all
she could
ever know
and when the police finally
came to her and asked
she wouldn't
even tell them
her name

* * * * * * * * *

"Sometimes I miss her so much."

"What spirit of woman am I?

We women of many shades and vibrant hues, often inhabit our homes, houses, hallways, and bedrooms with our silent rages. Not only is our silence family scripted, but we also receive legions of messages not to talk from our racial, ethnic, and cultural communities. Oftentimes, it is the community that knots the ties even tighter, and the taboo of breaking the silence bond is held in higher esteem than the truths that are lived by its prisoners. It is too much.

From our youngest days, and as a general rule, we are taught, trained, educated, programmed, drilled, conditioned, commanded, charged, regulated, domesticated, dominated, admonished, beseeched, implored, rebuked, disputed, berated, restrained, threatened, subdued, incarcerated, assaulted, raped, battered, and even murdered, not to break the chains, that choke...we...women...of sundry shades and rainbow hues. And while the Most Highs may rule the Kingdom of men, it is the Divine Mother Spirit that sways the tides of the ocean.

We have gained new voices to inhabit old bodies, and have acquired visionary solutions to rectify past embedded problems and break those iron chains. We have connected with new friends to help us on our paths to personal freedom. Obstacles no longer stay their course, and the rain has stopped falling on the just. We are now unbroken, unrestrained, undamaged, undaunted, unfettered, unhampered, unhindered, untouched, unswayed, unconditioned, unencumbered, unassailable, and impregnable in the face of external forces; and we are renewed by our indomitable spirits we have reclaimed, on this, our healing journey.

Peace be still. The Sea abides. The Women speak. And we are not afraid.

Dedicated to Kemba N. Smith @ 4/18/99

* * * * * * * * *

"My language is universal."

APPENDIX
GLOSSARY OF ACROMONYNS

CSA: Childhood Sexual Abuse

DID: Dissociative Identity Disorder

DNA: Otherwise known as deoxyribonucleic acid. In the most general of definitions, it holds the genetic information and instructions development of all living organisms.

DSM: Diagnostic and Statistical Manual of Mental Disorders

ER: Emergency Room

LGBTQ: Lesbian, Gay, Bisexual, Transgender, Queer, Questioning

MCWS: Misogyny, Chauvinism and White Supremacy

PTSD: Post-Traumatic Stress Disorder

SA: Sexual Assault

NOTE: The following resources for rape crisis centers, self-defense and martial arts centers and bibliography are a reference point from which to start for additional support, assistance and help in their expert areas.

ADDRESSES AND WEBSITES FOR THE NATIONAL COALITIONS AGAINST SEXUAL ASSAULT IN THE UNITED STATES AND U.S. TERRITORIES

NATIONAL SEXUAL ASSAULT HOTLINE
http://www.rainn.org
(800)-656-4673

NATIONAL SEXUAL VIOLENCE RESOURCE CENTER
http://www.nsvrc.org
(877)-739-3895

ALABAMA COALITION AGAINST RAPE
http://www.acar.org
PO Box 4091
Montgomery, AL 36102-4091
(334) 264-0123

ALASKA NETWORK ON DOMESTIC VIOLENCE AND SEXUAL ASSAULT
130 Seward Street, Ste. 214
Juneau, AK 99801
http://www.andvsa.org
(800)-478-8999

AMERICAN SAMOA
U'una'i Legal Services Corporation
http://www.nsvrc.org/organizations/248
PO Box 1353
Pago Pago, AS 96799
(684) 633-7224

ARIZONA SEXUAL ASSAULT NETWORK
http://wwwsacasa.org
1949 E. Calle de Arcos
Tempe, AZ 85284
(480)-831-1986

ARKANSAS COALITION AGAINST
SEXUAL ASSAULT
http://www.acasa.us
215 North East Avenue
Fayetteville, AR 72701
(866) 632-2272

CALIFORNIA COALITION AGAINST SEXUAL ASSAULT
http://www.calcasa.org
1215 K St., Ste. 1100
Esquire Plaza
Sacramento, CA 95814
(916) 446-2520

COLORADO COALITION AGAINST SEXUAL ASSAULT
http://www.ccasa.org
PO Box 300398
Denver, CO 80203
(877) 372-2272

CONNECTICUT SEXUAL ASSAULT CRISIS SERVICES, INC.
http://www.connsacs.org
96 Pitkin Street
East Hartford, CT 06108
(888) 999-5545

DELAWARE CONTACT Lifeline, Inc.
http://www.contactlifeline.org/contact.html
P.O. Box 9525
Wilmington, DE 19809
(800) 262-9800

DISTRICT OF COLUMBIA RAPE CRISIS CENTER
http://www.dcrc.org
PO Box 34125
Washington, DC 20043
(202) 333-7273

FLORIDA COUNCIL AGAINST SEXUAL VIOLENCE
http://www.fcasv.org
1311 North Paul Russell Road, Ste. A204
Tallahassee, FL 32301
(888) 956-7273

GEORGIA NETWORK TO END SEXUAL ASSAULT
http://www.gnesa.org
131 Ponce de Leon Ave., Ste. 122
Atlanta, GA 30308
(866) 354-3672

GUAM HEALING HEARTS CRISIS CENTER
http://www.safe4all.org
P.O. Box 1093
Hagatna, GU 96932
(671) 647-5351

HAWAII STATE COALITION FOR THE PREVENTION OF SEXUAL
ASSAULT
http://www.hscadv.org
P.O. Box 1093
Honolulu, HI 96816
(808) 733-9038

IDAHO COALITION AGAINST SEXUAL AND DOMESTIC VIOLENCE
http://www.idvsa.org
300 E. Mallard Dr., Ste 130
Boise, ID 83706
(888) 293-6118

ILLINOIS COALITION AGAINST SEXUAL ASSAULT
http://www.icasa.org
100 North 16th Street
Springfield, IL 62703
(217) 753–4117

INDIANA COALITION AGAINST SEXUAL ASSAULT
http://www.incasa.org
55 Monument Circle, Ste. 1224
Indianapolis, IN 46204
(800) 691-2272

IOWA COALITION AGAINST SEXUAL ASSAULT
http://www.iowacasa.org
515 28th St., Ste. 107
Des Moines, IA 50312
(800) 284-7821

KANSAS COALITION AGAINST SEXUAL AND DOMESTIC VIOLENCE
http://www.kcsdv.org
Topeka, KS 66603
(785) 232-9784

KENTUCKY ASSOCIATION OF SEXUAL ASSAULT PROGRAMS
http://kyasap.brinkster.net
PO Box 4028
Frankfort, KY 40604
(888) 375-2727

LOUISIANA FOUNDATION AGAINST SEXUAL ASSAULT
http://www.lafasa.org
1250 SW Railroad Ave., Ste. 170
Hammond, LA 70403
(888) 995-7273

MAINE COALITION AGAINST SEXUAL ASSAULT
http://www.mecasa.org
83 Western Ave., Ste. 2
Augusta, ME 04330
(800) 871-7741

MARYLAND COALITION AGAINST SEXUAL ASSAULT
http://www.mcasa.org
1517 Governor Ritchie Highway, Ste. 207
Arnold, MD 21012
(800) 983-7273

MASSACHUSETTS: JANE DOE, INC.
http://www.janedoe.org
14 Beacon St., Ste. 507
Boston, MA 02108
(617) 248-0922

MICHIGAN COALITION AGAINST DOMESTIC AND SEXUAL VIOLENCE
http://www.mcadsv.org
3893 Okemos Rd., Ste. B-2
Okemos, MI 48864
(517) 347-7000

MINNESOTA COALITION AGAINST SEXUAL ASSAULT
http://www.mncasa.org
161 St. Anthony Ave., Ste. 1001
St. Paul, MN 55103
(800) 964-8847

MISSISSIPPI COALITION AGAINST SEXUAL ASSAULT
http://www.mscasa.org
PO Box 4172
Jackson, MS 39296
(888) 987-9011

MISSOURI COALITION AGAINST SEXUAL ASSAULT
http://mocadsv.missouri.org
217 Oscar Drive, Ste. A
Jefferson City, MO 65110
(573) 634-4161

MONTANA COALITION AGAINST DOMESTIC VIOLENCE AND
SEXUAL ASSAULT
http://www.mcadsv.com
PO Box 818
Helena, MT 59624
(888) 404-7794

NEBRASKA DOMESTIC VIOLENCE AND SEXUAL ASSAULT COALITION
http://www.ndvsac.org
1000 "O" St., Ste. 102
Lincoln, NE 68508
(402) 476-6256

NEVADA COALITION AGAINST SEXUAL VIOLENCE
http://www.ncasv.org
P. O. Box 530103
Henderson, Nevada 89053
(702) 940-2033

NEW HAMPSHIRE COALITION AGAINST DOMESTIC AND SEXUAL
VIOLENCE
http://www.nhcadsv.org
PO Box 353
Concord, NH 03302
(800) 227-5570

NEW JERSEY COALITION AGAINST SEXUAL ASSAULT
http://www.njcasa.org
2333 Whitehorse Mercerville Rd., Ste. B
Trenton, NJ 08619
(800) 601-7200

NEW MEXICO COALITION OF SEXUAL ASSAULT PROGRAMS
http://www.nmcsap.org
3909 Juan Tabo Northeast, Ste. 6
Albuquerque, NM 87111
(505) 883-8020

NEW YORK COALITION AGAINST SEXUAL ASSAULT
http://www.nyscasa.org
28 Essex St.
Albany, NY 12206
(518) 482-4222

NORTH CAROLINA COALITION AGAINST SEXUAL ASSAULT
http://www.nccasa.org
183 Wind Chime Ct., Ste. 1000
Raleigh, NC 27615
(888) 737-2272

NORTH DAKOTA COUNCIL ON ABUSED WOMEN'S SERVICES
http://www.ndcaws.org
418 E. Rosser, #320
Bismarck, ND 58501
(888) 255-6240

OHIO YWCA H.O.P.E CENTER
http://www.ywca.org/site/pp.asp?c=hgLRJ0NNG&b=91698
1018 Jefferson Ave.
Toledo, OH 43604
(419) 241-7273

OKLAHOMA COALITION AGAINST DOMESTIC VIOLENCE
AND SEXUAL ASSAULT
http://www.ocadvsa.org/member_programs.htm
3815 North Santa Fe Ave., Ste. 124
Oklahoma City, OK 73118
(405) 524-0700

OREGON COALITION AGAINST DOMESTIC AND SEXUAL VIOLENCE
http://www.ocadsv.com/sa.htm
380 Southeast Spokane St., Ste. 100
Portland, OR 97202
(503) 230-1951

PENNSYLVANIA COALITION AGAINST RAPE
http://www.pcar.org
125 N. Enola Dr.
Enola, PA 17025
(800) 692-7445

PUERTO RICO COALITION AGAINST DOMESTIC VIOLENCE AND
SEXUAL ASSAULT
http://www.salud.gov.pr
P. O Box 193008
San Juan, PR 00910
(787) 721-7676

RHODE ISLAND: DAY ONE: THE SEXUAL ASSAULT AND
TRAUMA RESOURCE CENTER
http://www.dayoneri.org
100 Medway St.
Providence, RI 02906
(800) 494–8100

SOUTH CAROLINA COALITION AGAINST DOMESTIC VIOLENCE
AND SEXUAL ASSAULT
http://www.sccadvasa.org
PO Box 7776
Columbia, SC 29202
(800) 260-9293

SOUTH DAKOTA COALITION AGAINST DOMESTIC VIOLENCE AND
SEXUAL ASSAULT
http://www.sdcadvsa.org/Home.html
PO Box 141
Pierre, SD 57501
(800) 572-9196

TENNESSEE COALITION AGAINST DOMESTIC AND SEXUAL
VIOLENCE
http://www.tcadsv.org/index2.htm
2 International Plaza Dr., Ste. 425
Nashville, TN 37217
(800) 289-9018

TEXAS ASSOCIATION AGAINST SEXUAL ASSAULT
http://www.taasa.org
6200 La Calma Dr., Ste 110
Austin, TX 78752
(512) 474-7190

UTAH COALITION AGAINST SEXUAL ASSAULT
http://www.ucasa.org/home.html
284 West 400 North
Salt Lake City, UT 84103
(801) 746-0404

VERMONT NETWORK AGAINST DOMESTIC VIOLENCE AND SEXUAL
ASSAULT
http://www.vtnetwork.org
PO Box 405
Montpelier, VT 05601
(800) 489-7273

VIRGIN ISLANDS DOMESTIC VIOLENCE AND SEXUAL ASSAULT
COUNCIL WOMEN'S COALITION OF ST. CROIX
http://www.wcstx.com/rapeindx.htm
PO Box 222734
Christiansted, VI 00822
(340) 773-9272

VIRGINIA SEXUAL AND DOMESTIC VIOLENCE ACTION ALLIANCE
http://www.vadv.org
508 Monument Ave., Ste. A
Richmond, VA 23230
(800) 838-8238

WASHINGTON COALITION OF SEXUAL ASSAULT PROGRAMS
4317 6th Ave., SE, Ste. 102
Olympia, WA 98503
(800) 755-8013

WEST VIRGINIA FOUNDATION FOR RAPE INFORMATION AND
SERVICES
http://www.fris.org
112 Braddock St.
Fairmont, WV 26554
(304) 366-9500

WISCONSIN COALITION AGAINST SEXUAL ASSAULT
http://www.wcasa.org
600 Williamson St., Ste. N-2
Madison, WI 53703
(608) 257-1516

WYOMING COALITION AGAINST DOMESTIC VIOLENCE AND
SEXUAL ASSAULT
http://www.wyomingdvsa.org/index1.htm
PO Box 236
409 South Fourth Street
Laramie, WY 82073
(307) 755-5481

SURVIVOR WEBSITES

ARLETHER WILSON: SUPPORTING AND EMPOWERING WOMEN
http://rewritethescript.wordpress.com

FEMINIST MAJORITY FOUNDATION
http://www.feminist.org/911/assaultlinks.html

INCITE!
http://www.incite-national.org

LGBTQ COMMUNITY
http://www.ibiblio.org/rcip

SURVIVORSHIP
http://www.survivorship.org

THE VOICES AND FACES PROJECT
http://www.voicesandfaces.org/rape_links.asp

THE WOMEN OF COLOR NETWORK
http://womenofcolornetwork.org

SELF-DEFENSE AND MARTIAL ARTS

I strongly advocate that everyone take classes or workshops in self-defense. Full force impact classes allow you to use your total body strength in self-defense training. Other self-defense classes may also use full force training, but not all of them do. The following is a limited list of organizations that teach self-defense and/or self-defense with organizations that teach martial arts. Their websites and phone numbers and/or email are listed for contact.

If none are in proximity to your location, please take a self-defense class near you (you can check with your local rape crisis center for classes in their agencies or local police departments). In the case of taking self-defense classes at a martial arts organization, you might discover you want to take martial arts training. The overwhelming majority of self-defense classes teach both verbal and physical boundary setting, which is especially helpful in the healing process for survivors.

Many of the schools listed below practice the martial art style called Kajukenbo. This martial art was co-founded in 1947 at the Palama Settlements in Hawaii by five men who called themselves the Black Belt Society and the art evolved under the leadership and the recognized founder of the system, Sijo Adriano Emperado, known as the Kajukenbo Self-Defense Institute (KSDI).

HAND TO HAND KAJUKENBO SELF-DEFENSE CENTER
http://www.handtohandkajukenbo.com
(510) 428-0502

DESTINY ARTS CENTER (YOUTH)
http://www.destinyarts.org
(510)-597-1619

BONO'S JKD AND KAJUKENBO
http://www.bonosjeetkunedo-kajukenbo.com
(408) 298-2663

DRAGONS DEN KAJUKENBO CLUB
http://www.dragonsdenmma.com
 (510) 477-6800

FEMINIST ECLECTIC MA RTIAL ARTS
http://www.fema-wuchienpai.com
(612) 729-7233

FUJI RYU JUJUTSU
http://www.fujiryu.com/home.html
(718) 991-3723

GERRY'S MARTIAL ARTS
http://www.markgerry.com
Private lessons by appointment
(510) 886-3499

GINTS FIGHTING CLUB
http://home.att.net/~gints/home.htm
email: gints@att.net
Telephone Number not listed

GUANGXI CH'UAN
http://www.gxnapa.com
(707) 257-0873

HARPER KAJUKENBO
http://www.freewebs.com/kajupit/index.htm
(559) 732-4530

HOKKIEN MARTIAL ARTS
http://www.topekakarate.com/Chief
(785) 213-1576

IMPACT BAY AREA
http://www.impactbayarea.org
(510) 208-0474

JOHN BISHOP'S KAJUKENBO HOME PAGE
One of the most comprehensive websites on Kajukenbo
Bishop's Kajukenbo Academy
http://www.kajukenboinfo.com
(909) 839-7070

KAJUKENBO ASSOCIATION OF AMERICA
Great Grandmaster Charles Gaylord, founder of the
Gaylord Method of Kajukenbo
http://www.ggmgaylordkajukenbo.com
Telephone Number not listed

KAJUKENBO CAFÉ
http://www.kajukenbocafe.com/smf
Telephone Number not listed

KIDPOWER, TEENPOWER, FULLPOWER INTERNATIONAL
http://www.fullpower.org
(800) 467-6997

NATIONAL WOMEN'S MARTIAL ARTS FEDERATION
http://www.nwmaf.org
Telephone Number not listed

PACIFIC ASSOCIATION OF WOMEN MARTIAL ARTISTS
http://www.pawma.org
Telephone Number not listed

POWELL'S MIXED MARTIAL ARTS ACADEMY
Suisun, CA
(707) 344-1655
Website not listed

REALM OF THE TIGER KAJUKENBO
http://www.rottkajukenbo.com (in progress)
(503) 839-6359

SEATTLE KAJUKENBO & KUNG FU KIDS
http://www.seattlekajukenbo.com
(206) 329-5719

SEVEN STAR WOMEN'S KUNG FU
http://www.7starwomenskungfu.org/index.html
(206) 720-1046

SOLIS MARTIAL ARTS
http://www.solismartialarts.net
(510) 235-6565

TERRAZAS KAJUKENBO
http://www.freewebs.com/kajugurl
email: sifuserene@yahoo.com

THOUSAND WAVES
http://www.thousandwaves.org/index.asp
(773) 472-7663

WOODY SIMS KSDI
Vallejo, CA
(707) 644-2425
Website not listed

ADDITIONAL STATISTICS ON SEXUAL ASSAULT

This book is written for adult and teen survivors of sexual assault and incest. It is a strange sociological phenomenon, but when looking for information on sexual assault against women of different races, three groups consistently came up: Blacks, Latinas and Whites. The United States has diverse populations of many ethnic, cultural and racial strata, and we are still not listening to the voices, nor meeting the needs of all our sisters nor are we or they telling their stories.

Nonetheless, there are a few studies, notably the National Violence Against Women Survey of 1998 that represent categories similar to those found on rape crisis forms on racial and ethnic identity for women who disclose they have been raped as follows: 34% American Indian/Alaska Native, 24% mixed race (which could be all of the Black and White, Asian and White and, Latina and Black and Other categories such as Southeast Asian), 19% African American, 18% of White, and 7% Asian/Pacific Islander women.[9]

Of all the groups victimized by sexual assault and rape in the States, the most reluctant to disclose sexual assault, other than heterosexual males, tend to be from the Lesbian, Gay, Bisexual, Transgender and Queer community (LGBTQ), regardless of racial or ethnic identity. A 2000 report cited that between 16-30% of victims had been victimized by the police. In another study by the National Coalition of Anti-Violence Programs for the years 2001-2002, 20% of reports that victims wished to make were refused by law enforcement, although in 2002-2003 there was a decline in the refusals by law enforcement by approximately -12%, but at the same time there was an increase of sexual violence by 8%.[10] According to a 2001 study in Massachusetts on sexual harassment and assault on girls, the findings showed that compared to 6% heterosexual girls, 23% lesbian and bisexual girls had been victims of attempted rape or rape by their peers.

One of the main reasons victims of any demographic are reluctant to report the sexual assault other than personal shame and self-blaming, is the expectation that the police will be unsympathetic. There have been a number of changes in attitudes and education in law enforcement in regards to rape, yet changing old attitudes is a slow process, and sometimes it takes generations

[9] 2007 Rape Report CalCASA
[10] Ibid.

to substantially change the thinking patterns and beliefs of a society or its subgroups.

In a 2000 report, 25% of all female victims were assaulted by family members. Of these 25% victims, 44% were between the ages of 6 to 11 and 51% were between the ages of 0-6. If the assault took place in the residence of the victim, then more than likely the offender was an adult as opposed to outside the residence whereby the offender more than likely was a juvenile offender. Despite reporting these crimes of sexual assaults against youth ages 6 and younger, the offenders of these crimes were the least likely to be arrested or for the case to be cleared.[11]

These sexual crimes and the probability for the mental health recovery of these, our most vulnerable victims, are chilling considering that it is more than probable that it causes *lifelong* problems for its victims.[12] Such lifelong problems effect not only the survivor but every relationship she has or does not have. Until we can provide services to survivors that are affordable and effective, this lifelong aspect is like the falling domino effect. We are all impacted by the sickness of childhood sexual abuse, incest, sexual assault and rape in whatever forms they take upon victims and survivors. Survivors and victims are your family, lovers, friends, co-workers, employers and the people you have everyday dealings with. When survivors heal so does society.

[11] Ibid
[12] Ibid.

UPDATE: 20-year old Black woman, Michael Jackson and Warren Jeffs.

I will give her last name, which is Williams, because her mother and she wanted the world to know what crimes had been committed against her. **Ms. Williams** lived to see her offenders arrested and sentenced to long-term imprisonment. However, not without some controversy; firstly, some members of the Black community thought that the crimes committed against Ms. Williams should have been prosecuted as hate crimes. The district attorney's office differed in that they were looking for the crimes that were committed and would deliver the most severe punishments. Secondly, in October 2009, Ms. Williams recanted her story. Nonetheless, the district attorney commented that they did not depend only on Ms. Williams' story but also upon the physical evidence and the confessions of the offenders—all who pled guilty to the crimes they committed.

Of the six criminals, Alisha Burton and George Messer pleaded guilty to assault and kidnapping receiving up to 10 years; Frankie Brewster was sentenced to 10-25 years for second-degree sexual assault; Karen Burton was sentenced to 10 years for violating Williams' civil rights and 2-ten year sentences for assault, to be served consecutively. Bobby Brewster was sentenced 13 to 40 years in prison for conspiracy to commit kidnapping and malicious assault, and Danny Combs received 20 years for sexual assault, assault during the commission of a felony, and conspiracy to commit kidnapping or hostage holding.

Michael Jackson. August 29, 1958 – June 25, 2009
Michael died from a coronary attack. In 1993, the first allegations against Michael were investigated for molesting a young male, but Michael was not charged. However, he did make an out-of-court settlement for $22 million. As to the second and last allegations of child abuse in 2005, he was charged on 7 counts of molestation and 2 counts of administering an intoxicating agent to a child; Jackson was acquitted on all accounts.

Warren Jeffs.
On September 25, 2007 Jeffs was declared guilty of two counts of rape as an accomplice and was sentenced to 10 years to life at the Utah State Prison. Jeffs' conviction was reversed by Utah's Supreme Court on July 27, 2010 because of incorrect jury instructions. On November 15, 2010, the State of Utah ordered Warren Jeffs extradited to Texas, which is charging Jeffs with sexual assault of a child, aggravated sexual assault of a child. He is also charged with bigamy for a spiritual marriage he allegedly entered into in 2006 with a 12-year-old girl in Eldorado, Texas, and another underage girl to whom he allegedly fathered a child in 2005. If convicted on the Texas charges, Jeffs could face a maximum penalty of five to 99 years or life in prison and a fine of $10,000. Jeffs is now in Texas custody waiting for his hearing sometime in January 2011.

BIBLIOGRAPHY

Allison, D. 1992. *Bastard Out of Carolina*. New York: Penguin Books.

Bass, E. & L. Davis. 1994. *The Courage to Heal: A Guide for Women Survivors of Child Sexual Abuse*. New York: HarperCollins Publishers, Inc.

Bishop, John. 2007. *KAJUKENBO: The Original Mixed Martial Art*. Tennessee: IstantPublisher.

California Coalition Against Sexual Assault. 2007 REPORT: Research on Rape and Violence. Sacramento.

California. 1872. California Penal Codes 261. ed. O. C. L. Information. Sacramento: State of California.

---. 1901. California Penal Codes 288. ed. O. C. L. Information. Sacramento: State of California.

Free Health Encyclopedia (2007) Incest. http://www.faqs.org/health (last accessed November 11, 2007).

Freyd, J. J. 1996. *Betrayal Trauma: The Logic of Forgetting Childhood Abuse*. Cambridge: Harvard University Press.

Herman, J. L. 1992. *Trauma and Recovery: The Aftermath of Violence -from Domestic Abuse to Political Terror*. New York: Basic Books.

Lloyd, R. D. V. L. 1940. *How Green Was My Valley*. New York: Macmillan Publishing Company.

Nazer, M. & D. Lewis. 2003. *Slave: My True Story*. New York: Public Affairs.

NCVC (2004) Incest. http://www.ncvc.org/ncvc (last accessed November 19, 2007).

Oksana, C. 1994. *Safe Passage to Healing: A Guide for Survivors of Ritual Abuse*. New York: HarperCollins Publishers, Inc.

Persall J. & Trumble, B. 2003. *Oxford English Reference Dictionary: Revised Second Edition*. New York: Oxford University Press.

Pierce-Baker, C. 1998. *Surviving the Silence: Black Women's Stories of Rape*. New York: W.W. Norton & Company, Inc.

Robinson, L. S. 2002. *I Will Survive: The African-American Guide to Healing from Sexual Assault and Abuse*. New York: Seal Press.

Reuters. Accessed on November 29, 2010: http://www.upi.com/Top_News/US/2010/11/15/Jeffs-ordered-extradited-to-Texas/UPI-74741289871282/

San Mateo County. (2007) Rape Statistics. http://www.rapetraumaservices.org/rape-sexual-assault.html (last accessed November 19, 2007).

Shange, N. 1977. *For Colored Girls Who Have Considered Suicide When The Rainbow is Enuf*. New York: Macmillan Publishing.

Walker, A. 1982. *The Color Purple*. New York: Simon & Schuster.

Wilson, M. 1993. *Crossing the Boundary: Black Women Survive Incest*. Seattle: Seal Press.

INDEX

CPSIA information can be obtained at www.ICGtesting.com
Printed in the USA
BVOW01s0436160813

328571BV00009B/169/P

9 780979 863387